War Letters to a Wife

France and Flanders, 1915–1919

WAR LETTERS TO A WIFE

FRANCE AND FLANDERS, 1915–1919

by
Rowland Feilding

Edited by Jonathan Walker

SPELLMOUNT
Staplehurst

British Library Cataloguing in Publication Data:
A catalogue record for this book is available
from the British Library

Copyright © Rowland Feilding 1929, 2001
Introduction © Jonathan Walker 2001

ISBN 1-86227-119-4

First published in the UK by the Medici Society Ltd in 1929
This edition published in 2001 by
Spellmount Limited
The Old Rectory
Staplehurst
Kent TN12 0AZ

Tel: 01580 893730
Fax: 01580 893731
E-mail: enquiries@spellmount.com
Website: www.spellmount.com

1 3 5 7 9 8 6 4 2

The right of Rowland Feilding and Jonathan Walker to be identified
as the authors of this work has been asserted by them
in accordance with the Copyright, Designs
and Patents Act 1988

All rights reserved. No part of this publication may be
reproduced, stored in a retrieval system or transmitted in
any form or by any means, electronic, mechanical,
photocopying, recording or otherwise,
without prior permission in writing from
Spellmount Limited, Publishers.

Typeset in Palatino by MATS, Southend-on-Sea, Essex
Printed in Great Britain by
TJ International Ltd, Padstow, Cornwall

Contents

FEILDING PEDIGREE (Simplified)

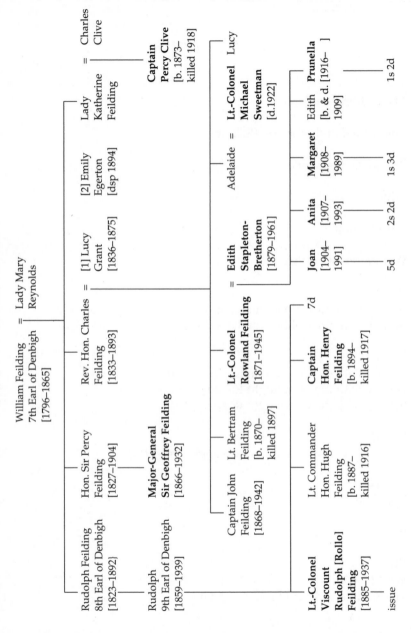

STAPLETON–BRETHERTON PEDIGREE (Simplified)

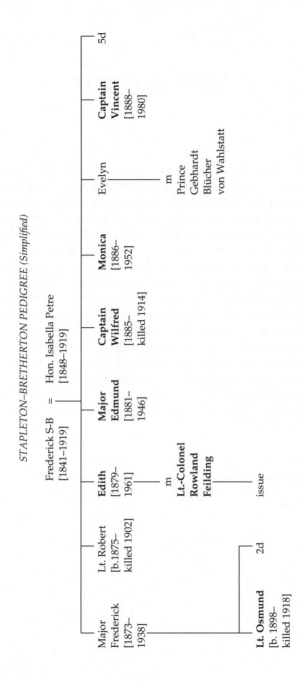

Frederick S-B [1841–1919] = Hon. Isabella Petre [1848–1919]

Major Frederick [1873–1938]

Lt. Robert [b.1875–killed 1902]

Edith [1879–1961]
m Lt.-Colonel Rowland Feilding — issue

Major Edmund [1881–1946]

Captain Wilfred [1885–killed 1914]

Monica [1886–1952]

Evelyn
m Prince Gebhardt Blücher von Wahlstatt

Captain Vincent [1888–1980] 5d

Lt. Osmund [b. 1898–killed 1918] 2d

Acknowledgements

In my quest to bring Rowland Feilding's moving letters to a modern readership, it was my good fortune to find that his youngest daughter was still living. I am grateful to Prunella Howard, on behalf of the Rowland Feilding Estate, for permission to publish her father's letters and for the help and encouragement she, and her daughter, Caroline Gordon-Duff, have given me. Anne Reyntiens, whose mother, Joan, was Rowland Feilding's eldest daughter and correspondent, has provided me with useful letters, sketches and anecdotes about her grandfather. My sincere thanks to her for her help and for permission to use her mother's letters.

I would also like to thank the staffs of the libraries of the Liddell Hart Centre for Military Archives, King's College, and the National Army Museum, London, as well as Trinity College, Dublin and The National Library of Ireland, for their assistance with background material. My special thanks to my wife, Gill, for correcting typescripts.

My appreciation also to Dr John Bourne, Ray Westlake and Dr Keith Chambers for their constructive advice and similarly my publisher, Jamie Wilson.

Editor's Note

While the sheer size of the Feilding correspondence has been reduced for publication, there has been no attempt to change either the spelling or style of the original letters. His liberal use of hyphenated words, such as 'shell-fire' or 'dug-out', has not been corrected to modern usage.

The original letters were inscribed 'OAS' (On Active Service) and postmarked with a Field Post Office number. Most were passed by a numbered Field Censor and did not contain sensitive information such as place names or units. These were later added by Feilding from information contained in his diaries, but they were the only amendments made. Where he omitted personal names for family reasons, these have been left blank. Similarly, where swearwords were originally indicated by asterisks, these have been retained.

All letters are from Rowland Feilding to his wife, Edith, and are dated together with an address. The exceptions are his letters, interspersed, to his eldest daughter, Joan, which open 'My darling Joan'. Feilding also sketched the landscape of the Western Front and often attached these pictures to his letters. Some have been reproduced in this book.

Modern notes are provided on the actions and most of the characters mentioned. The identity of 'the figure in black' may become clear to the reader by the end of the book.

Introduction

An officer's letter from the Western Front has an aura about it. Written in indelible pencil or Stephens' ink, on quarto paper, the only hint as to the writer's address is 'On Active Service' or 'BEF, France'. In reality, this address is usually a dank, smoky dugout in the front line and its fetid smell – that curious mix of tobacco, latrines, sweat, rum fumes and sodden wool – permeates everything. The letter is written by the light of a candle or lamp, and the distant 'crumps' of a bombardment can be heard in the background.

Many of Rowland Feilding's letters to his wife were written under these conditions. There is nothing exceptional about that. But while there exist many fine collections of officers' letters, most are either the work of subalterns or of more senior commanders. The Feilding Letters fill that gap. They were written, for the most part, while he was either a company or battalion commander, a position which enabled him to take part in not only the planning of military operations, but also their execution. Consequently, he provides some valuable insights into the problems of command on the Great War battlefield.

Because of his wide experience before the war, Feilding was able to write about life on the Western Front with a maturity and fineness of feeling, rarely seen in the letters of younger officers. His 'pen-portraits' of his brother officers and men are social history in themselves, and it is a bonus that he has so few of the prejudices normally associated with the age, which makes his writing so easily digestible to the modern reader.

The letters were written almost continuously from 1915 to 1919.[1] Those reproduced in this volume represent the bulk of his output, but he also wrote a series of letters to his eldest daughter, Joan. A sample of these have also been included, and they add another dimension to this soldier's tale. While he spares his wife little of the ghastliness of trench life, more importantly, he demonstrates the small rewards that gave men the will to survive. Given the constant action he saw, it is a miracle he survived at all.

Rowland Charles Feilding was born on 18 May 1871, the third son of five children of the Rev. Hon. Charles Feilding.

He had an illustrious and colourful pedigree. His father, who was Rector of Stapleton, near Shrewsbury, was the fourth son of the 7th Earl of Denbigh, a family who traced their ancestry back to the Austrian Hapsburg dynasty.[2] They played a prominent role in the English Civil War, one ancestor even accompanying King Charles to the scaffold. Another branch of the family had produced the famous novelist, Henry Fielding (who changed the spelling of his surname to suit artistic sensibilities). On his mother Lucy's side were the Earls of Elgin, famous for the 7th Earl's rescue of the Parthenon marbles.

Feilding barely knew his mother, as he was just 3 years old when she died in childbirth in 1875. Seven years later his father married Emily Egerton, and in 1885 Rowland followed his brother, Bertram, to Haileybury School. By all accounts, he excelled in Mathematics and Science, and when he left school in 1888, he went to Manchester to study Civil Engineering. Qualifying as an Associate of the Royal School of Mines in 1893, he travelled to Rhodesia and the Transvaal the following year, to pursue mining contracts.

It was during his time in Southern Africa that he first became involved in military operations, when the Matabele rebellion broke out. In 1896 he joined Gifford's Horse, part of the force raised to protect white settlers. After several skirmishes, his troop was ambushed at Fonseca's Farm, his horse being shot from under him, and he was wounded in the leg. Although the Matabele were never defeated in a major battle, they were worn down by the Rhodesians and soon capitulated. With the rebellion over, Feilding left Africa, and travelled in turn to every continent in the world, continuing his mining career. He soon became an expert in the techniques of tunnelling and drilling, and later, when he fought in the Great War, found that he was one of the few officers outside the Royal Engineers with an expertise in mining. Consequently, he was able to appreciate the extraordinary skill of the tunnellers on the Western Front.

Both Feilding's elder brothers had joined the Army; his closest brother, Bertram, was killed in a mutiny in Uganda in 1897. When he returned from his travels in 1898, he too obtained a commission, as a subaltern in the 6th Battalion, The Lancashire Fusiliers. He was promoted Captain in 1903, and in the same year, at the age of 32, he married Edith Stapleton-Bretherton. At this time, he converted to her faith, Catholicism, which was to have a great influence on both his private life and military career. Edith subsequently bore him five daughters, Joan (born 1904), Anita (1907), Margaret 'Peggy' (1908), Edith (born and died 1909) and Prunella 'Pru' (1916).[3]

When war broke out in August 1914, Feilding was a Captain in the 2nd Battalion, City of London Yeomanry (Rough Riders), a territorial unit of four squadrons, which had seen action in the Boer War. He spent the winter of 1914–15 at battalion headquarters in Finsbury Square and this was followed with periods at camp and on training exercises. But he was keen to see action, despite his age of 44, and lobbied his cousin, Geoffrey Feilding, for a transfer to the Guards. Officer casualties had been particularly heavy in the Spring of 1915, and Geoffrey Feilding, who commanded the 3rd Battalion, Coldstream Guards, needed little persuasion to effect the request. On 6 April 1915 Captain Rowland Feilding joined the Special Reserve of Officers, Coldstream Guards and by the end of the month he had left for France.

Edith Feilding made her husband promise that, in his letters from the Front, he would spare her nothing of the dangers he faced – she would know if he was hiding anything and would only imagine the worst. She had few illusions about the pity of war, having lost two brothers in battle, one in the Boer War and another in the first months of the Great War. Any lack of news this time would only increase her pain.

On arriving in France, Feilding was posted to the 3rd Battalion, Coldstream Guards – part of the 4th Guards Brigade, 2nd Division. After a brief period as second-in-command of a company, he was transferred on 13 May 1915, with his Company Commander, Guy Baring, to the 1/Coldstream Guards (1st Guards Brigade, 1st Division), where he was to spend the next eight months.

The reputation of the Guards Brigades[4] was formidable, but theirs was a world Feilding knew well. The Coldstream Guards included many members of the aristocracy and landed gentry and he could count his uncle and cousins, as well as many friends, in the regimental list. However, by the end of 1915, a year which had seen the carnage at Loos, this intimate society began to change. Losses continued to rise in the Guards and, while the effect of the 'Lost Generation' in the Great War can be exaggerated,[5] few families escaped. Feilding was fairly typical, losing three cousins, two nephews and a brother-in-law.

The replacements for these officer casualties began to be drawn from a wider social mix. When Feilding was transferred to command the 6th Connaught Rangers in September 1916, he noted that his mess boasted 'a racehorse trainer, a MFH, an actor, a barrister, a squireen or two, a ranker from the Grenadiers, a banker, a quarter-master from the 9th Lancers, and a Nationalist MP'.

A conscious effort was now being made in Southern Irish Regiments, where vacancies arose in battalion command, to employ competent Catholic officers. At the time when Feilding transferred to the Rangers, Irish politics were in turmoil. It was, after all, the year of the Easter Rising, and with one eye on battalion discipline, he was anxious to glean as much knowledge as possible about the 'Troubles'. Irish politics had already touched his family, as his sister-in-law, Evelyn, and her German diplomat husband were friends of the notorious Sir Roger Casement.[6] Also, during Feilding's service with the 1/Coldstream, he had spent much time in the company of Tommy Robartes, who, before the war, had been the first politician to embrace the idea of Partition in Ireland.[7] By 1916 politics within the 6/Connaughts had polarised, not so much from the 1916 Rising itself, but from the fallout from the resulting executions. Together with the threat of conscription in Ireland, this did much to alienate Catholic opinion and jeopardise recruitment.

The 6/Connaughts belonged to the 16th (Irish) Division, a unit serving on the Western Front. The division contained no fewer than five serving Nationalist (Irish Party) MPs, as well as many of their supporters, so events at home in Ireland were closely followed. There, two parties vied for the Catholic vote. John Redmond, the leader of the constitutional Irish Party, who had pledged loyalty to King and Empire, had tied his fortunes to the Home Rule Bill becoming law. He, and those who joined the British Army, believed that an identifiable Irish contribution to the war would help win Home Rule after the Armistice.[8] But by 1917 there seemed little hope of any compromise with Ulster that would save the cause. The younger, radical Sinn Fein party repudiated any attempt by a British Parliament to give dominion status or Home Rule to Ireland. With a policy of complete cultural and government independence from King and Empire, they heavily defeated Redmond's party in the 1918 General Election.

However, regimental loyalties often surpass national ones, and despite the political upheavals of 1916 and 1917, the 6th Connaught Rangers fought on until they were tragically destroyed in the 1918 German Spring Offensive.[9]

The sacrifice made by the Connaught Rangers and other Irish regiments was considerable, and it has been estimated that between 27,000 and 35,000 Irishmen were killed in the Great War.[10] Sadly, the collapse of moderate Irish nationalism meant the total eclipse after the war of all that the 10th and 16th (Irish) Divisions had achieved, and this sacrifice has been wilfully ignored in the Republic of Ireland ever since.[11]

It is immediately apparent from his letters that 'Snowball', as Feilding was known because of his shock of white hair, was a compassionate man. As with most regimental officers, he cared about his men, their morale and conditions, but his letters were unusual in that they included personal details about the men. He troubled to name them and discussed their foibles, their attitudes and most of all, their sense of duty, which he contrasted bitterly with the civilian profiteers at home.

This alienation with all things civilian even extended to trippers who visited the battlefields at the end of the war, and is indicative of the gulf between those who fought and those who did not. In many ways, Feilding reflects the feelings of Stuart Cloete, another Coldstream officer, who wrote in his memoirs, '*We* were the fighting soldiers. The ASC and RAMC, the padres and Army Pay Corps were a kind of social No Man's Land.

Neither one thing nor another. The staff were hated more than civilians. Civilians were despised and regarded rather like children who did not know the facts of life. They were *Them*, as opposed to *Us*. The Germans were *Them* too, but we were nearer to them than to civilians in many ways.'[12]

One reason for this empathy with the Germans was the common enemy – the frequently appalling conditions. Both sides were also in constant close proximity and the 'live and let live' policy was endorsed locally more often than brigade or division would care to admit. But Feilding's affinity with his foe was also born out of a curiosity that, fifty yards away in another trench, there must exist civilised men with a similar culture. He wrote:

> An officer has found the diary of a Bavarian Infantry soldier, Otto Arnesmaier – a wonderfully human document, into which the writer pours his full soul. He was a man of gentle disposition, who was no soldier by choice, and indeed hated everything to do with war; a lover of music, which he describes as 'the divine daughter of Heaven, and consoler'.
>
> His was one of the bodies that helped make the parapet of the Hohenzollern Redoubt.

One refreshing aspect of these letters is the consideration Feilding gives to the role of spirituality in warfare. Organised religion in the Great War has often been parodied, as if it was an irrelevance to men concerned with the very mortal business of fighting and killing. Yet Feilding finds, in his largely Catholic battalion, a strong need for the certainties that ritual can provide. His appreciation of faith as a great strength in war goes beyond the normal zealousness of a convert to a creed. Superstition may have played a part in some of the great legends of the war that he witnessed, like the leaning Madonna of Albert, but there is no doubting the strength he derived from other experiences – Christian symbols, such as the crucifix, surviving in villages almost completely destroyed, or the simple religious committal of dead comrades. The role of spirituality in maintaining morale was amply recognised by the priests of the 16th (Irish) Division and Father 'Happy Days' Williamson, whom Feilding later joined in the 47th Division. Displaying little fear at going into the front line, they appeared as comrades to the men – in contrast to the tales of remoteness often levelled at Church of England padres.

Although Feilding constantly praised the virtue and spirit of his men in his letters, he did conceal one colleague's resentment. When he went on leave from the 6/Connaughts in March 1917, he returned to find a regular, Lieutenant-Colonel Jourdain, had been placed in temporary command in his absence. Jourdain had a long service with the Connaught Rangers and took umbrage at the appointment of Feilding as CO of the 6th Battalion in 1916. Jourdain's private diaries[13] detail his extensive intrigues against, and perpetual rows with, his commanding officer. So Feilding was well aware of the problem, but perhaps not the scale of Jourdain's plot to have him removed. However, Jourdain's constant lobbying of both brigade and divisional commanders seems to have had little effect. In fact, Major-General Hickie, the divisional commander, was entirely satisfied with Feilding and ensured that it was Jourdain who was eventually transferred.

Feilding was held in high esteem, not only by senior commanders, but also by his junior officers. Captain CA Brett, one of his Company Commanders, recalled:

> He [Feilding] could always be trusted to be in the middle of the worst trouble the battalion was suffering, and could be trusted to see that the most ridiculous orders of High Command were interpreted in a sensible way. Those who took his place could not. He was a very good CO and a very great man. He was to all appearance, completely fearless, either of German shells or General Officers.[14]

One sentiment which may surprise a modern readership is Feilding's happiness with this extraordinary life, especially during 1915 and 1916. This feeling of well-being, which was often interspersed with sorrow, sprang from the intense camaraderie and selflessness of the trench world. The feeling was not uncommon. Indeed, Graham Greenwell, a Company Commander in the 1/4th Ox and Bucks, made similar comments in his Great War letters, first published in 1935 as *An Infant in Arms*. The mid 1930s was a fiercely pacifist period, and Greenwell was attacked by some reviewers for admitting that he had enjoyed elements of the war. Other letter writers and memorists, like Charles Carrington, Charles Douie and Sidney Rogerson, recorded those same mixed emotions. Sir John Baynes, in his study of morale in the Great War, concluded that stress made the emotions of elation and misery even stronger and 'within an hour, a man could easily say "this is fun" and "this is hell" and genuinely mean it both times'.[15] Reading Feilding's description of his transfer in September 1916, from the Somme to Flanders, as 'like moving from Hell to the Thames Valley in summer-time', we can appreciate his sentiments.

After the disaster that befell the 16th (Irish) Division in the 1918 German Spring Offensive, Feilding's last command was the 1/15th London Regiment (Civil Service Rifles). This appointment came towards the end of the war, and although the 'last hundred days' are often seen as some sort of blessed relief from trench stalemate, in fact the casualties were extremely heavy. Nevertheless, Fielding shows that the 'fighting character' of the British soldier was relentless, and in the end, contributed to the defeat of the German Army.[16]

His description of the relief of Lille in the last weeks of the war is revealing. He was genuinely shocked at the treatment meted out by the Germans to the inhabitants of Lille. Yet to modern readers, reared on later stories of Nazi and Balkan atrocities, this treatment seems almost benign. It demonstrates how totally indiscriminate war has become in two generations.

And when the Armistice finally came, it was not, surprisingly, the focal point as we know the eleventh hour today. To a weary army, it was almost an anticlimax.[17]

After demobilisation Feilding came home to his wife and family. Edith had endured not only four years of worry and fear of losing her husband, but also the very real risks from air raids when she and her family stayed in London.[18] Her joy at her husband's return was muted by the death of both her parents, who had supported her during the war, and who died within a few months of each other in 1919.

As Feilding predicted, life passed quietly after the war. The family moved to Stoke House, near Slough, then in deep countryside, where he involved himself in various business interests. With the explosion of interest in Great War books in the late 1920s, he was approached to publish his letters. A collection of these were published by Medici in 1929 as *War Letters to a Wife*, and received excellent reviews – in a climate hostile to objective views of the Great War. After the plaudits, he was content to retire and devote himself to family life. He always considered himself a fortunate man to have outlived his comrades who were killed – some of 'the dearest and the best' of a generation. He died on 5 September 1945. His devoted wife, Edith, died in 1961.

Jonathan Walker
August 2001

NOTES

1. With three intervals when he was invalided home.
2. A character in Anthony Hope's book, *The Prisoner of Zenda*, is reputed to have been based on a member of the family.
3. The daughters later married: Joan to Major (later Brigadier) Ian Bruce DSO, MBE; Anita to Basil (later Sir Basil) Mostyn; Margaret to Basil Feilding (nephew of Major-General Sir Geoffrey Feilding); Prunella to Major Charles Howard.
4. The Guards Division was not formed until August 1915.
5. It has been calculated that during the Great War, 19% of peers and their sons serving in the Army were killed in action. This rate exceeds even the casualties among peers during the Wars of the Roses, but the effect this had on the great estates, compared to Lloyd George's punitive tax measures, is debatable; see Jay Winter, *The Great War and the British People*, Macmillan, 1985, pp. 98–99.

6. Evelyn Stapleton-Bretherton, Edith's sister, married Prince Gebhardt Blücher von Wahlstatt in 1907. They lived in Berlin and became friends with Casement, who had been a diplomat with von Wahlstatt in Africa. Von Wahlstatt, who had influential contacts, told Casement that he could expect little practical help from the German government for an Irish uprising; see Casement Diary 1689, Casement Papers, National Library of Ireland, Dublin.

7. Captain Hon. TCR 'Tommy' Agar-Robartes (1880–1915); heir to Viscount Clifden of Lanhydrock House, Bodmin, Cornwall; Liberal MP for Bodmin 1906, later unseated; MP for St Austell 1908–1915; Partition of Ireland was first mooted by him in June 1912, when he proposed that the Home Rule Bill should exclude the four Ulster counties; 2nd Lieutenant, Buckinghamshire Yeomanry, 1914; transferred 1 January 1915, 1/Coldstream Guards; Mentioned in Despatches (MID), 1915; died of wounds, 30 September 1915.

8. There were early hopes that Catholics and Protestants could fight together in the same units. But the imperative for both sides to show a tangible and independent contribution to the war proved too strong. While the 16th (Irish) Division and 36th (Ulster) Division fought near each other in 1916, it was not until Messines in June 1917 that they actually fought side by side.

9. Albeit with a reduced Irish element. In June 1917 the 16th (Irish) Division comprised 60% Irish born. By August 1917 the percentage had started to fall; see Nicholas Perry, 'Maintaining Regimental Identity in the Great War: The Case of the Irish Infantry Regiments', in Stand To!, April 1998; also 'Recollections', CA Brett Papers, 7608–40, National Army Museum, London (NAM).

10. Earlier estimates of 49,000 are exaggerated as this figure appears to represent the total killed from Irish Regiments. Those killed, who were Irish born and served in other regiments and colonial armies, as well as Irish regiments, has been put at 27,405 (David Fitzpatrick in Bartlett & Jeffery, eds, A Military History of Ireland 1900–1922, CUP, 1996) and 35,000 (P Casey, 'Irish Casualties in the First World War', Irish Sword, Vol. XX, No. 81, 1997).

11. Even in British publications, these divisions have received scant attention. Despite the inspired editorship of Hugh Dawnay in the 1920s, The Army Quarterly only produced one article on Irish military operations during the period and even during the next forty-five years only two further articles appeared. However, much valuable recent research has been undertaken by Keith Jeffery, Terence Denman and Nicholas Perry.

12. Stuart Cloete, A Victorian Son, Collins, 1972, p. 292.

13. Lieutenant-Colonel HFN Jourdain, Jourdain Diaries, 5603–12, NAM.

14. CA Brett, 'Recollections', Brett Papers 7608–40, NAM.

15. John Baynes, Morale – A Study of Men and Courage, Cassell, 1967, p.6.

16. For a concise assessment of the 'fighting character' of British units in 1918, see Peter Simkins, 'Co-Stars or Supporting Cast? British Divisions in the Hundred Days, 1918', in Paddy Griffith, British Fighting Methods in the Great War, Frank Cass, 1996.

17. This attitude was widespread; see JC Dunn, The War the Infantry Knew 1914–1919, later edition, Jane's Publishing, 1987, p.567.

18. Anita, RCF's second daughter, later recounted her experiences as an 11-year-old during bombing raids in London; see Lynn MacDonald, 1914–1918 Voices and Images of the Great War, Joseph, 1988.

WAR LETTERS TO A WIFE

PART I : 1915

SERVICE WITH THE COLDSTREAM GUARDS

3rd Battalion (29 April–12 May)
1st Battalion (13 May onwards)

29 April 1915 [Harfleur]

We left Windsor the day before yesterday – a draft of 12 officers and 250 men. The regimental band led the way to the station at the foot of the hill, playing lively airs, as is the custom when troops are leaving for the front. A crowd followed, and men and women pressed forward to shake hands with their friends among the men. The latter seemed very cheerful and sang lustily as they marched along.

We left Southampton for Le Havre at 9 pm and berthed at 6.30 yesterday morning. Leaving the docks at 8.10, we marched about 5½ miles to the Reinforcement Camp, where we now are. It was very hot, and after a rough crossing, I think most of the draft found the march rather trying, as they were in heavy marching order. As for myself, it was the first time I had ever carried a pack, and felt as if it was filled with lead before we reached Harfleur. I am glad to learn that, as a Captain, it is not likely that I shall have to carry one again.[1]

3 May 1915 [Le Préol]

On May 1, I left the Base with Geoffrey Fildes, in charge of drafts for three line battalions, and reached Chocques, where we detrained at one o'clock yesterday (Sunday) afternoon.

On marching my draft to the village where the battalion was billeted, I found that, by a coincidence, the latter was being relieved by the 1st Batt. Coldstream Guards,[2] who were preparing to go into the trenches as I arrived. Arthur Egerton[3] and the two other officers of his Company were just sitting down to tea and eggs and asked me to join them, which I was very thankful to do, since it was my first square meal of the day and I was ravenously hungry. Afterwards, I returned to Chocques, where I was lent a motor car by a generous staff officer, which brought me through Bethune to the village of Le Préol, where the 3rd Battalion, to which I have been posted, is billeted.[4]

As I reached the village last evening I met a company of my new battalion returning from the trenches. It is an impressive sight to see for the first time. The men, led by an officer, were marching along the canal

1

bank with the stretcher-bearers bringing up the rear. Their clothes and boots were stained with the clay and dust of the trenches, but the rifles were spotless, as usual, and I thought their faces wore a strained and tired look such as men get when they have been a long time without sleep.

I dare say I shall cease to notice these details when I have been here longer, but I mention them since this, my first direct contact with the war, brought home to me its reality more than anything had done before. I felt I should like those thick-skinned 'home-service' young men of ours to see the sight too. It might perhaps bring home to them their duties and responsibilities.

We are 3 miles behind the firing line and, as I write, one of our heavy guns is blazing away every two or three minutes from close by, making the windows rattle and the ground shake. At night the glimmer of the rockets from the trenches indicates the position of the line, from which the sounds of battle come almost continuously:- the intermittent booming of the artillery, and the crack of rifle and machine-gun:- and yesterday, from 4.30 to 9 pm there was added the distant roar of a heavy cannonade:- our artillery, we have since learned, firing upon the Germans, who had attempted another attack near Ypres, with asphyxiating gas.

The country is looking lovely. All the fruit trees are in blossom and the banks of the railway cuttings are carpeted with primroses and cowslips. Everything looked so peaceful as we came along in the train that it was difficult to realise the war was on until we came within the sound of the guns. Even in this village the French children play about, apparently unconscious of the proximity of danger, and in the cottage where I am billeted there is a considerable family.

Unfortunately for me, Geoffrey[5] had left the battalion just before I joined, having got command of a Brigade. He has been through the recent fighting north of Ypres, and his Brigade is now, I believe, holding the point of the salient. In his place, Torquhil Matheson commands the battalion, and my Company Commander is Vaughan ('Little Man'), while Longueville is in the same Company. Rollo[6], also, is here, looking very fit and well, in spite of eight months of the trenches.

P.S. I have been watching the bombardment by the enemy of three of our aeroplanes which have been flying overhead. The shooting has been going on for half an hour, over a hundred shells having been fired. The sky is studded with little puffs of smoke from the bursting shells, which look like flecks of cotton-wool. Yet the pilots continue to circle round recklessly, in a manner most contemptuous and admirable.

Later – It is just beginning to get dark, and weird. The sky is lighting up from the star-shells which rise constantly from the trenches.

* * *

2

6 May 1915 [Le Préol]

On Tuesday evening, I went into the trenches for the first time and found them in a very sodden condition. Our bit of line ran through the village of Givenchy, practically nothing of which remains now, though the Germans continue to shell it, so that the little that is still standing of the church will soon have disappeared, and even the graves that surround it are giving up their dead.

We relieved the 1st Irish Guards by daylight, my Company being one of the two whose turn it was to man the front line. On either side of me I found relations. On my immediate left Percy Clive[7] commanded a company of Grenadiers, and the Coldstream Company on my right was commanded by Rollo. I visited Percy at 4.30 on the morning after our arrival. The last time I had seen him was at dinner at the House of Commons, and I was very glad to meet him again. While I was shaving, Rollo brought Henry Feilding to see me. He is with a squadron of King Edward's Horse, which is acting as Divisional Cavalry to a Territorial Division near here, and was paying a visit to Rollo in the trenches. You will think I have stumbled into a regular family party.

We were relieved, quite unexpectedly, after twenty-four hours, and ordered to a sector a few hundred yards further to the right, on the other side of the canal, and we spent last night at Le Préol, in our former billets.

6 May 1915 [Cuinchy]

My darling Joan,

Thank you for your letter. Yes, I went into the trenches just a week from the day I left Windsor. The German trench was about 70 yards away for half the distance, and never more than 200 yards away.

Your candles have been most useful. We should have been quite dark in the train without them, and what are left I use in my dug-out in the trenches. You can also tell Anita and Peggy that I use Anita's soap box every day, and I carry Peggy's chocolate in my haversack to eat when I get hungry in the trenches.

It is funny living underground. Perhaps, someday, when the war is over, I will take you to France, and show you where these lines of trenches were.

Best love, darling, to all of you. God bless you.

8 May 1915 [Cuinchy Brickstacks]

At 3.15 on the afternoon of the 6th, we fell in and marched to the Cuinchy Brickstacks. Some of these are held by the enemy and some by us, and our new trenches run between them.

Since I last wrote I have been transferred from No. 3 to No. 2 Company, which is commanded by Captain Guy Darell[8]. The other officers are Ernest Platt, Lord Ipswich[9], and Palmer. It was my new Company's turn for the firing line.

It is a tricky bit of trench, there being much sapping and mining from both sides. In the Company's section alone we have six saps, three of which are also mined and charged with high explosive, and the German miners, from their side, are suspected of being actually beneath us at one spot.

Two of our saps run to within 5 or 6 yards of a big mine crater, occupied by the enemy, between which and our No. 6 sap, a duel of hand grenades took place yesterday morning, supplemented by trench-mortar bombs and rifle grenades. It was a noisy affair that lasted about an hour and a half, but was harmless in so far as we were concerned. It was a blind fight at close range in the dark, so to speak, since neither side could see the other.

Many of the German hand grenades failed to explode, so it was possible to examine them. They are barbarous looking things – the shape and size of big square hairbrushes – the kind that has a handle, with a long jagged iron bolt wired on at each corner.

The dead that lie unburied between the trenches are becoming a source of trouble now that the hot weather is setting in. Many have lain there for months. At nights such of them as can be reached are fetched in and buried, or in some cases are covered with chloride of lime. Last night I saw it being done. It is a sickening job.

This morning, I paid a visit to the French who hold the trenches on our immediate right, and returned to my Company in time to receive my baptism of shell-fire. Thirty-six 'Jack Johnsons', spread over an hour and twenty minutes, were dropped upon us. The enemy started with our fire-trench, of which he showed that he had the range, repeatedly only just missing it, and obtaining at least one direct hit which blew in the parapet alongside the spot where Ipswich and I happened to be standing.

I confess the sensation is far from comfortable. You hear the shell from the moment it leaves the howitzer, and you can have no idea of the long time it takes to come, or of the weird scream it makes in doing so. When at last it bursts and you know that the danger is over, at any rate for the moment, there comes a highly satisfactory feeling of exhilaration and relief.

I was covered with showers of earth and dust time after time, and once was hit on the head by a big lump of dry clay. Ipswich, though he was not actually hit, was rather nearer than I to the shell which fell in the trench alongside of us, and has been a good deal shaken by it.

This afternoon, walking along the fire-trench, I came upon one of our bombers on the ground. A bomb had that moment exploded in his hand and blown off both his hands and forearms. He died in about twenty minutes. These bombs explode four seconds after lighting the fuse, and there is a tendency among the men to hold on for a second or two before throwing them, so that they cannot be used by the enemy to throw back again. It is a risky practice.

4

Later in the afternoon my Company was relieved from the fire-trench, and we moved some 300 yards back into support. Here we received orders for a great combined French and British attack, to be delivered tomorrow.

10 May 1915 [Cuinchy Brickstacks]

The orders for yesterday were that the 1st Division would attack on our left; the French on our right. We (the 4th Guards Brigade) were, at all costs, to hold the intervening sector, where it was considered probable that a counterattack would be delivered; and we were given to understand that we must rely upon ourselves alone. The artillery was to begin wire-cutting at 4.45 am in co-operation with the machine-guns. Infantry fire was to open at 5.40 am.

About 3.30 am, an English aeroplane flew very low over our lines and was met by a heavy fusillade of rifle-fire from the enemy, which brought it down between the trenches, close to the Germans. As it crashed, the latter raised a cheer and threw bombs at the machine, which burst into flames, burning the two occupants, who were probably already dead or dying.

Punctually, at 4.45 am, our artillery on the left opened fire, and, after two hours or more of continuous bombardment, the British attack was launched. A battalion of the Rifle Brigade (4th Corps) succeeded in rushing the first German trench and passing beyond it, but in their impetuosity, they passed over the dug-outs in which many of the enemy were taking shelter.

The latter came out when the first wave had passed over, and succeeded in holding the second wave which was not expecting opposition from this quarter, as well as cutting off the men who had gone forward.

On their right the 1st Division got hung up in the barbed wire, which the preliminary bombardment had failed to cut. Indeed, the shrapnel, which had been chiefly employed for wire-cutting purposes, had proved a hopeless failure, as also had the machine-guns (who could have expected otherwise?), and when our troops reached the wire they found it intact, and the enemy's trenches, which had been steadily reinforced in anticipation of the infantry assault, manned almost shoulder to shoulder.

The attack was repeated in the afternoon in glorious sunny weather after a second bombardment of two hours duration. On this occasion a Company of the 1st Black Watch reached the German fire-trench, and an officer with a few men got well beyond it, but there was heavy resistance. The survivors had to fall back after severe hand-to-hand fighting, and at the close of the day our line was as it had been in the morning.

The French, simultaneously, made a series of attacks on our right, preceded by a heavy bombardment. In fact, the roar of their artillery continued the whole of yesterday and a great part of last night. The rumour is that they have met with some success, particularly in the neighbourhood of Loos.

12 May 1915 [La Tombe Willot]

The battalion was relieved this afternoon by the Gloucesters and marched to La Tombe Willot, a short distance north of Locon, where we are billeted for the night, and shall take off our clothes for the first time for a week and sleep in sleeping-bags. The distance was about 6 miles, and we carried packs!

As we came through Le Préol we passed our 1st and 2nd Battalions. It was the first time in history that the three Coldstream battalions have met together on active service.

13 May 1915 [Le Préol]

Guy Darell (my Company Commander) and I have been transferred to the 1st Battalion[10], and this morning Darell said goodbye to the Company which was drawn up for the purpose. As he left, the men gave him three cheers, and then did the same for myself:- which I appreciated very much, having regard to the very short time I had spent with them.

Afterwards, Darell's eldest brother[11], who is on the Staff of the 7th Division, sent a car for us, which brought us to his Divisional Head-quarters at Hinges, where we lunched, and where I sat between General Heyworth[12] and Lord Bury, both of the Scots Guards. The elder Darell then motored us to Beuvry, from where we walked to Le Préol and joined our new battalion. The latter is commanded by Colonel John Ponsonby[13].

Each trench at Cuinchy is labelled with the name of some familiar London street, such as Dover Street, Half-Moon Street, Hanover Street, Edgware Road, Marylebone Road, Birdcage Walk. Even Leicester Square is represented. At the cross-roads (or rather cross-trenches) are signboards 'To London' or 'To Berlin'.

Where bricks are procurable – and that is almost anywhere since scarcely a house remains standing – the floors of the trenches have been paved with bricks. Here and there in the sides of the trenches or behind a brick stack, in fact wherever the situation has been considered suitable, dug-outs have been made, of varying stability, with roofs, some of which are strong enough almost to stand a direct hit from a light shell, while others would scarcely stop a splinter.

Some of the dug-outs bear fancy names, such as 'The Guards Club', 'Sylvan Villa', and so on. There are, or were, numerous villages and farm buildings scattered about the area where we are fighting. All are gone now. The churches in particular have been shelled to ruins. It is curious, nevertheless, how sometimes the holy statues have survived the wreckage. Two still stand on their niches in the roofless walls of Cuinchy Church, and, at a point where the communication trench passes an old cemetery, the great crucifix which dominates every graveyard in this part of France still stands intact against the sky, amid its shattered surroundings. I shall never forget the first time I saw it. I had plodded along many hundreds of yards of the communication trench, seeing nothing but the bricked floor and the clay walls – for there was nothing else to see. Then something above me caught my eye and I looked up, and saw this great crucifix towering above the trench, and facing me.

One of my duties is to censor the men's letters home. It is a duty I do not like at all, but it gives me an insight into the simple minds of the great majority of the writers. There are no heroics. And almost every letter begins and ends with the same formula: 'Dear Sister' (for example), 'I hope this finds you as it leaves me at present, in the pink'; and, at the end, are numerous children's kisses.

14 May 1915 [Bethune]

My new battalion was in reserve during the attack of last Sunday, and was lucky in having only twenty-one casualties. It has not always been so fortunate. Indeed, since the war began, its casualties have already reached 2,600 or nearly three times the full strength of the battalion. It has been badly cut up on four occasions – on the Aisne in September, at Givenchy in December, at Cuinchy in January, and it was almost annihilated last October at Gheluvelt, in front of Ypres, when, there being no other officer left, Boyd, the Quartermaster, brought the battalion out of action.[14]

It is still very short of officers, and was resting when I joined yesterday. Nevertheless, shortly after my arrival, we got orders to march at 9 pm for Bethune, which we reached about 11.30, and from where I write.

16 May 1915 (Sunday) [Sailly Labourse]

This morning Darell and I rode with the Colonel (John Ponsonby) to reconnoitre the trenches in front of Vermelles, which our Brigade has just taken over from the French. We found the left section manned by the 1st Cameron Highlanders, the centre by the London Scottish, and the right by the 1st Scots Guards. The German trenches are a long way off – quite 500 yards away in places.

There seems to have been a sort of tacit 'live and let live' arrangement between the enemy and the French, who, as you know, have several hundred miles of battle front to defend, and are probably not sorry when the opportunity occurs to do a bit of it on the cheap. Indeed, it is very necessary. At any rate John Ponsonby told us today that the French commander had assured him that it was a quiet sector, and had added, jokingly, 'We are very good friends here – the Bosche and ourselves. We never shoot at them, and they never shoot at us!' I wonder how long this 'Utopia' will last, now that we have come here? Our line, compared with that of the French, is short, and consequently every yard of it is strenuous.

*   *   *

20 May 1915 [Le Rutoire]

Last night after dark we relieved the 1st Scots Guards in the trenches east of Vermelles. My Company is in the reserve trenches for the moment, my headquarters being in a dug-out made by the French.

The exterior construction of this dug-out amounts to nothing, and would not stop anything heavier than a whizzbang, if that, but much care has been devoted to its interior decoration, which resembles that of a cottage parlour. The French are much more thorough in these matters than we are. It has a door, two windows with muslin curtains, a little fireplace with wax flowers on the mantelpiece, papered walls and ceiling, a boarded floor, a little crucifix, a big looking-glass, a sketch and poem by a former occupant nailed upon the wall. You must not suppose that all dug-outs are like it. Those in the fire-trench are, as a rule, only just large enough for one or two men to crawl into and lie down side by side.

Scattered about us are little graveyards – French and German; and now we are starting our own. Those of the French are easily recognisable, owing to the custom of placing the dead soldier's cap on his grave or perched above it on a stick. The grass is growing long and is beginning to hide the older graves. It is thick with all the wild flowers of an English spring – dandelions, thistles, daisies and buttercups.

Today has been fairly quiet for us, except for some shelling which killed two NCOs. We also had a man wounded by rifle fire. On our left, however, there was heavy shelling during the late evening.

We heard officially today of the Government's decision to retaliate on the enemy with asphyxiating gases. Every first opinion that I have heard is strongly opposed to this on the principle that two wrongs do not make a right, and we should do better to keep our hands clean, and partially I agree.[15]

Today the weather is beautiful, though lately it has been miserably cold and wet, and we have longed for the sun again. The lilac was lovely till the rain came; the country is full of it.

22 May 1915 [Fire-trench in front of Le Rutoire]

Tonight there has been another heavy bombardment on the French sector to our right. It was already dark when it began, and while the firing was at its height a thunder storm got up, producing an effect that was wonderfully vivid and inspiring. The forks of lightning mingled with the flashes from the guns, bursting shrapnel and the Véry lights, while the roar of the bombardment was punctuated and occasionally drowned by the loud crashes of the thunder. There then followed torrential rain, which soaked the men to the skin.

It is a healthy life and I have never felt better. It is worry that kills, and we have no worry here. We have practically no sickness. Do you remember the outrageous sick-lists at Putney? We have no sick-list here.

The men are quite wonderful, always cheerful under the most trying conditions; sleeping, when not in the trenches, crowded in such accommodation as can be got in a barn, or a cow-stall, or a loft. Sometimes their boots are so bad that their toes stick out, but they just laugh and patch them up with newspaper or cardboard, and carry on.

Our present trenches are largely in chalk – the most fascinating stuff to carve with a jack-knife – and it is like visiting an art gallery to walk through them. Model prayer books and hymn books and slabs of chalk carved with the regimental crest. The Star of the Garter and other devices adorn the parapet. There is also much doggerel, too long to quote, and bits of philosophy that show the trend of the men's minds, all written in that purple ink which is produced from a mixture of indelible pencil and spit.

Looking over the parapet, across No Man's Land, we see the German wire, and, a few feet beyond it, an irregular, built-up line of sandbags. That is the German parapet. These German sandbags are conspicuous by the diversity of their colouring. Some are jet-black; others almost snow-white. Some of the material used looks more as if it had been designed for petticoats than sandbags.

30 May 1915 [Support Trench, Le Rutoire]
Out in No Man's Land, close to the German line, grows a tree, which, though small and insignificant, is the only object in the broad and desolate and otherwise treeless space between the German trenches and our own. This tree, therefore, has achieved a notoriety which it most certainly would never have done otherwise. It is known as the 'Lone Tree' and, I dare say, is as famous among the Germans as among our troops. Last night a patrol of No. 1 Company, which was engaged in examining the enemy's wire, bumped suddenly into a hostile advanced post near it, and lost two killed, while a third man was wounded, but was got away.

Today has been very quiet. I lunched at Battalion Headquarters in the cellar under the ruins of Le Rutoire farm, and ate plovers' eggs from home.

31 May 1915 [Support Trench, Le Rutoire]
We have orders to hand over, tomorrow, to the 140th Brigade (London Territorials). We shall then have been five days in the trenches, and I shall be glad to get my boots off.

1 June 1915 [Le Rutoire]
I have been writing to the parents of a man in my Company who was killed this evening by shrapnel. He was a good lad but was where he should not have been. That is the trouble. They get incurably careless. His brother was with him when it happened. The two were inseparable.

10.45 pm. I have just returned from the burial of Private _____.
Arthur Egerton read the funeral service. The friends lowered the body,

9

wrapped in a blanket, into a grave which had been dug behind Le Rutoire farm. The poor brother sobbed on his knees by the grave side, while the guns flashed and boomed in the darkness. It is such sights as this that blot out the romantic and bring home the cruel side of war.

10 June 1915 [Bethune]

Ralph Burton was hit by a shell on the evening of the 5th, and Johnston being on leave, I was left without a single other officer, till Woods[16] – a young Canadian who joined the battalion the same afternoon – was posted to my Company.

Our withdrawal from the trenches and the subsequent long rest has given rise to many rumours as to our destiny, and has suggested a 'fattening for the slaughter', as it is commonly called; in short, that we are to take part in a fresh 'push' that is believed to be pending.

11 June 1915 [Cuinchy]

My dearest Joan,

I am sending you each a poppy to put in your prayer-books. There are masses of them growing just behind my trench, beside the ruins of a farmhouse which is the centre of my position. There are also roses growing there. It must have been the garden before the war came and everything was abandoned and destroyed. But where the roses grow, there are also many bullets, and it would be foolish in daytime, to go and pick them. I did try but gave it up.

Will you thank Grannyma for the translation of the French verse, and give her my love.

We have been having very heavy rain, and the trenches are full of mud. As I came into these trenches last night, the mud was just like very thick soup. I thought of Anita and Peggy, and thought it was good mud wasted. How they would have loved it. If only you could hear the sounds I hear as I write this. The Germans are sending over big shells and trench mortar bombs and rifle grenades and bullets.

Much love to all at Rainhill.[17]

12 June 1915 [Cuinchy]

Since I was here with the 3rd Battalion last month, the enemy has blown two mines – one alongside the other under our fire-trench, immediately north of Hanover Street.

When we were here before, the German miners could be heard burrowing at this point from one of the underground listening posts. Yet, somehow, they succeeded in getting their mine off first, with a cost to our side of ten miners and a listener killed underground, in addition to the infantry – probably twenty or more – who were manning the trench above.

The external visible result of the explosion is the total extinction of the trench for a length of about 50 yards, and its substitution by an enormous double crater. The incident took place about five days before we took over, since when all endeavours to repair the damage by digging round the lip of the crater have been frustrated, with considerable loss of life, owing to the bombing activity of the enemy, who is not more than 30 yards away.

I must say that I do not think the battalion we relieved was in a condition to take the initiative. It had suffered heavily in the recent attacks, was still only about half strength, and was commanded by the Adjutant, the Colonel having been killed.[18]

They were considerably dejected when I first saw them, and, together with the battalion on their right, were enduring what must be regarded as heavy casualties in the ordinary routine of trench warfare. The latter had just lost between forty and fifty men in a single day.

Without questioning the gallantry of these battalions, which ought to have been resting after their heavy trials instead of holding a very tricky piece of line, I should say that the enemy had got the upper hand. He was punishing them immediately and unmercifully for any small liberty they might take by way of retaliation.

14 June 1915 [Cuinchy Support Trench]

Johnston got a stray bullet through the leg last night (what the men would call a 'cushy' or 'blighty' one), so I am again with only one subaltern in the Company.

15 June 1915 [Cuinchy]

Today, at 1.30 pm, the Company Commanders were sent for by the Commanding Officer to his headquarters in Cambrin village, just behind here, and given preliminary orders for an attack which is to be delivered by the Brigade, though only in the event of the success of an operation (which takes place today on the other side of the canal, to our left) involving the capture of the high ground round Violaines.

My Company is to open the 'Ball' for the Brigade by seizing the Railway Triangle; after which the other companies will advance on the right, and capture the Brickstacks, etc. My 'jumping off' position will be in the fire-trench facing the Triangle, with my left on the canal – that is to say, in front of the famous 'Hollow', where Michael O'Leary won his VC[19]. This evening I have been looking at the objective with Captain Forrester, of the Black Watch, whose battalion is holding the front line opposite.

The bombardment by our artillery preparatory to the attack continued throughout today, and at 5 pm 'Mother','Grandmother', and other heavy howitzers and guns concentrated on the Brickstacks in front of us. At the same time our bombardment of the German trenches to the left of the canal became intense, continuing so till six o'clock, when the infantry were timed to go over the top.

11

The moment of the assault was signalised by the 'blowing' of a mine, after which all was hell and fury for two hours, when the firing slackened and continued on a reduced scale throughout the night.

These are thrilling experiences which make all things else fade into insignificance. How the men and masters, who, in spite of the critical times, are striking and squabbling at home, can belong to the same race as these heroic fellows here, beats me altogether. Over and over again it is the soldiers' duty to charge against barbed wire into almost certain death. Often no one comes back. Yet there is never any hesitation or questioning. I tell you that, as an onlooker on this occasion, when the guns were lifted, and from the burst of rifle and machine-gun fire I knew that the time had come for the rush over the parapet and across the open, it brought home to me this mighty contrast.

The old garden belonging to the dilapidated ruin which serves as my Company Headquarters is gaily asserting itself, and though thick with weeds and torn with shell-fire, the rose-trees and sweet-williams and other plants are bright with blossom; and No Man's Land is ablaze with scarlet poppies.

16 June 1915 [Cuinchy]

This morning I took Woods (my very gallant young subaltern whose duty it will be to lead the advanced platoons if the attack takes place), my Company Sergeant-Major Hill, and the platoon sergeants, to reconnoitre, or rather to look over the parapet, at our objective.

On arrival at the front line Company Headquarters, the first thing I learnt was that Forrester, who showed me round yesterday, had been killed by a sniper shortly after I left him. I remember him saying, while he was pointing out the features of the Railway Triangle, that it was quite safe to expose oneself while our shells were falling as thick as they were at that time, since the enemy must certainly be taking cover; and he and I, in consequence, stood upright on the fire-step for quite a time.

The more you look at this Cuinchy Triangle the worse it looks. The problem is anything but a joke really, but so hopeless is it universally regarded by those who know the Triangle, that it is treated as a sort of joke, and there is considerable chaff about it. 'Nipper' Poynter – a Major of the 1st Scots Guards – said to me when the orders first came out: 'The only chance you have is that the attack on the left of the canal may fail.' As a matter of fact it did fail yesterday, but they are going to have another try today. I am told that the Canadians, who made the assault on the immediate left of the canal, captured three lines of trenches, without casualties. Yet, this morning, out of a battalion, there are left only a major and sixty men, the rest having been knocked out during the night by bombs and shell-fire.

Apparently, more than one thing went wrong. The troops on the left of the attack seem to have been hung up, and there was also a hitch about the mine which synchronised with the first forward rush of the infantry. This mine unexpectedly blew back through the gallery leading to it, at the mouth of which were congregated the bombers as well as their reserve of bombs. All were destroyed, with the result that when the enemy counter-attacked, bombing along the captured trenches, there was no one to meet them except the riflemen, who were rapidly reduced, to a negligible quantity, and the few survivors that were left were compelled to fall back.[20]

17 June 1915 [Bethune]

The shelling of the German lines to the left of the canal began again yesterday afternoon at 3.30 o'clock. About 4.20, the bombardment became intense, and half an hour later, or less, the guns were lifted, and the attack was repeated. The storm of rifle and machine-gun fire that followed told us that once again the infantry had gone over the parapet and were making their wild rush across the poppies.

Again the attack failed, and as we left the trenches, having been relieved by a territorial battalion of the King's Liverpool Regiment, the small-arms fire was dying away, though the after-shelling continued fast and furious.

Then we marched to Bethune, where we billeted for the night;– the men in the local barracks, and the officers scattered about in different houses. It was a luxury to have one's boots off for the first time for six days and nights, to wash off the dirt, and to sleep in a bed with sheets.

23 June 1915 [Bethune]

We await orders to move, and in the meantime the battalion has been providing digging parties for the new Reserve defences that are under construction.

Today, I marched a party of my Company which had been detailed for this work to Cambrin, the little village behind Cuinchy, about a mile from the firing line. The village is much battered by shell-fire, but the church – I suppose because it is hidden behind trees – has escaped, except for a couple of shell-holes through the roof.

In the churchyard I found the graves of Senhouse and Brabazon, both of the Coldstream, who were killed last week.

The fields around are carpeted with cornflowers and poppies and were bathed in sunshine today, and as it was quiet in the line everything seemed very peaceful. I wandered backwards and forwards between the different places where the work was going on. In almost any direction one stumbles upon little and sometimes large groups of graves. I was reading the names, today, on the wooden crosses of one of these, when four stretcher bearers brought along a dead soldier of the Regiment, to bury him. He had been considerably broken by a shell. He was small, and was covered except for his legs. You could see just the puttees and part of his trousers and the crinkled-up marching boots as he lay upon his stretcher. It was a simple enough funeral – without parson or prayers or any paraphernalia – but for all that, coming upon me suddenly as it did, this funeral struck me as more impressive than most that I have seen, and made me feel a great respect for those who have given up their lives in the way that this little man had given his.

28 June 1915 [Burbure]

I overhear many funny conversations as I ride or march in front of the Company, and, though these are not always of the most edifying order, I must write down one. It was raining, and one of the men, feeling very miserable, was holding forth on the hardships of a soldier's life. 'I wish my father had never met my mother,' he said. There was silence for a moment; then a voice came softly from behind: 'Perhaps he didn't'.

13 July 1915 [Vermelles]

We came out of the trenches a few hours ago, and are in reserve, among the ruins of Vermelles. My two subalterns and I have just returned from roaming through what remains of the village. It amuses them (they are very, _very_ young), when they find a wobbly piece of wall still standing, to push it over, and certainly the game is rather fascinating, especially when the piece of wall happens to be high.

We explored the battered skeleton of the old church. The roof has collapsed and now litters the floor, mixed with the loose stones from the shattered walls. Strewed among the debris are broken chairs, confessionals, screens and pieces of priests' vestments, ragged and rotting. The Figure of Christ has been shot from the great crucifix or rood that hung before the sanctuary, and lies in bits upon the ground. The side altars have been demolished. The door has been torn from the tabernacle. Every particle of the church furniture has been gutted. Yet one thing alone remains intact, or practically so. This is a recumbent statue in marble of Our Lord which lies beneath the High Altar. Though a shell has actually passed through the centre of the altar that covers it, the Figure remains unharmed, except for a tiny fragment chipped from the beard. Even the fingers are perfect.

17 July 1915 [Right fire-trench opposite the Lone Tree]

Last night, the wind was blowing directly to us from the German lines, and at just about the right velocity for gassing. On our left the night started with a furious burst of fire, accompanied by a firework display that would have attracted attention even at the Crystal Palace.

The shooting was taken up by the enemy on our immediate front, and flights of their bullets came whistling overhead as I stood on the parapet, setting the men to their digging. It soon died away, but the general eeriness of such a night affects the men. They do not work with their usual vigour. They are wet through and uncomfortable, and they keep glancing over the parapet, while the covering party lying in the long grass in front shoots freely at whatever arouses its slightest suspicion.

20 July 1915 [Bethune]

At ten last night we were relieved and marched to Bethune, where, at 2.30 am, I got into an exceedingly comfortable bed in a house with a lovely garden, in which the owner – a kindly old Frenchman – takes the most lively interest. He showed me round the garden this morning. He made it all himself. Even the trees, which now are big, he saw planted fifty years ago.

He has a fascinating outdoor aviary which leans against an angle of the house. In it are quantities of canaries and other birds – Californian partridges, a Cardinal bird, etc.; and in a separate place he has thrushes, caught in the garden, to which he whistles, and which sing to him in return. There are some very ingenious contrivances for feeding the birds and for them to nest in, and there is a curious little passage by which the bantams, of which there are several, can leave the aviary and walk out into the back yard, where they scrape and scratch about.

The Germans have been shelling Bethune daily of late, and heavily. No doubt they would argue that the women and children ought to have been evacuated long ago, but it makes my blood boil to see this useless and vindictive shelling of the towns that the enemy has initiated.

This morning, as I looked out of the window, some fifty children were playing on an open space outside. Suddenly, the shells began to fall. There was immediately a general scuttle of the children to their mothers and their homes, but two little ones were killed. It is dreadful to think that men can drop shells callously on such surroundings.

This afternoon, the shelling was repeated. My host's old wife was out shopping at the time, which naturally made him anxious. I went down and talked to him in the garden, and he took me and showed me a shell crater just over his garden wall, made the day before yesterday.

23 July 1915 [Bethune]

Yesterday was a bad day here in Bethune. In the morning, at bombing practice, one of our officers was wounded slightly. In the afternoon, while practising with a trench mortar, three were killed and four or five wounded, the former including Mitchell, of the Black Watch, who took on Carpentier, the French boxer, last year.

In the evening there were in the town 128 casualties to our troops from shell-fire, including three men of ours. A great many casualties were caused by a shell which burst in the 'Ecole des jeunes filles', which we use as a barrack. I passed the door with John Ponsonby as they were bringing them out. Certainly, this place is becoming very unhealthy, and I wish the civilians would clear out. Yesterday, I am told, a woman and two children were killed.

The old man and his wife with whom I am billeted still cling on, though I doubt if they will stand it much longer. The poor old lady – a dear and very fat – sits down palpitating, each time the shells begin to fly, and counts them.

RCF goes on leave 1–5 August 1915, visiting his family, who are staying at Rainhill.

7 August 1915 [Bethune]

On my return from leave, on the 5th, I found the battalion just finishing a tour in the trenches in front of Cambrin, immediately south of the La Bassée road.

Two officers had joined during my absence. One – Captain Gregge-Hopwood[21] – had taken over the command of No. 1 Company, whose former commander, Digby, has come to me. The other, Dermot Browne[22], had been commanding my Company during my absence.

The trenches which the battalion was holding (Cambrin, Z2) were new to us, and were very lively; and the contrast between the peaceful life I was leading with you and the children last Wednesday and my occupation the following day and night could scarcely have been greater. Nowhere along the whole front are the Germans and ourselves more close together than there. Twelve to fifteen yards was all that separated us in the advanced portions of the trench, and the ground between was a shapeless waste – a mass of mine-craters, including two so large that they are known officially as Etna and Vesuvius.

The ragged aspect of this advanced trench I cannot picture to you. The hundreds of bombs which explode in and around it each day and night have reduced it to a state of wild dilapidation that is indescribable. There is not a sandbag that is not torn to shreds, and the trench itself is half filled by the earth and debris that have dribbled down. So shallow and emaciated has this bit of trench now become that you have to stoop low or your head and shoulders poke above the parapet, and so near are you to the enemy that you have to move in perfect silence. The slightest visible movement brings a hail of bullets from the snipers, and the slightest sound, a storm of hand grenades.

I did a bit of bombing myself during the thirty hours I was there – a rather different occupation to our tea-party in the grotto at Rainhill! Who would have imagined, two years ago, that I should actually so soon be throwing bombs like an anarchist?

Tommy Robartes'[23] Company has a band, and, the night before my arrival, being the anniversary of the declaration of war, he tried a 'ruse de guerre'. The band was posted in a sap leading from the fire-trench, and, at six minutes to midnight, opened with 'Die Wacht am Rhein'. It continued with 'God Save the King' and 'Rule Britannia', each tune being played for two minutes. Then, as the last note sounded, every bomber in the battalion, having been previously posted on the fire-step, and the grenade-firing rifles, trench-mortars, and bomb-throwing machine, all having registered during the day, let fly simultaneously into the German trench; and, as this happened, the enemy, who had very readily swallowed the bait, were clapping their hands and loudly shouting 'encore'.

On the evening of my arrival I tried to get into conversation with the enemy, as they had been very talkative the previous day, but they were disinclined to be drawn. The experience of the night before had evidently upset them, and we had also given them a severe 'strafing' during the day, which did not help matters. And at 10 pm, No. 2 Company band once more gave a recital. But there were no 'encores' this time, and no applause. When the band had exhausted their stock of tunes, they sang, but all was unavailing; their efforts were ignored.

Even Chapman – one of the Company wits – failed to get a reply. I tried a London Scottish machine-gunner who spoke German, and he could get no answer till he asked whether they had orders from their officers not to speak to us: when someone answered in a coy kind of way so that we could not hear what he said. My impression was that he had been promptly silenced from behind.

In these conversations the soldiers on both sides address one another as 'kamarade', or 'Tommy' or 'Fritz'. On the whole, the remarks made to men of my Company during the three days they were in these trenches were vacuous but rather amusing. Once the Germans called out 'Coldstream form fours': so they apparently knew who was opposed to them. Another time one of our men called, 'Do you know a man called Cooper?' It was just one of the catch sentences you so often hear out here, but the reply came: 'Yes, he's here'. One of our men asked: 'Aren't you sick of it, Fritz?' and got the answer: 'Yes, aren't you?' Another man shouted: 'Wouldn't you like to have peace?' to which the reply was: 'We aren't ready for peace, but let's have it tonight!'

Then they asked if we had lost a corporal who had been born at _____. This was a corporal of the Scots Guards who had crawled to the edge of one of the craters the night before we relieved his battalion, and had been bombed and killed at a range of two or three yards. His Captain, Harold Cuthbert[24], who is a very gallant fellow, had subsequently crawled out and collected some of his private belongings. Drury Lowe, of the same regiment, told me today he had heard that the Germans had put up a notice saying that they had buried this man properly. I cannot vouch for this, but the body had disappeared by the time I arrived from the very prominent position it had occupied on the lip of the crater.

And they also put up a notice board, which I saw, saying, 'Warschau is our' [sic] – which, I am afraid, is true. The men tried to shoot this down and eventually the rain washed it off.[25]

I enclose some weed which I got among the ruins of Cambrin. I picked it yesterday as I came out of the communication trench, after being relieved. It is 'Flos Crucis', or the flower of the Cross, so Egerton has told me. The legend is that it grew beneath the Cross, and the black spots are supposed to represent the stains of our Lord's blood.

16 August 1915 [Reserve Trenches, Le Rutoire]

The Brigadier (General Lowther) turned up suddenly in my dug-out this morning at 8.20. I was in bed, with my feet in sandbags to keep them warm. I had been up during the night. He told me that we are going back to the other side of St. Omer on the 23rd, to form a Guards Division.[26] He also said that the other day the Germans at Givenchy are reported to have called out: 'When are you ****** Guardsmen going to St. Omer? When you do, we are going to have these trenches back.'

26 August 1915 [Lumbres]

We marched from Vermelles on the 22nd, led by the battalion drums and fifes, which played for the first time during the war.

It was our final exit from the 1st Division, and General Rawlinson, the Corps Commander, and other Generals, stood by the roadside to see us off. As we passed them the band of the 1st Black Watch, with whom the 1st Coldstream has been brigaded since the war began, played us out. Colonel John fell out as we reached the Corps Commander and waited beside him. He told me later that he had never seen the battalion march past better, though he added: 'He didn't say much, **** him!' – I believe he (Rawlinson) seldom does say much on these occasions.

The heat was oppressive and the march was trying, and the packs are heavy, and the men's feet soft after the trenches. Besides, the boots often do not fit: they are in many cases the resoled boots of other men. No. 4 Company marched well. The Company feeling is strong. When they saw others fall out the men cried: 'Stick it, No. 4'.

What is going to happen next none of us know. There are bound to be lots of changes due to the organisation of the new Guards Division. If it is my lot to go elsewhere, I shall be sorry but not surprised. I have already overstayed the average. Before I came, No. 4 Company ran through, I believe, six Captains in six months. Anyhow, whatever happens, it will be nice to remember that I have commanded a company of Coldstreamers for over three months of the war. And they have been very happy months indeed.

At times I have felt some feeling of despondency and isolation, since I am an old man compared to the boys with whom I associate. But I have, I think, got on well with them, and I have had unswerving support from one and all, and there is much satisfaction in that.

RCF goes on leave, 7–11 September 1915.

13 September 1915 [Lumbres]
Returning from leave, the day before yesterday, they made everybody on the boat wear cork waistcoats, which, from force of habit, the men called 'respirators', and which is an innovation, designed of course to combat torpedoes and floating mines.

As usual, we landed at Boulogne, from which place the less experienced among the officers are wont to come up to the line by the night 'leave' trains – a very wearisome way of doing the journey I should imagine, although the orthodox way. We considered ourselves superior to 'leave' trains, and decided to spend a comfortable night at the Louvre Hotel and to chance finding a car in the morning.

16 September 1915 [Lumbres]
This morning Lord Cavan, who commands the newly formed Guards Division, reviewed the 2nd Brigade. Although he is a 'dug-out', he has a tremendous vogue, and induces quite extraordinary confidence among all ranks. We formed up in mass in a flat meadow by the brook here, and John Ponsonby, who is now Brigadier, sat on his horse in front and gave the order for the General Salute to the whole Brigade, which was very effective. We then marched past in column of half-companies, to the Divisional Band, the Coldstream in rear.

It was a memorable occasion. Two out of the four battalions, as you know, have been right through the war, and might almost have been excused had they got rusty in ceremonial: yet Cavan said he had often seen ceremonial in London after months of practice done not half so well; and he ought to know. The Prince of Wales was there.

Yesterday, the Corps Commander (General Haking) came over and met the officers and some of the NCOs of the Brigade, and told them about some stirring events which are about to happen. The meeting took place in my Company's drill field.[27]

He spoke very confidently, comparing the German line to the crust of a pie, behind which, once broken, he said, there is not much resistance to be expected. He ended up by saying, 'I don't tell you this to cheer you up. I tell it you because I really believe it.'

As he spoke of 'pie-crust' I looked at the faces around me, and noticed a significant smile on those of some of the older campaigners who have already 'been through it'.

Digby left No. 4 Company yesterday to take over the command of No. 3, and Charles Noel[28] has come to me in his place. So now I have Noel, Philipson, and Heathcote[29].

25 September 1915 [Houchin]

By the time you get this you will have heard that a great combined French and British attack was launched today. As we came within sight of the drifting battle smoke and looked upon the familiar flat landscape and the great cone shaped spoil heaps of the coal mines which stand up like the Pyramids against the sky, a message from Lord Cavan was passed round. It said 'that we were on the eve of the greatest battle in history'– 'that future generations depended on the result of it' – and 'that great things are expected from the Guards Division'. Later, we received the splendid news that our troops had broken through the German line and taken Hulluch, Loos, and Cite de St. Elie; all places that we have looked towards so long from the trenches in front of Vermelles.[30]

The road was frequently blocked, and halts were numerous. We met many ambulances returning with wounded, and once I had to halt my Company to allow a party of English and Indian troops to pass who had succumbed to our own gas. The 1st Cavalry Brigade overtook us at the trot on their way towards the break. It is really exciting, this wild rush towards the enemy, to exploit today's advantage.

The roads were very muddy, the rain heavy, and the day has been a hard one; but the men are in fine spirit. A private of my Company, when asked if he could manage the last few miles, said: 'If we can't do it on our feet, we'll do it on our hands and knees.' They are looking forward to a scrap in the open, when they know, man for man, that they can beat the Germans.

2 October 1915 [Verquineul]

My silence during the greater part of the past week will, I am afraid, have caused you anxiety, but it has been quite impossible to write. Our experiences during these days have been wonderfully exciting, and the results have been to some extent satisfactory: but we have seen much of the ghastly side of war, and our losses have been heavy – about 300 out of the battalion, including 13 officers, seven of whom are dead.[31]

We are now taking a 'breather', with so few officers that Company messes have been dispensed with, and those of us that are left mess together.

I am fit and well, my only 'adventure', apart from a blackened toe nail caused by a splinter of shell, having been a shrapnel bullet, which, after passing through a fat bundle of letters which I luckily had in my pocket, made a hole through the book containing my Company roll, and actually lodged in one of your letters to myself! I did not discover it, or know that

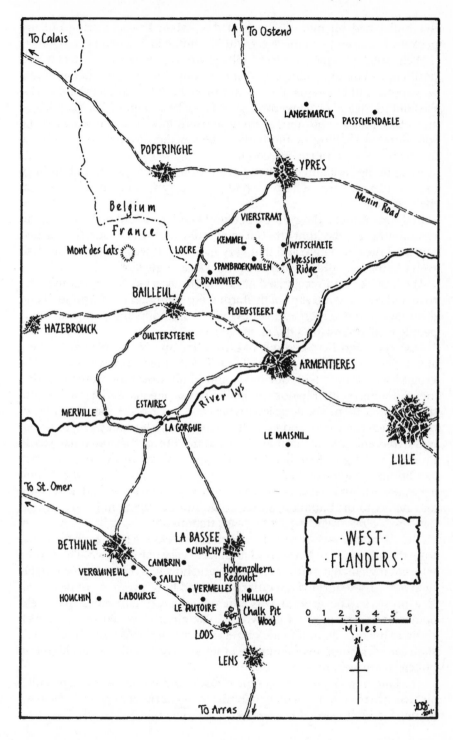

To Calais

↑ To Ostend

LANGEMARCK
PASSCHENDAELE

POPERINGHE

YPRES

Menin Road

Belgium

France

VIERSTRAAT

Mont des Cats

LOCRE

KEMMEL

WYTSCHAETE

SPANBROEKMOLEN

Messines Ridge

DRANOUTER

BAILLEUL

PLOEGSTEERT

HAZEBROUCK

OULTERSTEENE

ARMENTIERES

River Lys

ESTAIRES

MERVILLE

LA GORGUE

LE MAISNIL

LILLE

To St. Omer

LA BASSEE

·WEST·
FLANDERS·

BETHUNE

CUINCHY

CAMBRIN

Hohenzollern
Redoubt

VERQUINEUL

SAILLY

HOUCHIN

LABOURSE

VERMELLES

HULLUCH

LE RUTOIRE

Chalk Pit
Wood

0 1 2 3 4 5 6
·Miles·

LOOS

N

LENS

To Arras

this bullet had hit me, till the next day, when I was clearing out my pockets. I will send you the letter with the bullet in it, when I get a chance.

Well, to tell you the story! The village we were in occupies an elevated position, and the sun being bright and the day clear, a splendid panorama was spread out before us. We sat and picked out the familiar landmarks: the famous 'pylon' or 'Towerbridge' of Loos; Fosse Eight[32]; the slag-heaps, and other places, and among them and around them we watched the concentrated shelling of the battle – begun the day before – with the feeling that we should soon be in it.

At 2 pm the battalion marched to Le Rutoire, the ruined farm buildings in front of Vermelles, where we had previously spent so many weeks in the trenches.

In the meantime, 'Bing' Hopwood and I had been sent on in advance to reconnoitre, by daylight, the German trenches which our troops had captured the day before and that very morning. It was the first time I had seen a battlefield after an attack, and it was an ugly sight.

The first person I recognised at Le Rutoire was Geoffrey Feilding. The road and ruined courtyard of the farm were crammed with wounded and dead men. No one seemed to know what was happening in front. Some people were optimistic. Others, the reverse.

Hopwood and I crossed our old front line and No Man's Land – here about 500 yards wide – past the Lone Tree to the German trenches. The ground was strewn with our dead, and in all directions were wounded men crawling on their hands and knees. It was piteous, and it is a dreadful thought that there are occasions when one must resist the entreaties of men in such condition, and leave them to get in as best they can, or lie out in the cold and wet, without food, and under fire, as they often have to do for days and nights together. We had some timbers thrown over a trench as a bridge for some of them who said they had been trying all day to find a way across; but we had our own work to do, and we also had to get back and report to the battalion, so we could not do much; indeed, it would have been a never ending job had we attempted it.

The German trenches which for so many weeks we have looked at only from the other side of No Man's Land, were very like our own. The barbed wire entanglements in front of them were, however, far more formidable than ours. These formed a regular maze, and how our men got past them is a mystery. The ground was littered with German rifles, bayonets, bombs and equipment of every sort. The air still reeked of gas, which clung to the ground and made our eyes smart; and every now and then a shell came crashing over from the other side, or a flight of machine-gun bullets made us bob.

The battalion arrived about nine o'clock, and we spent the night, till 3 am, lying in the open. We then marched to the German trenches, which we manned, and proceeded to convert for our own use.

At four in the afternoon the Colonel gave us orders for an attack which he explained was to be made half an hour later upon the Chalk Pit and Wood, a mile and a quarter in front of our position;– the 2nd Irish Guards in front, the 1st Coldstream supporting.

This attack was launched punctually, but the Irish Guards met with heavy opposition, and though the 1st Scots Guards, who were on their right, came to the rescue, it was some hours before the position had been forced.[33]

Meanwhile I, with my Company waited for the order to advance. A certain number of shells were falling around us, but beyond wounding Captain Guy Darell (then second in command of the battalion) who was with me, these did very little damage.[34]

At last our turn came. Since it was already getting dark, I went out in advance to keep touch with the leading Companies. As I did so I met a stream of battle stragglers. Many were wounded, but with them was also a liberal accompaniment of unwounded 'friends' and others who obviously should not have been there. In reply to my questioning, the latter gave the well-worn excuse that 'an officer had given the order to retire'. I called on them to turn, but they were in no mood for that: they were surely and sullenly bound for home.

I had no time to waste, so left these men to the tender mercies of young Dermot Browne, who had just then walked up, and who began to deal with them very thoroughly, as they deserved, with a heavy hunting crop, which he carried.[35]

By the time No. 4 Company was well launched, it was dark and rain was falling. I had warned the men that if they met any stragglers as they went forward they were to sweep them along with them, if possible, or failing that, to allow them to pass through their ranks. I am proud to say that they carried out this order literally, not a man turning to right or left; though, as all will understand who have had such an experience, the temptation to some of them must have been considerable.

The darkness was soon like pitch, so that we lost touch with the advanced Companies, and with the firing from the front having become very heavy, I decided to leave the men under an officer (Heathcote) behind the wood, in what happened to be more or less sheltered ground. I myself went forward with an orderly to explore. It was impossible to see a yard, but we picked our way step by step, and, after tumbling once or twice painfully into shell-holes, we reached the Chalk Pit Wood and felt our way through it.

All the while, the wounded, who were lying pretty thick on the ground, kept calling to us to fetch them away. I felt a beast for not being able to help them, but we had no stretchers, and after promising to do what I could, I pushed along, for from the sound of digging in front it was clear that we were on the track of what we were looking for.

Then, to my relief, a voice called out from the slush, 'Hullo, Rowland'. It was Cecil Trafford.[36] There they were – all mixed – Scots Guards, Irish Guards, Grenadiers, digging in for dear life. It was the new front line on Hill 70. I knew then that my people could not be far away, and after following the line a short distance towards the left we came upon them.

Then I returned, having been away about an hour, to fetch up the men I had left behind the wood. During my absence Heathcote – the only officer with this party – had been shot through the spine by a stray bullet and lay paralysed. It was his first time under fire. I sent him back on a ground-sheet, and with the men rejoined the battalion. On the way I met Arthur Egerton, who is now Colonel. He said I had been reported killed and that a stretcher had been sent out to bring in my body!

By this time the Chalk Pit and Wood were well in our hands, but there was no sign of the 1st Guards Brigade, with whom we should have been in contact on the left.[37] I found myself at the danger-point of what was a very precarious situation. I therefore set out with two orderlies, if possible to find the 1st Brigade.

At a point some distance along the road towards La Bassée, my attention was attracted by four wounded Englishmen, who, as they heard our steps, called out for water. They had already lain two days in the muddy ditch by the roadside, where they had been left behind when our forces had retreated the previous Saturday. Having lent them our water bottles, and promised to send for them later, we continued our search for the 1st Brigade, but eventually having failed to find any trace of it, and having been a long time absent from the Company, I decided to return and report what I had found out – or rather had failed to find out.

As we repassed the wounded men in the ditch they again called to us, but seeing no object in stopping then, I was for hurrying on, when their calls became so urgent that I decided to hear what they had to say.

It is typical of the chivalrous character of the British soldier that in spite of the wretchedness of their position, it was not about themselves, but about us, that these men were concerned. They wished to warn us about a sniper, who, they said, was in a tree in front of us. They had heard him shooting at intervals all the time they had lain there.

Though it was unlikely that any sniper would be perched in a tree on so dark a night, we were proceeding with caution, when from some bushes on the left there came groans as if from a wounded man. My orderlies were convinced it was some enemy device to draw us into a trap, but I thought I would chance that, and following the direction of the groans, I soon came upon a dying German soldier.

He sat propped up in a sniper's pit – a grotesque figure, with his ridiculous pickelhaube tilted over one eye. As I approached he muttered some sort of imprecation. I promised him he should be looked after. He was quite a lad and so frail and light and his face so pale and artless as I lifted him out of the pool of rainwater in which he sat, that it was hard to believe that he had been engaged upon so dirty a trade. He died as I moved him; and I left him lying by the edge of the pit from which he had been sniping English soldiers. He was evidently the man referred to by the wounded men in the ditch.

Early in the morning the expected German bombardment began, and during the day – until the late afternoon – we collected the wounded of last Saturday, and otherwise lay in the narrow holes, like shallow graves, which the men had dug during the night.

At five minutes to four an orderly reported that the Commanding Officer wished to see me, so I went towards a lime kiln which did duty as Battalion Headquarters. This consisted of two underground chambers, with a vertical flue at one end, and a staircase leading to the surface at the other end which was nearest to the enemy.

As I walked across the open towards this place, the German shelling became intense. A shell pitched within 3 or 4 yards of me, but by a miracle did me no harm. I met Digby hurrying back to his Company. He said things were pressing and I had better run. I found Egerton giving final instructions to young Style[38], of No. 1 Company, who fell wounded and was captured a few minutes later while leading his Company to the assault.

The Colonel told me that we were to attack Puit 14 immediately; that Nos. 1 and 2 Companies were to make the attack, and that No. 4 was to occupy the trench vacated by them.

I ran back to my Company and found many of the men dozing after the strenuous work of the past few days and nights. Already, the enemy had spotted what was happening, and a storm of fire had burst out. I swept the men out of the rifle-pits and called to them to follow me to the forward trench. The noise had become so great that no order could be heard; and the men were half dazed by the suddenness of the change in the situation.

Immediately we showed ourselves we were met by a terrific hurricane of machine-gun and rife fire from Bois Hugo – a wood on our left front – and by shell-fire of every description. All was howling Inferno. The trees were crashing. I ran forward to the trench I had been told to occupy, but found when I reached it that I had got there alone. I went back, but the general din drowned all individual sound. I could not even hear my own voice. I found Charles Noel and young Philipson preparing to make a dash with the Company across the open, and presently in the face of the storm of bullets this was done, and the forward trench was manned.

By this time the assaulting Companies were returning, having lost practically all their officers and over a hundred men apiece during the few minutes they had been out of the trench. Riley, commanding No. 2, came in wounded, and Holmesdale also appeared. He was with the machine-guns. He was on his way back to Battalion Headquarters and offered to take a message for me. He made a dash across the exposed strip of ground that separated the trench from the lime kiln; but he had no luck, for just as he reached the other side, he fell, with a bullet through the leg. He is a charming boy, and it gave me a considerable qualm to see him fall, especially as I could not tell from where I was, whether his wound was slight or serious.

The attack had failed.[39] We spent the next two nights in improving our newly dug trenches, during the daytime being subjected to heavy shell-fire, which came from the flanks as well as from the front, and was almost continuous. The strain upon the men was heavy, but they bore it splendidly and cheerfully. To make matters harder, there was a pene-trating rain which soaked us all, and the cold was bitter, so that we were not only practically sleepless, but wet and shivering all the time. We never lay down: there was nowhere to lie but the watery trench. Of course we had no hot food or drink, but mercifully a rum ration was got up which was a Godsend to all.

Occasionally, the moon shone out, lighting up the chalk like snow, and showing up the bodies of the dead that lay in the great pit.

I was visited the first night by the Brigadier, who is always there when he is wanted, and glad I was to see him.

While he was with me a couple of whizz-bangs burst low over our heads, and a few minutes later, when he had gone, were repeated. I was still standing at the same spot, talking to a young sapper officer who had come up to put out some wire. He collapsed into the bottom of the trench. He was untouched by the shells, but so blinded by the shock that he was barely conscious of the fact even when I flashed an electric torch in his eyes. I confess I began by thinking he was making too much of it, as the shells had burst as close to me as to him. But he was still 'hors de combat' two hours later, and was sent away.

One night a C of E Chaplain came up, and I took him over the ground, and he said a prayer over each group of the dead – representing many regiments – that lay around the chalk-pit. It was a melancholy sight.

Contrary to all expectations and in spite of constant alarms the enemy never counter-attacked, and early yesterday morning we were relieved and got to billets here, and I to a bed, at seven o'clock am. After six nights and days my first real sleep.

Our crowning tragedy occurred on Wednesday. During the morning a message was passed along the front line, where I was in command, to the effect that some of the troops on our right were leaving the trench. I immediately sent an orderly to report this to the Colonel, who presently sent for me.

I moved along the trench to a point opposite the lime kiln, which served as his Headquarters, so that I could talk to him across the intervening open space. I reported the situation and mentioned that the enemy's shells were enfilading the trench. He laughed and answered, in the same strain, 'It's very unpleasant'. This finished our conversation, and they were the last words he ever spoke. As he said them he was killed. A shell burst. I knew it was close to him, but direct hits are rare, and believing him to be safely under cover from splinters (he was standing with Dermot Browne, the Adjutant, in the doorway at the top of the staircase), I thought nothing of it, and returned to my place in the trench.

Soon, a message was passed that someone was calling me. I turned back along the trench, but could hear nothing. Then an agonised voice moaned out something which the men said was my name. I went to the edge of the Chalk Pit just behind the trench and there saw an officer. He said that the entrance to the lime kiln had been blocked by a shell, and that the Colonel, Adjutant, Second in Command, and all the Headquarter Staff were buried!

I called for six volunteers with picks and shovels, and we crept across the open to the lime kiln. At the back of the kiln I saw the Colonel of the 2nd Irish Guards, who confirmed the bad news. At the rear of the kiln there was the flue or chimney, and through this, by means of a piece of telephone wire which he lowered to the chamber below, he got out Hopwood, who was now acting Second in Command.

I went round to the main entrance. I found a horrible state of things. The orderly whom I had sent with my message to the Colonel, lay buried, all but his head and shoulders, his head soaked in blood, and both his legs broken. Egerton and Dermot Browne were dead, and the three were jammed together under a mass of earth and fallen timber. Two of the volunteers – an oldish man named Robins and Murphy, an Irishman – were especially to the fore with the digging. Yet it seemed we should never get them out. For each shovelful of the loose crumbling rubbish dug out another slid in. The living man's feet were hopelessly wedged, between a balk of timber and the two dead bodies.

After an hour's ceaseless work, during which the shelling continued, we extricated the living man. The other two were not got out till after dark. We buried them at night behind the wood. I read the burial service over Dermot Browne from your prayer-book which I always carry.

I had fifty-five casualties in my Company, including some of my best men. C_____, one of the Company wags, got shot through the leg and was last seen hopping towards the rear, with a beaming face, and calling to his friends that he'd got a cushy one at last! I was afterwards told that he had jokingly suggested shooting his Company officers also through the leg, because he did not want to have them killed. You should have seen me when I got back to billets. At the Chalk Pit we were cut off from water (except the rain), so could not even wash our hands. My clothes were torn and caked with clay from head to foot: my face black from powder smoke and brown from the showers of earth which were constantly poured upon us by the bursting shells. I was unshaved. I was shivering in a man's greatcoat which a corporal had brought me, picked up on the battlefield, my own having been lost; as also was my mackintosh, my ground-sheet and my pillow, which I had given to a dying man in the Company.

I hope and believe we shall continue to hold the ground we won. It had previously been taken last Saturday, and lost again. It was strewn with the dead of that attack; and with the wounded, who had been lying out ever since in the cold and rain, without food or water.

This is the most horrible aspect of this horrible war. You hear the wounded calling for help, or blowing whistles; you see them waving their handkerchiefs; doing anything and everything to attract attention; and you have often to ignore their appeals. One's first attentions are due to one's own wounded.

Yet, I am glad to tell you that we were able to collect a large number of last Saturday's wounded – between 100 and 200 men I should think, including an immense Major of the Buffs who had defied all previous efforts to remove him. Indeed, when our men found him he said: 'It's no use unless you have a stretcher; it's been tried several times.' In spite of the days and nights he had lain out, foodless, and in the rain, he was quite cheerful.

I am sorry to say we lost some good men in this rescue work. Tommy Robartes and Fair were both killed in this way.[40] In fact, it became so dangerous that the Colonel stopped it after a time.

I feel that we are beginning to see daylight now. Goodbye, and God bless you.

4 October 1915 [Vermelles]

Last night we (the Company Commanders) went out to reconnoitre the trenches which we shall have to occupy in the event of certain contingencies. The trenches were packed with troops in course of relief, walking wounded and wounded on stretchers, all coming away from the firing line, so that it was a very slow and tedious affair working one's way forward. After we had finished our explorations there was a lull, and we were able to get out of the trenches and return across the open without danger.

The weather is very cold, and we lay shivering all last night. Tonight we have rigged up a fire. I now have three officers besides myself in the Company – Jackson, Roland Philipson, and Daniell (the last from Windsor).

Father Knapp,[41] came here yesterday. There was such a din, however, that it was hardly possible to hear him speak, and he decided not to attempt a service, but gave his blessing.

This morning we marched from Sailly Labourse, which village, after six nights in the fire-trench facing Hohenzollern Redoubt (a place of which I expect you have read a good deal lately), I reached only yesterday morning at 4.30, feeling so tired that I went straight to bed and stayed there till 3 pm. Jackson and I had spent a night longer in the trenches than the battalion, having volunteered to get certain work finished.

The trenches we have left were not in such a nice condition, as when we took them over. They had been the scene of several bloody attacks. The weather was wet: the place deep in mud and filth. They were strewn with every kind of discarded equipment, rifles and bombs. In front, the dead lay thick. Inside the trenches there were also still a few. There were no dug-outs to speak of. The outlook, altogether, was most undesirable; but, fortunately, the weather cleared up after we got in.

As I look upon such scenes as these it occurs to me what a good thing it would be to bring some of our professional hypochondriacs – male and female – that they might witness the appalling wastage of our best manhood. Could they go back and still worry about their own wretched unhealthy minds and bodies after seeing the prodigality with which these healthy young men have given their lives away?

Nevertheless, I confess that the first sight of the reckless slaughter brings a sense almost of shame. I find myself half wondering if the people at home can possibly realise what is going on here?

The dead seem to have a strange and subtle fascination for the living. I noticed that at Loos. When we were advancing over the old fought-over ground, the whole Company would turn and look each time we passed a dead body. Perhaps they were thinking that they might soon be looking like that themselves; but they would not touch the bodies. I soon found out that a night burying party would always shirk its job.

3.15 pm. I have just returned from parade. You may be surprised to hear that I have only learnt today from the 'Daily Mail' that the heavy bombardment of last Friday was the accompaniment to the big German counter-attack of that day, in which it is claimed that we killed 8,000 men: an estimate upon which I cast doubt. Such is our ignorance of things that are going on even a few hundred yards away from our immediate surroundings!

14 October 1915 [Prière de Ste Prie]

Jackson and I bicycled into Bethune yesterday, and arrived at the outskirts to find 15-inch shells plunging at intervals of about a quarter of an hour, into the centre of the town. These were something new, and heavier than anything I had experienced before. Certainly, the effect was very shattering, and the pieces were flying wide, and falling several hundreds of yards from the point of impact of the shells.

The population, who had seemed almost to have grown accustomed to their 'iron ration', were evidently startled by this ponderous stuff, and were crowding into the streets; and most of the shops, and even the famous 'Globe' (where our officers meet and pow-wow over cocktails), were closed for the time being.

Yesterday afternoon, the second great British attack was launched – though the Guards took no active part in it – a sort of repetition of September 25. The news we have received so far is very fragmentary, but they say it has been successful.[42]

The fact that this attack has been made unseals my lips, and I can tell you now of the mysterious work we were doing in the trench opposite Hohenzollern Redoubt, and at which I could only hint before. We were excavating emplacements under the parapet and filling them with cylinders of chlorine gas, in preparation for yesterday's attack. We stored 420 of these cylinders in our bit of trench.[43]

On the night I stayed behind, the Germans started shelling at a time when the trench was packed with cylinders, to say nothing of the men who were bringing them in; and, when I explain that these cylinders are big and heavy and each requires four men to carry it (two carriers and two reliefs), you will be able to picture the congestion that was produced in the narrow trench, and you can imagine what the effect would have been if a chance splinter of shell had happened to puncture a cylinder and let out the gas: and this condition of things continued during two nights.

19 October 1915 [Reserve Trenches opposite Hohenzollern Redoubt]

On Friday, the 15th, we got orders at 2 pm, to be ready in half an hour to march from Prière de Ste Prie to the trenches, and we arrived in position in front of Hohenzollern Redoubt at midnight. We found ourselves immediately to the right of the sector we had occupied a few days previously – in the portion which was then held by the Irish Guards.

On our way up we saw the Prince of Wales, who stood by the roadside as we passed.[44] We found the trenches greatly changed since we had left them. The big attack of Wednesday the 13th had been made and contrary to the first messages that came through, had failed with very heavy losses. Only a part of the trench which had formed the front of Hohenzollern Redoubt was still held by our troops; the rest of the Redoubt was in German hands, with the exception of such part of it as had been trans-formed into No Man's Land, having been blown sky-high by the artillery.

This bit of trench we proceeded to occupy, as well as the old front line in which we had placed the gas. The cylinders were now empty. The communication trenches – and in many parts the fire-trenches also – had been blown in by the enemy's shells. Both were littered with the sweepings of war, gas-pipes and cylinders, discarded rifles and equipment, bombs, small arms ammunition-boxes, and the dead. On the ground in front lay hundreds of our dead. The narrow communication trenches were also crowded with living men, scrambling in the dark to pass one another.

I suppose there is nothing in the world where theory differs from practice so much as in war. Contrast the practice trenches in Windsor Park with the trenches here. Since this battle began, Brigades and more have been squeezed in where battalions used to be. The communication trenches are very long and very narrow. They are crossed and re-crossed and threaded by telephone wires, many of them loose and dangling – which trip you up, and catch you by the head; and during the period which has elapsed since the war began, a perfect maze of trenches has evolved, in which no amount of organisation will prevent men losing their way, especially in the dark.

The congestion in the trenches at night, during this time of battle, must be seen to be appreciated. The communication trenches, except where blown in by shells, are generally just wide enough for two men with packs to squeeze past one another with difficulty. Picture what happens when – as is often the case – a Company or Battalion going in takes the wrong turn and meets another coming out! The chaos becomes more bewildering still when they meet in a tunnel; and when, as last night, one is being relieved by people who make such a noise that the relief is spotted and the enemy opens fire with shrapnel, the climax is reached.

The shambles (you can call it nothing else) is about 200 yards in front of our old fire-trench. The part of it which we hold and the communication trench leading to it have been so shelled that, at the time we took them over, they were no longer trenches but ditches, very wide and shallow, with frequent upheavals in the floor, indicating the positions of dead men, now wholly or partly covered with earth splashed over them by the bursting shells and the passage of troops.

It would, I suppose, be an exaggeration to say that the parapets at this place are built up with dead bodies, but it is true to say that they are dovetailed with them, and everywhere arms, legs and heads protrude.

At one place an arm and hand stuck out and dangled across the trench. On one of the fingers was a solid looking gold ring, and owing to the narrowness of the passage, each man that passed it had to brush the hand aside. It spoke well for the battalion, I thought, that to my knowledge, the ring still remained untouched for more than twenty-four hours.

The artillery certainly did its work well here. The surface of the ground over a large area has been reduced to a shapeless jumble of earth mounds and shell-holes. The formidable wire entanglements have gone. On all sides lie the dead. It is a war picture of the most frightful description; and the fact that the dead are all our dead, arouses in me a wild craving for revenge. Where are the enemy's dead? We hear much of them, but we do not see them. During this fighting I have seen thousands of British dead, but the dead Germans I have seen I could almost count upon my fingers.

At 5 am, while we were standing to, the Commanding Officer (Guy Baring)[45] came hurrying along my trench. He said the plans had been changed, that we had just been detailed to take the place of the 3rd Grenadiers, and that we were to attack immediately. I asked for instructions. He replied: 'There is no time for instructions. You must use your discretion'. Thus, as at the Chalk Pit, we had only a few minutes in which to organise our arrangements. Charles Noel's bombers (No. 3 Coy.) and mine (No. 4) made the assault. I immediately reinforced Noel by sending one platoon under Jackson into the Redoubt, another to the communication trench leading to the Redoubt, and my remaining two platoons, under Daniell, to the first support trench. I myself, having seen the men into position, went into the Redoubt.

In spite of the unexpected suddenness of the order, there was no crowding and no vestige of undue hurry or excitement. The orders were obeyed in perfect silence, the men filing steadily along the trenches to their positions. At each end of the main communication tunnel I posted sentries to keep it clear, so that it might be available for further reinforcements should they be needed, and for getting out the wounded.

The bombers went in with dash, and to start with, made good progress. They rushed the barricade separating us from the enemy, and bombed their way for a considerable distance beyond it. The trenches were, however, so flattened by shell-fire that they gave very little protection. At this spot they are, moreover, a regular tangle. There came a point where the party should have taken a turning to the left, but in the darkness they bombed straight on. The trench they followed became so shallow that presently it ceased to give any cover at all. The Germans, who are always quick to spot a weakness of this kind, lost no time in making good their opportunity. They brought a machine-gun into position; and that ends the story.

Our losses were not severe, but bad enough. I do not know what the casualties amounted to in the battalion. Those in my Company, since we came up this time, are twenty-four. These things begin to tell. I have lost, I suppose, ninety men, or half the Company, since we left Lumbres, and Nos. 1 and 2 Companies have lost considerably more, though the gaps have already been almost filled by drafts from home.

A good deal of sniping was indulged in by both sides, in which most of those present took a hand. The opposing troops were, however, so close to one another that this was a tricky game. It was impossible to search for a target with a periscope, for so hot was the sniping that no periscope survived more than a minute or two. The only way was to peep over the parapet and snap from the shoulder, and though anyone exposing himself in this way for more than a second would most assuredly be shot, there was plenty of light-hearted rivalry whenever a target did offer.[46]

Once, a party of the enemy had been spotted digging among the shell-holes, not more than 30 yards in front of where I was standing. One of the men who had mounted the fire-step to shoot, recoiled the very instant he exposed himself, with a German bullet through his cap which lifted the latter clean off his head. The self-conscious grin he gave as he stepped back into the trench was very comical to see.

There was one wonderful dug-out which the men had rather avoided, from a feeling, I think, that there was some thing uncanny about it. I went down and explored it with an electric torch. It was like an old clothes shop. It was 20 or 30 feet deep, excavated in the chalk, with two entrances, and with a chamber quite 40 feet long at the bottom. In the latter were wooden bunks for sleeping, two deep, ranged along one wall and the floor was almost knee deep in clothing, equipment, medicine cases, tinned food, and other stuff.

One dead man also was there; again, not a German, but a British casualty from a previous attack, who either had crept in, or to give them their due, may have been carried in by the enemy to die.

Our bombing attack brought on the heaviest bombardment I have yet sat under. It was at about its zenith at a quarter to ten am. It lasted for over nine hours, and was intense during a great part of that time. The stream of German shells was continuous. They came in 'coveys', whistling through the air like a storm at sea. Often they were falling at the rate of a hundred a minute.

But our trenches here are like network: they are repeated parallel after parallel, till not only are they confusing to the German gunners, but the area over which the fire is distributed is fortunately extended, and therein lies our chance of safety.

It is of course bewildering to be shelled like that. There is no denying that when such shelling happens to be concentrated on the particular bit of trench you are in, as it often is for an hour or more together, it is extremely disagreeable; but, on the whole, the damage done by these huge bombardments is out of all proportion to their cost, and they do not produce the demoralising effect, which is their sole object.

Once it is over, you shake yourself and recover, and if you are healthily minded you soon have forgotten it, just as you forget the other disturbances of life. Yet, to tell the truth, I marvel myself sometimes how human nerves can stand the strain of our existence; day after day, night after night, hour after hour, being shelled; sometimes, for hours at a time, a heavy shell falling every few minutes within a few yards of you, shaking the ground beneath you, half stunning you with the crash of the explosion, and covering you with earth.[47]

I wrote you a short letter towards the end of the bombardment of which I have been speaking. Just after I had finished it, a shell burst outside the door of the dug-out where I was writing, upsetting everything. My dug-out was blown right in, and my trench was smashed in over and over again.

On Monday it was quiet until 2.30 in the afternoon, and we were hoping inwardly for a day of comparative peace, when our artillery aroused the sleeping lion by opening fire. Personally, I am all for bombarding the enemy and strafing him on every possible occasion, and I am sure I speak for the great majority when I say that, so long as we feel that our guns are doing him some damage, we are willing to sit and receive the retaliation which almost certainly follows.

On this occasion, however, our artillery began by dropping shells upon our own support trenches, including my own. This is a practice for which some of the new batteries are becoming famous. I have myself reported it over and over again. It is annoying enough in itself, but on Monday it was doubly so, as the Germans immediately took up the challenge, and instead of a restful afternoon, we had to sit through a heavy hate. The same morning, while I was shaving, I got my face scratched by a splint of shell which drew blood.

I have mentioned tunnels in this letter. A feature of the communication trenches leading towards Hohenzollern Redoubt is that some of them are in the form of tunnels, burrowed through the chalk, 2 or 3 feet below the surface of the ground. These Russian saps, as they are called, are peculiar to this part of the line. But for the fact that they have been penetrated here and there by German shells, they would be pitch-dark; and, as they are only wide enough for men to pass along comfortably in single file, they are apt to produce a very choky feeling when they get crowded, particularly if you are inclined to claustrophobia.

20 October 1915 [Reserve Trenches opposite Hohenzollern Redoubt]

The Colonel told me today that we are to be here till the 26th, when we go back for a rest. They are beginning to issue steel helmets to our men. They look like that kind of suet pudding which we used, as children, to call 'Plough-boy's hat'; and they are painted mottled green to make them inconspicuous. There are not, as yet, enough to go round, so they are doled out to the men in the most forward positions.[48]

You can tell 'M'[49] that I do not think the trenches would suit her. They are full of mice and rats, which run about like lapdogs. Last night, while we were dining, our food being spread upon the floor, a mouse ran about among the plates, and was not at all abashed by the burning candles, or ourselves. They run up and down the earth walls of the dug-outs and at night have violent scuffles overhead, shaking the earth into our eyes and ears as we lie beneath.

The amusing thing is that we all take care not to tread upon them or injure them in any way. In some mysterious way the war, while making one more callous to the sufferings of men, seems to increase one's sympathy with the lower animals. Perhaps it is that in the scheme of creation, the animals are coming out so much better than the men.

The days of the old famous dug-outs are over. What was not good enough for a Company Headquarters in those happy days is now too good for a Battalion and good enough for a Brigade. We are no longer critical in such matters. We do not look for chairs or tables, but sit and eat and sleep upon the hard ground, with a more or less splinter-proof roof, if we are lucky, just high enough to allow kneeling.

It is cold at nights and more so in the early mornings. Speaking for myself, I lie shivering but exceedingly healthy. Yesterday, I rigged up a coke fire in my dug-out, which is a great boon. I have no clothes other than those I wear, except a man's greatcoat, a man's ground-sheet, and a waterproof cape, all picked up in the trenches since I lost my own at Loos.

Philipson and Daniell have gone home, sick. I remain, and thank God, stick it wonderfully. I have never felt better in my life.

An officer in the battalion has found the diary of a Bavarian Infantry soldier, Otto Arnesmaier – a wonderfully human document, into which the writer pours his full soul. He was a man of gentle disposition, who was no soldier by choice, and indeed hated everything to do with war; a lover of music, which he describes as 'the divine daughter of Heaven, and consoler'.

His was one of the bodies that helped to make the parapet of Hohenzollern Redoubt.

22 October 1915 [Fire-trench (Guildford Alley): Hohenzollern Redoubt]

Nothing more unlike the talk of soldiers, as depicted on the stage or in the classics, could be imagined than the real thing as we get it here. There are no heroics. In fact, it is rather etiquette to grumble and pretend to be frightened. It is, I imagine, a sort of protective bravado.

The men can be philosophic too. The following is a snatch of conversation between two privates of the Scots Guards which I overheard in the trench the other day. Their talk also was of the war.

'If you gets wounded', said one, 'and it's a cushy one, you gets sent 'ome; and if you gets killed, well, it's **** all'.

The enemy snipers here are very active. They have killed two of my men and badly wounded a Welsh Guardsman since last night. These snipers are very bold. It is a common sight to see two or three of the enemy exposing themselves in a most reckless way. I have myself seen many, and I must admit that they do not look at all downhearted, but spruce and clean and full of confidence. One cannot but admire their audacity. It is, of course, possible that these men are new to the game, but it is just as likely that they are put up as decoys, to tempt us to expose ourselves.

It is getting colder and colder at nights. Last night a half-starved dog crawled into the trench and slept beside me, and I was glad of his company for the warmth it gave. We are to be relieved tonight and go out, I believe, for a fortnight's rest, of which we shall be very glad. We have had eight days and nights of the worst in these trenches, which have cost the battalion about a hundred casualties, and my Company twenty-six.

24 October 1915 [St. Hilaire]

I have just been sent for by the Commanding Officer and told that in view of my strenuous duties during the past month I can go home on extra leave on the 29th – in five days time!

24 October 1915 [St. Hilaire]

Darling Joan,

This is a German soldier's shoulder strap, which I got for you myself from the famous Hohenzollern Redoubt.

Your loving Dada.

RCF goes on leave, 29 October–4 November. On arrival in England, he visits two of his daughters, Joan and Anita, at their boarding school, The Convent of the Assumption, Sidmouth, Devon.

6 November 1915 [St. Hilaire]

As the result of twelve hundred men having missed the boat of the night before, the one by which I crossed was packed. We were cautioned not to crowd to one side for fear of overbalancing the boat, but this caution was unnecessary, as the decks were so blocked with humanity that it was next to impossible to move in any direction. General Maxse was on board with his ADC, Fred Montague of this regiment, and I had tea with Montague in the saloon.

I failed to get a lift on a motor car from Boulogne and was obliged to travel on the 'leave' train which, like the boat, was overcrowded. There were nine in my compartment, and I was the ninth, so had to balance on a dividing armrest. I travelled with a Captain of the Irish Guards whom I only know under the name of 'Nosy'. The train crawled and we reached our detraining station, which was Lillers, at 2.30 in the morning, having left Boulogne, after much waiting, at 8 pm. From Lillers, 'Nosy' and I walked off together through a thick fog and reached my billet here about 3.30. I found my bed occupied by one of two new subalterns who have joined the battalion from the London Scottish and had been posted to No. 4 Company during my absence. I had not been expected back as it was so late. However, room was made for me and I managed to get a sleep.

Guy Baring asked me this morning if you would undertake some of the visiting of the men's families about London and I said I was sure you would delight in it. I told him that you were the most unselfish woman on earth – which you are.

11 November 1915 [La Gorgue]

The trenches – or rather breastworks – which we are to take over have been held by Gurkhas, so that they may be expected, with luck, to reach to our men's waists, and we shall have plenty of work to do in building them up.

The bands of the different regiments of the Division are to take it in turn to come to France, and the Grenadiers are already here, and have been playing in the square today, just outside my billet.

The joint mess (Nos. 1 and 4 Companies) is a very cheery place. Last night we had a dinner party and a crowd in after, and it will be the same every evening till the end of this week. Our dinner party this evening consisted of Alfred Yorke (an old member of White's; forty-four and an ensign!); Lionel Tennyson,[50] Hylton Philipson, Sam Woods, etc.

17 November 1915 [Merville]

The battalion went into the trenches last night, but a most humiliating thing has happened to me. I have had a fall from a common push-bike and have injured my knee. The day before yesterday Hopwood, Charles Noel and I again went up to reconnoitre our new trenches, Hopwood riding, Noel and I on bicycles.

When we got within view of the Aubers Ridge we took to our feet and saw some very pretty shooting as we made off towards the trenches. The German gunners were firing at a house about 100 yards to the right of our starting-point, and hitting it every time. It was empty! We returned to the spot where we had left the bicycles after dark, and in mounting I missed the pedal. The miserable machine lurched into some deep mud by the roadside and I came down with a sickening thud upon my knee on the hard road. When I got home the doctor came to see me and found that I had a temperature of 102. The following morning my knee had stiffened and filled, and I could not walk without pain.

In the evening I was sent by ambulance to the Casualty Clearing Station at Merville, and here I am in bed, with an Australian Army doctor suffering from influenza on my left, a padre with a rheumatic knee on my right, and in front of me the same Irish Guards Captain whom I travelled with on the sixth, and who now has a shell-wound in the arm.

I have learnt during the last few days that the most exaggerated stories of Flemish winter mud do not exceed the reality. The mud varies in consistency from the creamy variety to the adhesive kind which holds you fast like birdlime and would suck off the long india-rubber hip boots with which the troops are now provided, were they not strapped to the waist belt.

The country we have come to is flat, low lying, and swampy. So sodden is the surface soil that trench digging is out of the question, and the defences consist of lines of breastworks built up of sandbags.

These breastworks are irregular in design and many shells having burst against them, are ragged and dishevelled in appearance. The older bags have rotted and the earth has slipped and shrunk with the weather. The ground in front and behind is thickly pitted with shell-holes, among which occasional little wooden crosses appear, marking the graves of soldiers.

The prevailing impression is one of chaotic freshly turned slimy earth, and the general scene is one of desolation such as I tried to describe to you when speaking of Hohenzollern Redoubt.

The communication trenches leading to the front line are half full of mud and water, which generally reaches your knees, and sometimes your waist. They have in fact ceased to be of any practical use, and most people travel to and from the fire-trench across the open, by night, which apparently is not so dangerous as might be supposed.

RCF's knee becomes badly infected and he is invalided home in December. He remains confined to bed and is incapacitated until March 1916.[51]

NOTES

1. For the service record of Rowland Feilding (hereafter RCF), see PRO WO339/48941. Unfortunately, the records were 'weeded' in 1955, leaving mainly medical details in the file.
2. The Coldstream Guards descend from Monk's Regiment of Foot, raised by Oliver Cromwell in 1650. They later changed allegiance, marching from Coldstream to support the restoration of Charles II. They were known as the 2nd Foot Guards until 1817, when they assumed their present name.
3. Major (later T/Lieutenant-Colonel) AGE Egerton (1879–1915); grandson of Lord Egerton and cousin of Emily (née Egerton), RCF's stepmother; commanded 1/Coldstream; wounded 1914, killed in action 29 June 1915.
4. At this time the 3/Coldstream formed part of 4th (Guards) Brigade, 2nd Division.
5. Brigadier-General (later Major-General) Sir Geoffrey Feilding (1866–1932); son of Hon. Sir Percy Feilding, who was present at Balaclava; cousin of RCF; DSO, Boer War 1900; commanded 3/Coldstream until April 1915; commanded 149th Brigade, April–June 1915 and 1st Guards Brigade (formally 4th Guards Brigade), June–December 1915; wounded December 1915; GOC Guards Division, January 1916–September 1918; MID seven times.
6. Major (later Lieutenant-Colonel) Viscount Rudolph (Rollo) Feilding (1885–1937); heir to 9th Earl of Denbigh, first cousin once removed of RCF; DSO, Landrecies 1914; Special Reserve, Coldstream Guards; 3/Coldstream.
7. Captain PA Clive (1873–1918), cousin of RCF; MP for South Herefordshire 1900–1910; 1/Grenadier Guards; later T/Lieutenant-Colonel commanding 1/5 Lancashire Fusiliers; killed in action 5 April 1918.
8. Captain GM Darell MC (1883–1947); later Lieutenant-Colonel (staff); 3rd son of Sir Lionel Darell Bt; 3/Coldstream; later 2nd in command, 1/Coldstream; wounded at Loos.
9. Viscount Ipswich (William Henry Fitzroy) (1884–1918); son of 8th Duke of Grafton; Lieutenant 4/Coldstream, later 5/Coldstream; later attached RFC; killed in flying accident 23 April 1918.
10. The 1/Coldstream were part of 1st (Guards) Brigade, 1st Division (General Officer Commanding (hereafter GOC), Major-General Richard Haking).

From 30 August 1915 1/Coldstream were transferred to 2nd (Guards) Brigade, in the newly formed Guards Division.

11. Lieutenant-Colonel WHV Darell (1878–1952); later Brigadier-General; MID, DSO 1915; AA and QMG, Guards Division, August 1915–December 1916; commanded Irish Guards 1924– 28.

12. Brigadier-General FJ Heyworth (1863–1916); DSO, Boer War; OC 3/Scots Guards; GOC 3rd (Guards) Brigade; killed by a sniper on Menin Road, 19 May 1916; see PRO WO95/1190.

13. Lieutenant-Colonel (later Major-General Sir John) Ponsonby (1866–1952); son of Rt. Hon. Sir Henry Ponsonby, equerry to Queen Victoria, and cousin of Earl of Bessborough; OC 1/Coldstream 1913–15; wounded 1914; GOC 2nd (Guards) Brigade, 1915–17; Haig had misgivings about him in 1916, and when Ponsonby was promoted Major-General in 1917, he was given command of 40th Division, a part 'bantam' unit; see Haig Diary, 19 January 1916, National Library of Scotland, Acc. 3155/97/9; also FA Pile to Edmonds, 25 October 1926, PRO Cab 45/186.

14. The Battle of Gheluvelt, 29–31 October 1914. The German attack at 5.30 am on 29 October was just north of the Menin Road and fell on the 1/Coldstream and 1/Black Watch. The British line was broken and these two battalions were almost destroyed.

15. In retaliation for the use of gas by the Germans at Ypres in April 1915, Lord Kitchener ordered the Royal Engineers to proceed with the development of gas warfare. The first trials commenced on 13 May 1915.

16. 2nd Lieutenant (later T/Captain) JR Woods; 1/Coldstream; died of wounds 16 September 1916.

17. The Hall, Rainhill, Lancashire, was the home of Edith Feilding's family – the Stapleton-Brethertons – a prominent county family. Her maternal grandfather was 12th Lord Petre.

18. The 1/Coldstream War Diary confirms that they relieved the 1/4th Royal Welsh Fusiliers, who were down to their last 100 men, on 10 June 1915; see PRO WO95/1263. The operation of consolidating and defending craters was extremely difficult and the later 'Actions of St. Eloi Craters', in the Spring of 1916, would highlight the problems; see Tim Cook, 'The Blind Leading the Blind', *Canadian Military History*, Autumn 1996; also 'Consolidation of Localities and Craters after Assault and Capture', General Staff, War Office 1916.

19. Lance-Corporal (later Major) Michael O'Leary (1888–1961); served in Royal Navy and Canadian North-West Mounted Police before returning to the Irish Guards at the outbreak of war; single-handedly, he stormed and captured two enemy barricades at Cuinchy on 1 February 1915, winning the VC; later served in WWII with the Middlesex Regiment.

20. A 3,000 lb ammonal mine was blown at the 'Duck's Bill', near the junction of the Canadian and 7th Division fronts. It was fired simultaneous to the infantry assault, on 15 June 1915, as part of the 'Second Action of Givenchy, 15–16 June 1915'; see PRO WO95/1263.

21. Captain EBG (Byng) Gregge-Hopwood (1880–1916); celebrated rider, cricketer and shot; later T/Lieutenant-Colonel commanding 1/Coldstream; wounded twice, killed in action 20 July 1917; his only brother, Captain Robert Gregge-Hopwood, was killed in action 24 August 1916.

22. Lieutenant Hon. HD Browne (1894–1915); 2nd son of Earl of Kenmore; 1/Coldstream, MID; killed in action 29 September 1915.

23. Captain Hon. TCR Agar-Robartes; see biog. in Introduction notes; his later

death in action was a severe blow to the family estate, Lanhydrock, Bodmin, Cornwall.

24. Captain JH Cuthbert (1876–1915); married (1) Anne Byng, niece of General Sir Julian Byng; High Sheriff of Northumberland; DSO, MID, Boer War 1901; killed in action 27 September 1915.

25. The subject of unofficial truces is examined by Denis Winter in *Death's Men*, Allen Lane, 1978, pp.217–22.

26. The Guards Division was formed on 30 August 1915. It comprised 1st Guards Brigade (renumbered from old 4th Guards Bde), 2nd Guards Bde and 3rd Guards Bde. The Guards Division was immediately incorporated, together with the New Army 21st and 24th Divisions, into the newly created XI Corps (Haking). This Corps remained with First Army during the whole of RCF's service with the Coldstream Guards.

27. Haking was referring to the impending Battle of Loos, 25 September–8 October 1915. Harold Macmillan, serving with the 4/Grenadier Guards (Guards Division), was surprised that Haking should exhort the Guards officers before the battle, in an open meeting in a village square. Haking's detailed account of what was in store was clearly audible to anyone in the vicinity; Harold Macmillan, *Winds of Change 1914–1939*, Macmillan, 1966.

28. Captain CHF Noel (1885–1948); 2nd son of 3rd Earl of Gainsborough; later Major 1/Coldstream.

29. 2nd Lieutenant JS Heathcote; 1/Coldstream; later wounded and paralysed, removed to base hospital in London, where he died 28 August 1917.

30. By nightfall on 25 September the British had indeed captured the defences around Loos, but Hulluch and Cité Ste Elie remained in enemy hands.

31. Another casualty of these actions was T/Captain Lionel Lord Petre, cousin of Edith Feilding, who died of wounds 30 September 1915.

32. In this important mining area of Loos, '*Fosses*' were principal pit heads and '*Puits*', auxiliary shafts. Their buildings and wheel houses, together with nearby slag heaps, afforded the Germans excellent observation posts.

33. During this attempt to capture Chalk Pit Wood, Lieutenant John Kipling, 2/Irish Guards and son of Rudyard, was killed in action. Just 18, he had sailed for France with his battalion one month before; for a classic account of this action, see Rudyard Kipling, *The Irish Guards in the Great War Vol II*, reprinted, Spellmount, 1998.

34. Darell was badly wounded in the face. HRH Edward Prince of Wales, who knew him, ensured his speedy evacuation from the front and this probably saved Darell's life. He returned to France in 1916, as a staff officer; Brigadier Sir Lionel Darell to Editor, 18/7/00.

35. At Loos, Haking's XI Corps formed the reserve (the 21st and 24th Divisions to the front, Guards Division to the rear). After much delay, the 21st and 24th Divisions were brought forward into the battle on 26 September. Their attack failed and after heavy casualties, four brigades began streaming back towards their lines. They were eventually rallied by the 1st and 2nd (Guards) Brigades coming forward. Although RCF and his fellow officers had little sympathy for these men, the failure of the operation was largely the fault of poorly trained commanders losing direction. Haking's later defence of his own conduct was inconsistent; see Haking to Edmonds, PRO CAB 44/28.

36. Captain Cecil Trafford MC (1884–1948); Scots Guards; cousin of Edith Feilding.

37. The Chalk Pit soon became HQ for the 1/Coldstream.

38. 2nd Lieutenant O Style was captured on 26 September 1915 and eventually repatriated on 22 November 1918.
39. This assault took place on the afternoon of 26 September 1915. Two companies of 1/Coldstream attacked German positions, believed to be in the buildings around Puit 14. In preparation, Corps and Divisional artillery bombarded these buildings. In fact, the German positions were 150 yards to the east, on the edge of Bois Hugo. As the Coldstream attacked the empty buildings, they were annihilated by crossfire from the enemy machine-guns in Bois Hugo; PRO WO95/1219.
40. 'Tommy' Robartes ran 100 yards out to drag back L/Sergeant A Hopkins, who had himself been wounded while rescuing another man. Having brought Hopkins back, Robartes was shot by a sniper and died of wounds the following morning. Buried in Lapugnoy Military cemetery, his original wooden cross was returned to his home at Lanhydrock, and still lies outside the estate church; see A Hopkins to Lady Clifden, 17 December 1915, Robartes Papers, Lanhydrock House, National Trust Cornwall.
41. Rev. Simon Knapp (1858–1917); educ. St Edmunds Catholic College, Ware; served Boer War; attach. 2/Irish Guards, DSO and MC; died of wounds 1 August 1917. There is a stained glass window in his memory, in the Carmelite Church, Kensington, unveiled by the Earl of Ypres (then Viscount French).
42. This attack by XI and IV Corps on 13 October, formed part of the 'Actions of the Hohenzollern Redoubt, 13th–19th October 1915'. The Redoubt was a large closed entrenchment, wired all the way round, with a front of about 300 yards. Lying one mile to the north of Loos, it was one of the strongest positions in the German line.
43. The total number of cylinders brought up for the attack was 3,170. Only one third of these were discharged, and to little effect.
44. HRH Edward, Prince of Wales was 21 years old and a Lieutenant in 1/Grenadier Guards. He was also ADC to the Commander-in-Chief.
45. Lieutenant-Colonel Hon. Guy Baring (1873–1916); 4th son of Lord Ashburton; MP for Winchester 1906–16; commanded 1/Coldstream, MID twice; killed in action 15 September 1916.
46. The Germans often used sharpshooters from Jaeger battalions, who in peacetime had been gamekeepers or guides. As the tally of British officer casualties mounted, many officers drew Other Ranks (OR) uniform from the quartermaster; with only woven shoulder stars to mark them, they stood a better chance of survival. The role of snipers in the battalion, is examined by Paddy Griffith in *Battle Tactics of the Western Front*, Yale, 1994, pp.73–4.
47. Within groups of officers and men, the feeling of identity was strong. The ability of each individual to hide fear under the stress of bombardment helped group morale; see 'The Influence of Group Life', in WN Maxwell, *A Psychological Retrospect of the Great War*, George Allen & Unwin, 1923.
48. This must be one of the first references to steel helmets in letters from the front line. A few helmets were first tried out in trenches near Hooge on 9 August 1915. This reference relates to the GHQ order for the issue of fifty helmets per battalion in October 1915. These were passed on by troops coming out of line. By March 1916 140,000 had been issued and their success during the actions of Spring 1916 ensured full-scale production.
49. Monica Stapleton-Bretherton; sister of Edith Feilding, living at The Hall, Rainhill.
50. Captain Hon. Lionel H Tennyson (1889–1951); grandson of Lord Alfred Tennyson, Poet Laureate; later Major 1/Coldstream; wounded three times,

MID twice; inherited title of Lord Tennyson when both his brothers were killed in action; later captained and played cricket for England.

51. 'Proceedings of a Medical Board', 9 December 1916; PRO WO339/48941.

WAR LETTERS TO A WIFE

PART I : 1916

SERVICE WITH THE COLDSTREAM GUARDS

1st Battalion (9 April–14 April)
4th Battalion (Pioneers) (15 April–6 September)

On 6 April 1916 RCF is declared fit for service and returns to France.

9 April 1916 [Harfleur]

We got here a little before one yesterday afternoon, after the 5½ mile march from the landing stage at Le Havre.

The sea was like glass, and the scene was very picturesque and rather spectral as our ship lay to, outside the great submarine net, waiting for darkness before setting out. The sun sank into the horizon a gorgeous red, and was followed by the flashes of signals from the destroyers and other craft which surrounded us, while the searchlights played upon the sky, looking for German aeroplanes. I was OC Troops on board, and was invited by the Captain to sleep in his cabin; so I was very comfortable. He wanted me to take his bed, but I could not do that.

I am in the same camp where I was this month last year. It is now the Guards Divisional Base Depot. There must be nearly twenty officers here, including members of all the regiments of the Division.

10 April 1916 [Harfleur]

My dearest Joan,

This letter is to wish you a very happy birthday. How I wish I could drop in to tea this evening and see you all. I have left my present for you with Mother. It is what you asked for – the cap star which I wore all through the tremendous fighting of last September and October.

I was posted last night, back to my old battalion, at which I was delighted: but so far, I have no orders as to when I am to join them.

The officers passing through have, in their spare time, made flower beds which now glitter with daffodils and other flowers. The coats of arms of all the Guards regiments have been planted in flowers. It makes the camp, which is on the side of a steep hill, very pretty.

Best love. Your loving Dada.

*   *   *

14 April 1916 [Harfleur]

I hear I am to go to the Entrenching Battalion, to take over the Coldstream Company.[1] It is a kind of advanced Depot, a stepping-stone to the trenches, where the young officers and soldiers are near enough to the front line to get used to the smell of gunpowder and the noise of shells, before actually joining their battalions.

I have a new servant from the 3rd Battalion called Glover, who seems a good fellow. He tells me he had never been a servant until he came to Harfleur: in fact, he had never been allowed to be. 'You see, sir,' he said, 'I'm a dare devil kind of a chap. I don't care what I do. I'll go out on patrols or anything.' And Acland Hood, who shared my hut, says that this description of Glover is correct.

19 April 1916 [Bois des Tailles, near Bray-sur-Somme]

We left Rouen at half-past three yesterday afternoon with 1,400 troops on board. I was OC train, so had a reserved compartment, which I shared with one of my subalterns. I had never seen Rouen before and was greatly impressed by the Cathedral. I visited the 'Place du vieux Marché', where Joan of Arc was burned, the spot – a couple of yards or so from a butcher's stall – being marked by no more than a slab, over which people walk.

I reached the Entrenching Battalion this afternoon, about forty-four hours after leaving Harfleur, after a wet and muddy march of 6½ miles. The camp is 4 miles behind the firing line, from the direction of which the rumble of the guns can be heard.

The battalion is commanded by Major Kirby Ellice,[2] of the Grenadiers, who is extremely nice and kind to me, and I hope my first jaundiced impression of the place will prove to have been influenced by my disappointment at not having been sent straight back to 1st Battalion, as I had hoped.

26 April 1916 [Bois des Tailles]

The horrible weather, rainy and cold, which I encountered on my first arrival, has gone, and given place to a period of glorious sunshine. What a difference it makes!

This Camp is pitched a few hundred yards from the Somme, where lie the gun-boats, on the top of the high escarpment which rises abruptly from the river on the north side. It is hidden among trees, many of which, wild cherries, are now thick with blossom.

The men sleep in canvas huts; the officers in tents. The officers' mess and ante-room are in a wooden shack – rather like a Newfoundland timberman's rig-out. I sleep on a canvas cot and am sitting on it now, as I write, since chairs do not exist.

On Easter Sunday I rode with Kemes Lloyd[3] to Albert, which is about 5 miles from here. The town has been well bombarded, though in the

On the Somme
by G.P.Fildes & R.Cf.
May 1916

outskirts the houses are still mostly standing. The most pronounced devastation is in the Cathedral square, which, with the exception of the Cathedral itself, has been completely flattened.

The greater part of the Cathedral, which is a modern building of extremely solid construction, still stands precariously, though seamed with cracks and fissures. But what immediately arrests the eye is a colossal gilded statue of the Blessed Virgin and Child which crowns the summit of the tower. This great effigy has been hit and knocked over, and though it lies poised horizontally in mid-air, in the attitude of diving, it still clings to its pedestal and continues to defy all efforts of the German gunners to dislodge it.

The sight is a very remarkable one, and it is not surprising that a superstition has grown up among the French that the ultimate fall of this statue will be the signal for the downfall of the enemy.

As with many religious emblems in the fighting line, the chance action of the shells has rather added to, than detracted from the impressiveness of this one, and as one looks up at it today, the Child, with its hands outspread, seems to be looking down from the Mother's arms in blessing on our soldiers, in the ruined square below.

General Maxse told me that when he first came here, the figure leant at an angle of about 45 degrees and that it has gradually sagged to its present position. So perhaps it will not be so very long before the actual crash comes.

28 April 1916 [Bois des Tailles]

Last Wednesday I dined at General Maxse's headquarters, and sat next to the General.[4] We had whitebait for dinner, which is caught by a very persevering mess cook, who sits on the bank of the Somme, with a gauze net at the end of a pole. He waits till the minnows and small gudgeon swim over his net; then lifts them out of the water; and it takes several hours to get a plateful. But they are very good, and I shall adopt the idea.

Montague took me by car yesterday to visit a part of his Divisional Front where the Somme forms a loop, almost completely enclosing a large tract of swampy ground, some 2,000 yards by 1,000 yards in dimension, so water-logged, that it cannot be trenched; and which consequently has become a sort of neutral territory, where the patrols of both sides wander by night and frequently encounter one another.

The sun was shining brightly, and the nightingales were singing for all they were worth, and all seemed very restful as we visited the outposts. One of those silent lulls was on, when both sides seem to have gone to sleep.

One sees here as elsewhere frequent illustrations of the huge divergence between theory and practice in war. For example, one of the things we used to learn was that you should avoid woods and villages on account of the target they offer to the enemy's artillery. Yet here, skirting the fringe of the marsh I have described, are three villages – Frise, Curlu, and Vaux, the two first occupied by the enemy; the last by our troops. As the ground on either side of the river rises precipitately, each army can look down upon the roofs of the other.

Frise was demolished during the great enemy attack on the French last January 28, and Vaux is more or less battered too, though not greatly so;[5] but from what I could see of Curlu, it is still in a good state of preservation. After all, these villages are small fry, garrisoned perhaps by a Company or less apiece, and though it would be easy to blot them out, they are left alone, probably not being considered worth the risk of bringing down the inevitable retaliation upon the populous villages behind the line on either side, where very much greater numbers of troops might be involved.

We visited the château at Suzanne, a large pretentious building which was much damaged by the bombardment of January 28. It presents an extraordinary mixture of the old and the new; of marble and gilt and glass of the most lurid modern French style; and such things as an old family coach emblazoned with coronets; with heavy velvet trappings round the coachman's seat, and a footboard behind for the lackeys. The little house chapel looks well cared for still, though it is damaged by shell-fire.

*   *   *

8 May 1916 [Bois des Tailles]

Four parcels arrived from you today, containing two pies, a cake, pâté de foie gras, plovers' eggs and smoked salmon. Thank you so much. We had the plovers' eggs and smoked salmon at dinner tonight. Kemes Lloyd, who returned from leave today, began by asking who the new mess president was, so that he might congratulate him. I said, in justice to my Lady, that it was she who had provided these luxuries. To which he answered, 'If only I could find a woman like that, I'd marry her'!

So we have conscription at last! It is about time too. The Conscripts have not, of course, reached us as yet, but some Derby (commonly pronounced 'Durby') men have. It is funny how these latter are despised by the other men, more so than the conscripts, who are regarded as having at least shown the courage of their convictions.[6]

To be called or even thought to be a 'Durby man' is in fact an insult. A few days ago I was at Commanding Officer's 'orders' when a man was brought up for giving an insubordinate reply to a corporal. He had been told to dig, but his spade, he said, was broken, and he had replied: 'I ain't no b***** Durby man'.

16 May 1916 [Bois des Tailles]

The parcel of ham, two dozen plovers' eggs, and the children's sweets arrived today. Thank you all.

I have had to go to a new place to start some work, and took with me one of the sergeants, Deakin, by name. He was working for a fruit grower and seedsman before he enlisted, and being intelligent besides an excellent NCO, I found his conversation very entertaining.

The ground is becoming strewn with a great profusion and variety of wild flowers. Few and far between are wild Lilies of the Valley in bloom, which are much sought after by officers and men, and are therefore difficult to find.

28 May 1916 [Station Hotel, Hazebrouck]

I left camp yesterday at noon with a mixed draft of Grenadier, Coldstream, and Irish Guards, and marched to the railway. It was the first time I had made the trip since the day I first arrived. Do you remember my description? Then the trees had no leaves; the fields no verdure; the whole horizon was a sea of mud, and sheets of rain were falling.

Yesterday, the whole scene had changed. The fields were green with young corn, or yellow with mustard, or crimson with clover. Woods and plantations, the existence of which before I had not noticed, sprung out in all directions, in masses of luxuriant colour. On the hills and in the valleys, villages now peeped out, which before I could not see because of the rain; and the big winding Somme graced all. In fact, I discovered that the country I had been living in for six weeks is really very beautiful in spring.

None of the Division are in the immediate locality, and the battalions are very scattered. Consequently, I have seen nobody I know except Guy Darell, who now wears red tabs, and who came buzzing along in a big staff car, but pulled up when he saw me. The last time I had seen him was at the moment he was bowled over by a shell, just as we were about to start off for our attack on the Chalk Pit Wood on September 27.

He advised me to ring up Divisional Headquarters, which I did, and was answered by his brother, Billy Darell, who is AA and QMG,[7] and who arranges the posting of officers. He recommended me to write to Guy Baring, and to ask him to apply for me. Apparently, they make a point that there should always be a Captain of each regiment with the Entrenching Battalion. Consequently, they may not release me until they get some one else.

Anyhow, I wrote to Guy Baring. I have considered the matter as much as I can. I have sometimes felt that I should not add to your anxieties at this time by pressing to be returned to my battalion, but on the other hand, I have thought that if every married man in my position were content to remain in a safe place, it would be a poor look out for the Army. Finally, if I inspire any confidence in the men, it is certainly right that I should be with them, and I am sure you will agree with me in this.

Do write me your views. God knows how I felt for you in the anxiety you must have endured last autumn, and I dread to repeat that.

29 May 1916 [Grand Hôtel du Rhin, Amiens]

My little scheme to get back to the 1st Battalion has failed so far, and I return to the Entrenching Battalion tomorrow somehow, either by motor car or train.

I visited the Cathedral, here, this evening. The approaches are barricaded with sandbags, to save them from the fate of Rheims. It is beautiful, particularly the stained-glass windows, but I still think our English Cathedrals can hold their own against the Continental; and if the war lasts much longer, they will be the only ones left.

6 June 1916 [Bois des Tailles]

I have been thinking things over today, and I feel I should not have worried you by telling you I was bored here, and wanted to get back to my battalion. I ought to have thought more of you and been contented to stay here. My efforts to get away have failed so far, and I shall not renew them. I shall wait until they send for me, though, if I see a chance of getting some more interesting job, I shall still take that.

But my anxiety to get a more dangerous job is over. I had a walk with my CO yesterday, and he told me more or less plainly that he had heard I was too chancy. Anyhow, that is over for good and all. I can say, before God, that I have never risked a man's life unless I was ordered, or thought it necessary: and I have never asked an officer or man to do a thing which I was not prepared to do myself. He was good enough to say that I was too brave (meaning, I suppose, foolhardy); but, never mind, I won't be brave in future. I shall hate it, but I will take any safe billet they may offer me.

When they say these things it makes me feel I have been unfair to you. But I have tried to act as I have thought you would like me to act. Besides, my inclinations are to be in the swim. You must be most careful about yourself. Don't tire yourself, and you need not worry about me, because I am absolutely safe here.

27 June 1916 [Corbie]

We (the Coldstream Company), 390 strong, paraded at 7.15 on Sunday morning, and marched 8 miles to this place, which is a town with a big church – almost a Cathedral, and an old hospital, something on the lines of St. Cross at Winchester, established eight hundred years ago.

We are in billets. For the officers' mess we have a room over an ironmonger's shop, with chairs, a big table, a piano, and a stuffed heron. The officers sleep in different houses about the town. The men, too, are very scattered. We are all very comfortable, and speaking for myself, I have a fine bedroom with a feather bed, in a brewery.

Yesterday evening I had a bath in the old Convent hospital. While I was still in nothing but my shirt, an old nun walked in, quite unembarrassed;

and began to tell me about Ste. Collette, whom I confess I had not heard of before. She was born here, in a house still standing a few doors from where I am writing, and the nun explained, has the town, and particularly the hospital, under her special protection.

She added that the Germans were here for fifteen days at the beginning of the war; and though they misconducted themselves elsewhere, they behaved like lambs when they came to the Convent, where the nuns were nursing the French wounded.

28 June 1916 [Corbie]

Today the Trench Mortar officer of the 30th Division (Captain Edwards) invited me to lunch at his Artillery Battle Headquarters, in front of Bray, to see the bombardment. It was in full swing, as it has been, day and night, since the 24th. It was an impressive sight.

The Germans must be having a horrible time, I should think. All our valleys are thick with guns and howitzers. In one small valley alone, which I know well, I was told today we have more guns concentrated than were employed by our army in the whole South African War.

1 July 1916 (Saturday) [Corbie]

This has been a great day, as you will have learnt from the newspapers. The battle, for which we have for some months been preparing, has begun, and thanks to a newly made friend, Thornhill, and his car, I have been able to see a lot of it.

The culmination of our bombardment – that is the infantry attack – took place this morning. It was originally planned for Thursday, but was postponed for forty-eight hours owing to the bad weather, which makes most of the roads, which in this part of France are not cobbled, impassable for heavy transport. The same rule no doubt applies to the roads on the German side.

The weather yesterday had become fine. Today, it was perfect. Between 6.30 and 7.30 am our bombardment was intensified. To give you an idea of what it then became, Major Watkins, a Coldstream officer, told me that on his Corps frontage alone (about 3,600 yards), 42,000 shells were sent over by our artillery in sixty-five minutes, or nearly 650 shells per minute. I hear we have 366 guns on this sector, including 8-inch, 12-inch, and 15-inch howitzers. At 7.30 the infantry went over.[8]

Thornhill called for me between 9 and 9.30. We motored to Bronfay Farm, which is just behind Maricourt, opposite Mametz and Montauban. The battle was then in full swing, and the sight was inspiring and magnificent. From right to left, but particularly opposite the French, where the more rugged character of the country is, the whole horizon seemed to be on fire, the bursting shells blending with the smoke from the burning villages. As I have said before, this is essentially a district of long views. Never was there a field better suited for watching military operations, or for conducting them.[9]

As we looked on, the shells from our heavier guns were screaming over our heads, but still, strange to say, the enemy was not replying.

The wounded – those who could walk – were streaming back, some supported by others; crowds of them. Parties of German prisoners too. I counted over seventy in one group, who were being marched under escort to the rear. They were pitiful objects to look upon; some with beards; all unshaven and dirty; some big, some small with spectacles; most with bare heads; a few wounded; all unkempt, dejected, abject, and dazed. Some looked up as they saw us. Most hung their heads and gazed at the ground.

As Thornhill said, 'Though our ambition is to kill as many of these people as we possibly can, when you see them beaten, like that, with that look in their eyes, you can hardly restrain a feeling of pity. I suppose it is the English sporting instinct asserting itself.'

We stayed half an hour or so at Bronfay; then Thornhill, remembering that we were 'joy-riding', and becoming a little anxious about his car, we motored to other parts of the line, passing through Méaulte and Albert, where the statue on the Cathedral is beginning to look very shaky. Here we saw many more wounded, and more German prisoners. I stopped and spoke to some of the former, most of whom looked tired but cheerful. All were smoking the inevitable 'fag'. Then we came home, stopping at various points along the way to watch the progress of the battle. Our artillery was still busy, and I counted twenty English and French observation balloons up together. Not a single German balloon was to be seen. All had been driven from the sky, for the time being, by our wonderful airmen.

It is said that the Germans were unprepared for an offensive in this locality; that the last place they expected to be attacked was opposite the point of contact – between the French and British armies;– that in consequence, they had no great concentration of artillery to meet our troops.[10] If so, they must be blind. Our preparations have been so immense that any photograph from the air must have revealed them. We have made new railways and new roads. The whole landscape has been altered, to say nothing of the fact that for weeks past, every valley has been filled with troops, horses, guns and transport.

I hope and believe our people have got the best of them this time, but do not expect to get much definite news for a few days yet. The wounded I have seen have mostly been hit by machine-guns. Judging from the numerous loaded ambulances I have passed, there must I fear be many casualties.

It has been a wonderful day, and my first experience of a battle as a sightseer. I feel rather a beast for having done it in this way, but shall continue to see all I can of it, for the sake of the experience, which may be useful later.

2 July 1916 (Sunday) [Corbie]

The wounded are still pouring into Corbie by ambulance, in French peasant carts whose owners have picked them up on the road and on foot. The last arrive, straggling along the road, white with dust; and generally bareheaded. The town is beginning to reek of iodoform and carbolic acid.[11]

4 July 1916 [Corbie]

Yesterday morning Kirby Ellice came over to visit us, and after seeing the Company at drill, he made a little speech.

In the afternoon, with three of my officers, I visited the battlefield of three days ago. We lorry jumped to Bray. From there we struck off on foot along the road towards Mametz, one of the villages captured by our troops. The fighting was still continuing in front, but in the ruined village itself all was quiet. Our heavy guns were firing over our heads as we walked, but beyond an occasional shrapnel burst in the distance, the German artillery was quiescent, and we were able to explore the surface in safety.

After proceeding 3½ miles we reached what last Saturday was the British front line. It was very battered, and scarcely recognisable as a fire-trench. Then we crossed No Man's Land, where we found infantry at work, salving equipment, and collecting the dead. Of the latter I counted a hundred in one group – a pitiful sight.

Then we came to what had been the German wire entanglements. Here our guns had certainly done their work well. The wire was completely demolished. Not one square yard had escaped the shells.[12] Then we came to the German fire-trench. It is difficult to understand how any living creature could have survived such bombardment. The trench was entirely wrecked, and so flattened that it could have given little if any cover at the end. Leigh-Bennett,[13] who was with me and who has been fighting in Gallipoli, when he saw this, his first view of a French battlefield, said: 'I see now, that what we thought was heavy shelling in Gallipoli, was mere child's play'.

Fifty yards beyond the German fire-trench was their Support trench, and about the same distance further on, their Reserve trench. Both had suffered severely. The ground is strewn with unexploded shells of ours, mostly of heavy calibre.

I went into some of the dug-outs, but as I had neither electric torch nor matches, it was not possible to see much. They are of varying depths, some being quite 20 feet below the surface, and are well made, the sides and roofs being strongly supported by timber. I saw only one that had more than one entrance, and it was on fire.

After exploring these remains of the German trenches we went on into Mametz village where living man was represented by the Salvage folk and a few infantry making their way up to the new front line. Scarcely a wall stands, and of the trees nothing remains but mangled twisted stumps. The ruins present an appalling and most gruesome picture of the havoc of war, seen fresh, which no pen or picture can describe. You must see it, and smell it, and hear the sounds, to understand. It brings a sort of sickening feeling to me even now, though I consider myself hardened to such sights.

To give an idea of the long period of time which the line, at this point, has remained stationary, I may say that in No Man's Land I saw two skeletons, one in German uniform, and the other in the long discarded red infantry breeches of the French.[14]

5 July 1916 [Corbie]

About midday yesterday, a thunderstorm burst out, and for a couple of hours there was torrential rain, so that the roads became like rivers. Thornhill and I motored to Bronfay Farm; and from there struck out on foot to our old front line. This brought us to the right of where I had been the day before.

The experience was practically a repetition of what I have described to you; the sordid scenes the same. The scaling ladders used by our troops to climb out of the trenches at the moment of assault were still in position – most suggestive to the imagination. The dead in many cases still lay where they had fallen. Less than a mile along the valley a furious fight was going on around Fricourt and Fricourt Wood. On our right the French were hard at it, and continued so throughout the night. For the time, I have seen enough of battlefields – I am 'fed up' as a sightseer.

6 July 1916 [Bois des Tailles]

I was up this morning at 5.30, and at 6.45 we marched from Corbie to rejoin the Entrenching Battalion in the Bois des Tailles.

I came across some officers of the 15th and 11th Hussars, with a party of men, burying Germans, most of whom they had to drag out of the dug-outs, where they lie, crunched up in fantastic attitudes: a very unpleasant duty after so long an interval. As I looked down the steep staircase of one of the deep dug-outs, and saw a dead German standing on his head at the bottom, I thought, 'Imagine if his mother could see him'. I suppose our enemies, too, have mothers, to whom they are all the world.

I saw a big 'minenwerfer'[15] very cunningly concealed in a deep excavation. A piece of paper was attached to it, with the following words: 'Captured by the Minden boys', i.e. the Suffolk Regiment.

Our heavy artillery is being pushed forward and you never know where or when you may stumble into a battery. Often the first intimation that one is there – for they are well concealed – is the crack of a gun, and the swish of a shell that feels like shattering your eardrums.

*   *   *

8 July 1916 [Bois des Tailles]

Yesterday I went off alone to visit Fricourt, which our troops captured last Monday. There was a picture of the village two or three days ago in the 'Daily Mirror', which I saw yesterday. The picture showed a church and a street of battered houses. It was not the Fricourt of today, which has no church, nor even a house standing. There remain just fragments of walls: that is all.

As you enter the village from this side you pass the cemetery. The tombstones practically all have been shattered and scattered broadcast. Scarcely a grave could be recognised by its nearest and dearest, save through its position. In one case, near the roadside, a shell has fallen upon one of those elaborate and rather pretentious family vaults so much in vogue in France, pulverising the great black granite slab which covered it, and exposing the coffin shelves below.

Heavy rain began to fall at midday, and continued in torrents at intervals throughout the afternoon. I had gone to Fricourt to look for Percy Clive, but when I reached the place I found that heavy fighting was in progress before Mametz Wood, about a mile in front, and that his battalion was in it.[16] So I had to postpone my visit.

The wounded were being carried back in streams, all covered from head to foot with the mud in which they had been fighting, slimy and glistening like seals. It looks more and more as if Hell cannot be much worse than what our infantry is going through at the present moment.

I mentioned to a machine-gun officer, whom I met, that I might be going on leave in a day or two, and should like a souvenir from Fricourt. Said he, 'I think I can help you then', and took me to a place his men had just discovered. I have seen many dug-outs, but this beat them all. It might almost be described as an underground house, where instead of going upstairs you went down, by one flight after another, to the different stories. There were three floors, the deepest being 60 feet or more from the door by which I entered. The entrance hall was the brick cellar of a former house.

The German occupants had evidently abandoned the place in a hurry, in the fear, entirely justified, that they might be buried alive if they stayed there. They had left everything behind. The floors were littered with every kind of thing, from heavy trench mortar bombs to grenades, the size of an egg, and from steel helmets to underclothing. Many rifles hung from the wooden walls of the first flight of stairs: The nooks and corners of the rooms were occupied by sleeping bunks, and from one of these I picked up the French 'Alphabet de Mademoiselle Lili', par 'un papa', delightfully illustrated, which I will send home to the children.

One meets nowadays on the roads many wagons returning from the direction of the line, loaded with 'swab' equipment. The troops of the new army wear pieces of cloth of different colours to distinguish their

Divisions and Brigades. A battalion – I think of Royal Fusiliers – which I saw marching up, fresh and clean and full of life and vigour, a day or two before July 1, had pieces of pink flannel over their haversacks, displayed in such a way as to be recognisable in battle by our aeroplanes.

A few days later I passed a wagon load of salved equipment returning from the line. It was interleaved with the same pink flannel, now no longer fluttering gaily, but sodden and bedraggled, and caked with sticky clay.

10 July 1916 [Bois des Tailles]

Yesterday, I went and explored the line of trenches captured this week between Mametz and Fricourt. It is one of the most mined sections of the whole of our front. For a length of 800 yards a practically continuous line of huge craters, some 50 feet deep at least, occupies the full width of No Man's Land from the British to the German parapet. Most of these contain water, which in some cases is red with blood, even today, a week after the battle.

The contrast between the two front trenches is remarkable. Though the line has remained stationary so long, ours gives the impression of a temporary halting-place; the German of a permanent defence. The effect of the suicidal German practice of having deep dug-outs in their front line is illustrated here, for most contain dead, who never could have fought, but must have been killed like rats in their holes.

Many French dead – skeletons now – still lie unburied in No Man's Land, dating from the period before our troops took over this part of the line. I saw some even between the German fire and support trenches, which, one would have thought, the enemy would have buried for the sake of their own comfort, if for no other reason.

12 July 1916 [Bois des Tailles]

German prisoners keep coming back all the time in driblets, and most of the cages hold a few. In one I passed today there were about a dozen, big, fine looking, fit men, apparently quite happy. They were chatting and laughing among themselves, and smoking cigarettes and eating bully beef supplied to them by our soft-hearted soldiers, who, though fierce enough in action, seem to take delight in feeding their enemy and giving him smokes once they have him safely caged. I even saw one man go to the trouble of opening a tin of beef before handing it through the wires.

14 July 1916 [Bois des Tailles]

This afternoon I visited the ruins of Montauban, which was captured by our troops on the 1st. The village is set on a hill, with long views in all directions. In front, in the distance, I could see the woods round the Bazentins, in which this morning's battle was fought, and where fighting was still in progress.

As General John Ponsonby used to say, 'A battle three or four times as big as Waterloo is fought a few miles away, but nobody thinks it worth while to ring up and tell you the result'. You, in London, hear much more quickly than we do; if indeed the result can be gauged at all, for in truth, bloody though they are, these almost daily battles represent but one move apiece in the deadly game.

17 July 1916 [Bois des Tailles].

I took a working party to Carnoy today. While I was there, a Tunnelling Officer asked me if I would like to see one of the German mines. Of course I said 'Yes'. There were several entrances – mostly blown in by our shell-fire, and we entered by an undamaged one from the enemy support trench.

First, we descended an incline to a vertical depth of about 15 feet below the surface. Then we climbed 60 feet further down a perpendicular ladder, through a shaft so narrow that it was possible to rest one's back against the wall. From the bottom of this we followed a close-timbered tunnel to the 'transversal' gallery, from which other galleries led towards our own front line. The excavation was in chalk, and perfectly dry. An electric cable passed down the shaft, and the officer who escorted me told me that, when the workings were first entered, an electric plant (dynamo, petrol engine, etc.) had been found, which had since been salved.[17]

By the time I saw them, the galleries had been surveyed by our engineers, and, to satisfy their curiosity, connected up with our own, so that it was possible to walk from the German support line to ours, or vice versa, at a depth of 75 or 80 feet below the surface. My guide told me that on July 1st, at a minute before zero (the moment of assault), his Company alone had exploded thirteen mines, beneath or near the German trenches!

I got a lift back to camp on an ambulance, with the usual cargo behind. I sat in front, and found myself beside a young private of the South African Brigade, wounded by a shell in the leg and ankle. He was all in a quiver. He had been lying out, waiting for the stretcher-bearers, from eight o'clock last night till this afternoon, and was in great pain. His Brigade had caught it very badly, and he said there were few of his battalion left. He spoke a good deal. His father, he said, had fought in the Matabele and Boer Wars, and is now fighting in East Africa, where also his brother is. He himself had come on to France from the S.W. African campaign. Before the war he was a hunter in the Transvaal and Rhodesia.

19 July 1916 [Bois des Tailles]

Captain George Lane (Coldstream Guards), who is Camp Commandant to the Guards Division, and Colonel Balfour turned up today, having come over in a car to see this battlefield.

Kemes Lloyd and I went with them. We motored first to Albert, then to Fricourt. Then we walked along the line of craters to Mametz. From there we motored to Mametz Wood, which was the scene of very heavy fighting a week or ten days ago. Here we were fortunate enough to come upon two French 75-mm. batteries in action, firing at top speed. I had always wished but had never seen this before at close quarters. The 75 is the French field gun, and though it looks almost like a toy, is the best balanced and the most perfect of weapons. It is the terror of the enemy, and worked as it is worked by the French gunners, is probably the quickest firing gun of its type in the field[18]

The Captain, a Frenchman possessing very striking features, after the 'cease fire', seeing how interested we were, walked up to us, saluted grandly, then ordered one more round to be fired – 'to demonstrate the mechanism'. Then, saluting again, he picked up the last shell-case, and with a bow, offered it to Colonel Balfour. It was a pretty little piece of by-play, and I shall never forget his face, or the grandiloquent manner in which he presented the souvenir.

21 July 1916 [Near Fricourt]

Yesterday, I was at work, all day, on what has now become one of our main lines of communication in these parts; beginning to convert a quagmire into a road fit for transport of the heaviest kind.

The conditions were something like what it would be if one were repairing Piccadilly during the height of the season without being allowed the privilege of roping off half the street in that aggravating way they have in London. In short, traffic innumerable was passing to and fro all the time.

Part of the backward traffic consisted of a unit of a famous New Army Division – the Highland Brigade – in course of relief from the battle. They have an advantage over us in that when they come out they are met by their bagpipes and drums. Each Company is preceded by pipers.

It was a sad sight to watch them yesterday, however, because scarcely a Company was more than 60 or 80 strong, compared probably with the 180 they had taken into action three days previously; but it was inspiring to see these men. On their faces they showed little sign of the appalling ordeal they had undergone.

The weather today has been gorgeous, and the enemy aeroplanes have taken advantage of it and become active. Our anti-aircraft gunners are active too, and hundreds of little puffs from their bursting shells speckle the blue sky.

24 July 1916 [Near Fricourt]

How sad the world is. One of my men has just been before me, almost in tears. He handed me a letter, just received, telling him that the eldest of his two little girls has been run over and killed by a motor-car. He has been out here, and has not seen his family since August last year. I luckily struck the Commanding Officer at an opportune moment, and he has promised to forward an application for special leave for this man, but it will probably fail.

There are so many hard cases, and the Higher Authorities are likely to argue, in this one, that since the child is dead, the father can do no good by going home – which is logical if brutal.

25 July 1916 [Near Fricourt]

This morning, I walked with two other C.G. Officers to a point opposite Contalmaison and Pozières, and watched a terrific bombardment by the enemy's artillery.

The Australians and some of our Territorials had attacked once more during the night, and I hear, had gained the remainder of the village.[19] Hence the fury of the enemy, whose heaviest shells were crashing tempestuously against the ruins, sending up great clouds of earth and brick dust, and producing a Gehenna-like impression, which I confess I felt thankful to be clear of.

Then, my companions being bent on sightseeing turned off to the left, while I struck out alone in the opposite direction, across country towards Carnoy, where I had some men at work.

Then suddenly, the enemy opened one of those promiscuous hurricane bombardments, and I found myself in the middle of the picture! I was out in the open when it started, but continued in the direction I was going, trying to look dignified, though in reality feeling rather foolish as I walked among the flying pieces towards some heads which I saw silhouetted against the skyline, some 400 yards away.

These I found belonged to two Gunner Officers and about five men who were sheltering in a trench. By the time I reached them the shelling had become heavy. They invited me into an old German observation post which they were using as a telephone dug-out, and which, being covered with a layer of rails and sandbags, was at least splinter-proof.

I went in, expecting to remain perhaps a quarter of an hour: I stayed, marooned for 3½ hours! Shells of every calibre – thousands of them, often many in the air together, high explosive and shrapnel – burst on the ground and in the air. They plunged all around our little shelter. One burst on the parapet, 3 feet from the door. Another, a dud, landed a foot or two short of the dugout, penetrated deep into the ground, and made the place shiver. Over and over again, bits of steel and a deluge of soil from bursting shells rattled into the trench outside. What folly, to get killed sightseeing, and what a fool to have risked it just as I was going home on leave.

At last there was a lull. One of the men suggested that Fritz had 'packed up'. I climbed out of the trench and made my way onwards, over the surface. Almost immediately the shelling started again but I was determined to chance it this time, and in half an hour or less, I found myself amid silent surroundings, among the ruins of Mametz. It was very restful to be out of the shelling, which had been really hot, and reminiscent of the worst days of last September and October.

Shall I analyse my sensations during a long and heavy bombardment? If I tried to do so I think I should say that for the first hour the feeling is one of apprehension: for the second, of indifference; and for the third and after, of sleepiness. The soporific effect of a bombardment is very strange.

26 July 1916 [Near Fricourt]

My servant[20] is always asking me to take him with me, 'in case', as he puts it, 'anything should happen to me'. So today I took him to Carnoy. He is like a wild man, and is always thirsting to 'pop over the sandbags'. He assured me this morning that if ever I have to do so, he would like to be by my side; and this, I think, is not mere talk.

He is a very gallant fellow, and last year I believe was recommended for a decoration, though it was refused (he says) because of his previous character. He has not always been a paragon of virtue. But what a reason, if true, to refuse a man recognition of his bravery! He has been out ever since August 1914, and was at Landrecies in the 3rd Battalion. He has never been more than a private, though he has soldiered all his life, having enlisted at sixteen under a fictitious age. His father claimed him back on that occasion. He is now twenty-six. He told me today that he would never be a corporal. Knowing that many men refuse the stripes for various reasons, I asked him what was his? He answered, characteristically, that it was because he would never then be able to ask even his best friend, if the latter were a private, to go into a pub with him and have a drink!

He describes to me his 'crimes', which according to him, were mere peccadilloes, such as, 'Looking contemptuously at the sergeant-major', but I have little doubt that he has given much trouble on occasion.

This morning I took him along the old German front line, past the craters, where the whole surface has been so violently distorted by the mining operations and the shell-fire of nearly two years, and where the trenches are battered almost flat.

We passed a group of four French skeletons – or rather what had been skeletons till the receding tide of war left them exposed to the traffic in the 'fairway'. Until July 1, they had lain undisturbed in No Man's Land, in their old uniforms of two years ago. Today, after the passage of many troops, their bones are scattered, though identifiable by the scarlet rags which still adhere. Tomorrow I shall send my servant to bury them, as well as any others he can find. I know of many.

*   *   *

28 July 1916 [Near Fricourt]

A message came this evening, saying that I have been granted seven days leave;- papers arriving tomorrow. So I shall leave here on Sunday morning.

I have a German rifle in my tent which I thought of bringing home, in spite of the regulations to the contrary, but I abandoned the idea on account of its bulkiness. Upon telling my servant this today, he offered to take the rifle home for me, when he goes on leave. I asked him how he proposed to do it, adding that he would certainly be stopped. 'I should carry it instead of my own rifle, sir,' he said. 'And how would you account for not having a rifle on landing in France again, after your leave?' I asked. 'Oh,' said he, with a grin, 'you've got to risk something in this world if you are going to have any success. You should just see me play nap, sir!'

RCF goes on leave 2–7 August and stays with his family at Wheler. He returns to France on Monday 7 August.

9 August 1916 [Near Fricourt]

I left Boulogne at nine o'clock on Monday evening, and spent most of the night in a crowded train, carrying French troops. The latter filled even the 1st class carriages – 'poilus'[21] rather merry – returning to the trenches after six days 'permission'.

Yesterday, I worked my way back here, about 25 miles by road, getting lifts on sundry motor-cars and an ambulance and walking a mile or two of the way. To finish up with I was picked up by the Camp Commandant of Rollo's Division, who sent me right up to this camp in his car.

13 August 1916 [Near Fricourt]

Yesterday afternoon I visited the Guards Division, which lately moved to this area.

Just as I was arriving in a Staff car on which I had been given a lift, I passed Humphrey de Trafford[22] and Hugh Kennedy.[23] They were just going out riding. Humphrey is leaving to take over the Adjutantcy of the Machine-Gun School at Grantham, and had been left out of the trenches, where the rest of the 1st Battalion were. He walked with me to Divisional Headquarters, where I saw Geoffrey Feilding, and several of his staff.

Geoffrey was in the best of form. He lent me his car to go and see General John Ponsonby, inviting me to return to dinner at 8.15. So I motored off to John Ponsonby's Headquarters and had a great welcome from the General and several others who were there – Guy Baring, who still commands the 1st Battalion, Sherrard Godman, commanding the 1st Scots Guards, 'Boy' Brooke,[24] now commanding the 3rd Grenadiers, 'Bart' Bartholomew[25] and others.

They were just sitting down to a Commanding Officers' Conference, so

I did not stay long. Then I went back to Divisional Headquarters, where I sat with Geoffrey, in his hut, for half an hour before going into dinner. After dinner Geoffrey sent me home in his car. No headlights are allowed, so as a heavy bombardment was in progress all along the front, the flashes of the guns were very vivid and imposing. Tonight is quiet. It is a night of flares – white and coloured – and we have been sitting out since dinner, watching what might almost have been a professional firework show.

16 August 1916 [Near Fricourt]

My darling Joan,

I enjoyed my stay at Wheler tremendously, and it was very sad coming away from you all. We have been having a good deal of rain lately, but today it has been beautiful and clear, which has brought out a lot of observation balloons, or 'sausages' as they are called. Twenty-six English and French balloons were counted from here today, and twelve German; thirty-eight in all.

Geoffrey Feilding who commands the Guards Division, came over to tea yesterday and I took him to see the huge mine craters and the battered trenches which we captured from the Germans on July 1.

Your loving father.

18 August 1916 [Near Fricourt]

This afternoon I watched a huge battle between Martinpuich and Guillemont. I watched from the high ground just south-east of Fricourt, which commands a wonderful view of the country.

It was a big show – far bigger, I dare say, than anyone might suppose from reading the newspaper reports of it, which will no doubt appear tomorrow.

Later – I hope today was a success. Anyhow, I have already seen a batch of prisoners (wounded) in the cage below this camp.

Unwounded German prisoners are employed on the roads in safe places several miles behind the line. I saw a good many the other day at Corbie. It was funny to see parties of them – great big fellows, including Prussian Guards – being shepherded by our 'Bantams'. The latter, with their top-heavy rifles and fixed bayonets, look very businesslike all the same, in spite of their small stature.[26]

23 August 1916 [Near Fricourt]

This, evening, to my joy, I have received orders to rejoin the Guards Division (starting at seven tomorrow morning).

25 August 1916 [Naours]

I was up at 5.45 yesterday morning, to catch the train at Méricourt. Five other officers were with me, including, however, only one Coldstreamer

(Walpole). We had an early lunch at Amiens, and afterwards, there being no immediate train out, we managed luckily to find a Flying Corps tender going our way, which brought Walpole, myself, our servants and kits to the Guards Divisional Headquarters at Vignacourt; where we found Geoffrey Feilding and his Staff having lunch.

They invited us in, and I was told that an application had been forwarded for me to go through a course, with a view to my becoming Divisional Trench Mortar Officer. I met Colonel 'Billy' Darell, George Lane, Dalkeith, Seymour, Jack Stirling (who was passing), and others. Darell afterwards motored me via the different Brigade Headquarters which he was visiting, and finally dropped me here with the 1st Battalion.

I have met so many friends that it would bore you if I named them all. I had tea with Colonel Skeffington Smyth (4th Battalion), and in the evening met General John Ponsonby, who took me along with him for a walk. He said he had heard about the Trench Mortar proposal, and gave me some advice as to the duties it would entail.

I saw Father Knapp (you will remember he comes from the Carmelites in Church Street). He has the Military Cross now. He is a splendid fellow, and has been with the 2nd Irish Guards ever since Loos. He said he was going to give Benediction at seven o'clock (last night) at the village church. So I went. It is a beautiful church – inside and out. I think almost the prettiest small church I have seen in France. But perhaps I say that because I am in such a happy mood at getting back to the Division.

26 August 1916 [Morlancourt]

We marched 4 miles to the station at Canaples yesterday, starting at 2 pm. I marched at the rear of the battalion with Humphrey de Trafford, who, until he leaves for Windsor, is a supernumerary, like myself. He and I stood on the short causeway leading to the village church, as the battalion moved off, and as No. 4 Company went by, I was greeted by broad grins of recognition by the men – that is to say those of them who were with me last year.

All through the day I kept meeting old friends – officers, NCOs and men. It is surprising what a change eight months have made in some of the younger ones. I left them boys, and return to find them men.

29 August 1916 [Morlancourt]

Yesterday morning I went to early Communion. Crowds of soldiers of the Division were there. Father Knapp has certainly succeeded in whipping up his flock. He is now assisted by another priest. He is a very successful Chaplain, has a very pleasing manner, and is very popular with the men. His brother was with me in Matabeleland, but was killed afterwards, in the Boer War.

Last night I dined with the Brigadier (General John Ponsonby). His latest joke is that if anyone makes a 'faux pas' in conversation he has to stand on a chair; the unfortunate remark being recorded against him in a book which is kept for the purpose. Most people fall into the trap. I did not escape. I said I had just read a splendid novel – referring to 'The Turnstile' by Mason. They asked me where it was. I said I had sent it to you. The Brigadier at once said this was a case for 'the chair'. I explained, by way of excuse, that you were 'in the wilds' of England, thirsting for literature, which you could not get. I was asked to explain what I meant by 'in the wilds'. I said Leicestershire. This just put the lid on it. Of course, John Ponsonby was delighted with his joke.

I sat next to him and told him how I had got side-tracked in the Entrenching Battalion. He said he had no idea that I was in France till he saw me a fortnight ago, which shows how little people know of one another's movements here. He suggested that I ought to get command of one of the New Army battalions, and asked me to come round this morning to talk it over. This I did. I feel I cannot decide upon this point myself. I do not want to leave the Division. But it was arranged that he should discuss the whole thing with Geoffrey, whom he was going to see today.

30 August 1916 [Morlancourt]

I told you in my letter of yesterday how things stood with regard to myself. This afternoon I got a message to go and see the Brigadier as soon as possible. He told me he had had a talk with Geoffrey, and also with Guy Baring. Geoffrey apparently had approved of the idea of a battalion for me, and thought it would be much to my advantage, and that I would do it well. The Brigadier added that it is practically certain that I shall be offered the job of Divisional Trench Mortar Officer, but they are now also going to write up and recommend me for the command of a battalion. So you see things are going well with me. Moreover, you need have no anxiety, because it is hardly likely that my new battalion (if I get it) will have to make any more attacks this year. Indeed, it is extremely unlikely, because the attacking season will be practically over by the time I get there.

I wonder what you will think of my news today. I have always said before that I would rather command a Coldstream Company than a battalion elsewhere. But the difficulty is my age. There is no getting away from the fact that, although physically I am well fitted for the strain and hardships, I am, in years, very old as Company Commanders go. I am double the age of all or nearly all the other Company Commanders of the Division, and there is practically no chance of promotion here.

Do write and tell me what you think.

*   *   *

1 September 1916 [Morlancourt]

The air is thick with balloons and aeroplanes nowadays. Yesterday, I counted thirty aeroplanes at least, and, if I had had glasses, I could no doubt have seen more.[27]

3 September 1916 [Morlancourt]

Still no orders. Bewicke-Copley[28] has just come out again, and he and I are riding out this afternoon to a place where Geoffrey is inspecting ideas from the different Brigades, with a view to determining how best the men can be equipped for the attack.

This morning (Sunday), at ten o'clock, I went to Mass. As I was leaving the Church I met Cecil Trafford, who asked me to his mess (Headquarters – 1st Scots Guards).

The latter is a house with a sort of garden or small yard in front of it. As we were crossing this there was a sudden loud explosion, and bits flew through the air about us. We looked round and saw Leach,[29] the bombing officer of the battalion (who had just come from visiting my own mess), on the ground, 5 yards away. He lay on his back, in a pool of blood, his arms outstretched and both his hands blown off. His brother officers soon began to collect around him, so I left, but I do not think he then had more than a short time to live.

Later – I have learnt some particulars about poor Leach's accident. He was detonating a bomb in the orderly room, which is a shed opening on to the yard, when the safety-pin slipped. Seeing that it was going to explode, and some of his men being in the shed, after ordering them to lie down, he picked up the bomb and dashed outside to get rid of it. He then had less than four seconds in which to decide what to do. I can only suppose that seeing Cecil and myself in the middle of the yard he came to the conclusion that his one chance of throwing it safely away was gone.

So he turned his back to us, faced the wall, and hugging the bomb in his hands, allowed it to explode between his body and the wall.

It is impossible to speak much of such courage and self-sacrifice. He is since dead. He was only twenty-two.

4 September 1916 [Morlancourt]

For better or for worse I have some interesting news for you today, though I wish I had had an opportunity of talking it over with you beforehand.

This afternoon, after tea with No. 2 Company, Bewicke-Copley and I rode to see the Grenadier Boxing Competitions. I rode a 'hairy' on a snaffle, which tried to bolt most of the way. Halfway, we passed in the distance two Staff Officers, one of whom called to me. They turned out to be Colonel 'Billy' Darell and Hermon Hodge. The former told me that I had been recommended for the command of one of the New Army battalions, and that today, in running through the correspondence, he had seen that I had been appointed to a battalion of the Connaught Rangers. It was not official yet: he had only had time to glance at the papers; and not even Geoffrey knew about it.

After the boxing I called on John Ponsonby and told him what Darell had told me. He is confident, and so, he told me, is Geoffrey, with whom he has again discussed the matter that I shall do right to accept. Being only a Special Reserve officer, you see, and an amateur soldier at that, I can never rise higher than a Company Commander here.

I then returned to the mess, where I found 'Bing' Hopwood, who, in Baring's absence, is commanding the battalion. I told him also what I had heard, and he and I went for an hour's walk, and talked things over. He is an extraordinarily silent fellow, and in the early days of our acquaintanceship I confess I never understood him. But the last fortnight, living with him, I have got to know him, and have acquired great confidence in him.

As I have said, I do so wish I could have talked it over with you, and got your opinion. It would have been such a help to me could I have done so. As it is, I feel very diffident as to whether I can command a battalion efficiently – let alone a battalion of Irishmen, of whose characteristics I am completely ignorant. You must continue to pray hard for me, and that whatever I may have to do I do it well;– and all will come right, I am sure. It will be a strange feeling, jumping up to find myself a Colonel.

5 September 1916 [Morlancourt]

Tonight I have been with others to see an exhibition of the 'Somme film', which was shown upon a screen, erected in a muddy field under the open sky. Presumably by way of contrast, Charlie Chaplin was also to have appeared, and I confess it was chiefly him I went to see. However, I came too late, and saw only the more harrowing part of the entertainment.[30]

This battle film is really a wonderful and most realistic production, but must of necessity be wanting in that the battle is fought in silence, and moreover, that the most unpleasant part – the machine-gun and rifle fire – is entirely eliminated. Of the actual 'frightfulness' of war, all that one sees is the bursting shells; and perhaps it is as well. I have said that the battle is fought in silence; but no, on this occasion the roar of real battle was loudly audible in the distance.

I must say that at first the wisdom of showing such a film to soldiers on the brink of a battle in which they are to play the part of attackers struck me as questionable. However, on my way home, my mind was set at rest upon this point by a conversation I overheard between two recruits who were walking behind me.

Said one, 'As to reality, now you knows what you've got to face. If it was left to the imagination you might think all sorts of silly b***** things.'

I wonder where his imagination would have led him had he not seen the Cinema. Would it, do you think, have gone beyond the reality? Hell itself could hardly do so. I think sometimes that people who have not seen, must find it difficult to comprehend how undisturbed life in the trenches can be on occasion: equally, how terrible can be the battle.

6 September 1916 [Morlancourt]

There was Brigade Battle training today, and on my return to billets, I found my orders. I am to assume temporary command of the 6th Connaught Rangers, belonging to the 47th Brigade, 16th (South Irish) Division, who, I find, are not far from here, at Carnoy – a place I knew well when I was with the Entrenching Battalion. It is the only battalion of the Connaught Rangers on the Western Front, and I am to join it this afternoon.[31]

NOTES

1. This entrenching formation appears to be the 4/Coldstream (Pioneers) Battalion, the pioneer unit for the Guards Division. Although a Coldstream battalion, it became a hybrid for other Guards battalions. For a detailed history of the Coldstream and its battalions, see Lieutenant-Colonel Sir John Ross, *The Coldstream Guards 1914–1918*, OUP, 1921.
2. Major EC (Kirby) Ellice; born 1858; joined Grenadier Guards 1876; Captain 1886, retired 1892; served Boer War with Lovat's Scouts; MP for St Andrews Burghs, 1903–6; rejoined Grenadiers 1914, promoted Major 1915. Whilst commanding the Guards Pioneer Battalion, he learned that both his sons had died of wounds, within a month of each other, in Autumn 1916.
3. Captain MKA Lloyd, 2/Grenadier Guards; wounded at Ypres, 1914; killed in action, 15 September 1916.
4. General Sir (Frederick) Ivor Maxse (1862–1958); Captain 2/Coldstream, 1891; 2nd in command 3/Coldstream, 1903; OC 2/Coldstream, 1903–7; Regimental Lieutenant-Colonel Coldstream Guards, 1907; GOC 1st (Guards) Brigade, 1914; Major-General commanding 18th Division, 1915–17; promoted General, 1923. Maxse was regarded as the finest trainer of troops in the war; see John Baynes, *Far From A Donkey*, Brassey's, 1995.
5. In a simultaneous attack, the Germans captured Frise from the French, but failed in their assault against the British at Carnoy, north of the River Somme.
6. On 11 October 1915 Lord Derby was appointed Director-General of Recruiting and immediately introduced the 'Derby Scheme'. It was a last ditch attempt to obtain recruits voluntarily, after the War Office gave notice that voluntary enlistment would cease in December 1915. The scheme attracted 215,000 men, but this was insufficient to defer conscription, which was introduced in January 1916 for single men, and May 1916 for married men; see Dr Ian Beckett, Keith Simpson (eds), *A Nation in Arms*, Tom Donovan, 1990, pp.115–18; for a general study of the conscription issue, see Ilana Bet-el, *Conscripts – Lost Legions of the Great War*, Sutton Publishing, 1999.
7. Assistant Adjutant and Quartermaster-General.
8. Much criticism has been levelled at GHQ over the timing of the attack – 7.30 am, full daylight on a summer day. However, the British wanted to attack in the dawn half-light, but deferred to the wishes of their senior French

partners, who wanted as much light as possible for their artillery; see John Terraine, '1916: the year of the Somme', *Army Quarterly & Defence Journal*, October 1986.

9. In front of Maricourt, the 30th Division (Shea), advanced ½ mile and the 18th Division (Maxse) advanced one mile, capturing Montauban by midday on 1 July. Their comparative success on the first day was partly due to straightforward terrain and clear objectives.

10. The British 30th Division were on one side of the allied boundary, the French 39th Division on the other side. The Germans mustered only twenty-three combined gun batteries in this southern sector against the sixty-eight they ranged against the British to the north. The British 30th and 18th Divisions were also helped by the heavy batteries of the neighbouring French XX Corps.

11. Antiseptic and disinfecting agents.

12. The 7th and 21st Divisions (XV Corps), who were charged with capturing Mametz and Fricourt, received effective supporting artillery from XV Corps. The GOCRA made extensive and effective use of the new creeping barrage; Major AF Becke, 'The Coming of the Creeping Barrage', *Journal of the R.A. Institution*, April 1931.

13. 2nd Lieutenant HW Leigh-Bennett; born 1880; 1/Coldstream Guards; his brother, Arthur, was killed in action 3 October 1915. His cousin, Olliph, died of wounds, a week after the armistice. Both were officers of the Coldstream.

14. From the outbreak of war, in 1914, the French Army persisted with the red pantaloons and *képi* of the old Second Empire uniform. By 1916 these had been phased out in favour of the *horizon bleu* uniform.

15. German trench mortar, which had its weaknesses – the heavy and medium types were prone to burst in cold weather. In average soil, their projectiles made a crater six metres deep and ten metres wide.

16. The bitter contest for Mametz Wood chiefly involved the 38th (Welsh) Division; for a detailed study, see Colin Hughes, *Mametz – Lloyd George's 'Welsh Army' at the Battle of the Somme*, Gliddon Books, 1990 and the classic by David Jones, *In Parenthesis*, Faber & Faber, 1937.

17. For further reading on the story of tunnelling, see *The Work of the Royal Engineers in the European War, 1914–19: Military Mining*, Chatham RE Inst., 1922, and Alexander Barrie, *War Underground: The Tunnellers of the Great War*, Tom Donovan, 1990; reprinted Spellmount, 2000.

18. The '75' had excellent mobility and was quick-firing but because of its lightness, was often ineffective against solid enemy redoubts. The life of a French artillery battery, similar to the one described by RCF, was evoked by Paul Lintier in his superb memoir, *My Seventy-Five*, Peter Davies 1929, previously published as *Ma Pièce*, Plon-Nourrit, 1916.

19. Brigades of the Australian Imperial Force (AIF) 1st Division (Walker) attacked the remaining enemy positions through the night. The Territorials referred to may be the adjacent 48th (South Midland) Division, who were in action on 23 July 1916.

20. Historically, 'servants' were civilians hired to take charge of baggage horses. By the end of the Great War, officers' servants became known as batmen (from the French *bat*/pack or saddle). One of their more unpleasant duties was to sometimes act as runner for their officer, in the event of a raid or attack. Fatalities were high.

21. *Poilu* – literally, 'hairy one'. The nickname given to French infantrymen, on account of their fashion for unkempt beards. Its usage predates the Great War

– references can be found in the papers of General Balzac, a Napoleonic commander.

22. Captain Humphrey de Trafford MC; born 1891; 1/Coldstream; succeeded to baronetcy, 1929; known to RCF because his cousin, Agnes Feilding, married into the de Trafford family.

23. Lord Hugh Kennedy MC; born 1895; 4th son of 3rd Marquess of Ailsa; Lieutenant, 1/Coldstream; served in RAF during WWII.

24. Lieutenant-Colonel BN Sergison Brooke (1880–1967); served Boer War; DSO, 1915; wounded in the Guards attack at Lesboeufs, 15 September 1916; later Brigadier-General; later ADC to the King, 1933, and Major-General, 1934; Lieutenant-General, 1939 and head of Red Cross with British Army of Liberation, 1944.

25. T/Captain C Bartholomew MC; 1/Scots Guards; OC 3/Grenadiers; killed in action 15 September 1916.

26. The extraordinary idea of 'bantam' units arose in March 1915. To avoid the minimum height restriction for enlisting in the Army, these units were formed to enlist physically fit men, between five feet and five feet three inches in height. The 'bantam' system became unworkable after the Battle of the Somme.

27. On 31 August 1916 de Havillands of the RFC had a number of dogfights with fast German scouts. On this day Captain Albert Ball, in his Nieuport, broke up a German formation of twelve Rolands. Ball's engine was damaged in the fight but he managed to land near Serre; see HA Jones, *The War in the Air Vol. II*, OUP 1928, pp. 267–8.

28. 2nd Lieutenant RLC Bewicke-Copley; later Captain 2/Coldstream; killed in action 21 December 1916.

29. 2nd Lieutenant G de L Leach (1894–1916); educ. Uppingham; 1/Scots Guards; died of wounds, 3 September 1916; awarded Albert Medal in Gold, posthumously, for saving life on land. The Gold (1st class) medal was succeeded by the George Cross.

30. The War Office had only just relaxed its ban on filming at the Front, and there were still only two official cine-cameramen. *The Battle of the Somme* was first put on general release in London on 21 August 1916, to much acclaim; see *Battle of the Somme* (IWM's first video publication, 1987), together with viewing guide; also Lieutenant Geoffrey Malins, *How I Filmed the War*, IWM/Battery Press, 1993.

31. The 1st Battalion (amalgamated with 2nd, 1914) served in Mesopotamia; the 3rd (absorbed the 4th, 1917) served in Ireland and England; the 5th were sent to Gallipoli with the 10th (Irish) Division, being transferred in August 1918 to the 66th Division in France.

WAR LETTERS TO A WIFE

PART II : 1916

SERVICE WITH THE CONNAUGHT RANGERS

6th Battalion (7 September onwards)

7 September 1916 [Carnoy]

I reported to my new Brigadier (47th Brigade) last evening: He is General George Pereira, Grenadier Guards – an elder brother of Cecil Pereira, whom you know.[1]

I had tea and dinner with him, and found that he knows many of the family well. He has told me to put up a Major's crowns. I am of course on probation, and I have not an easy task before me; therefore, I shall require all your prayers. What would I not give for the opportunity of a few words with you! I have hated having to make this great change without consulting you, and even without your knowledge.

My new battalion is one of the two which captured Guillemont four days ago – as hard a nut to crack as there has been in this battle so far. It was the battalion's first attack, so it has not done badly; though the casualties have been heavy, both the Colonel and Second in Command having been killed.[2]

I think we shall very soon be going out for a long rest, which I understand is overdue.

7 September 1916 (Evening) [Carnoy]

My new battalion, or rather the remnant of it, was bivouacking when I joined it, on a slope alongside the ruins of Carnoy, amid a plague of flies, reduced (apart from officers) to 365 other ranks, and very tired after the capture of Guillemont, in which it had taken a prominent and successful part, though the toll had been so heavy.[3]

Since General John Ponsonby had first suggested the possibility of my being appointed to the command of a New Army battalion, I had hoped that I should, perhaps be allowed a week or two with the officers and men, to get to know something of them before taking them into action: and certainly, in ordinary times, one would not expect a battalion straight out of one exhausting attack, and so punished as was this one, to be ordered back without rest, into another. Yet such is the case.

Today, within twenty-four hours of assuming command, I am to move up in front of Ginchy, preparatory to attacking that village the day after tomorrow. My orders are to take 200 fighting men, plus signallers and

Battalion Headquarters – about 250 all told. The few remaining are to be left behind, as a carrying party, to keep the fighting line supplied with water (a great difficulty nowadays) and ammunition.

8 September 1916 [In Trenches, facing Ginchy]

At 5.50 last evening I paraded my 250 Irishmen, who before moving off were addressed by the Senior Chaplain of the Division. Then, kneeling down in the ranks, all received General Absolution:– after which we started to move forward, timing our arrival at Bernafay Wood for 8.20, when it would be dark.

At Bernafay Wood we were met by a guide, who led us through Trônes Wood, that evil place. Thence, to what once was Guillemont.

All former bombardments are eclipsed by the scene here. Last year, in the villages that had been most heavily bombarded, a few shattered houses still stood, as a rule: last month, occasionally a wall survived. But today, at Guillemont, it is almost literally true to say that not a brick or stone remains intact. Indeed, not a brick or stone is to be seen, except where it has been churned up by a bursting shell. Not a tree stands. Not a square foot of surface has escaped mutilation. There is nothing but the mud and the gaping shell-holes;– a chaotic wilderness of shell-holes, rim overlapping rim; and, in the bottom of many, the bodies of the dead.

The guide was leading: I came next, and was followed by the rest of the party in single file. The moon shone brightly, and as the enemy kept sending up flares from his trenches at intervals of a minute, our surroundings were constantly illuminated, and the meandering line of steel helmets flickered, rather too conspicuously, as it bobbed up and down in crossing the shell-holes.

The guide soon began to show signs of uncertainty. I asked him if he had lost his bearings – a not uncommon thing on these occasions. He admitted that he had. I crawled past the body of a dead German soldier into the doorway of a shattered dugout, and with an electric torch studied the map.

As we started off again the shelling increased, and once I was hit by a small splinter on the chest, which stung. The men began to bunch in the shell-holes. They are brave enough, but they are untrained; and 91 of my 200 fighting men were from a new draft, which had only just joined the battalion.

I shall not forget the hours which followed. Remember, I had only the slightest acquaintance with the officers and as for the rank and file, I did not know them at all.

The shells were now dropping very close. One fell into a group of my men, killing seven and wounding about the same number. My guide was hit and dropped a yard or two in front of me. I told him to lie there, and I would have a stretcher sent for him, but he pulled himself together, saying, 'It's all right, sir', and struggled on. About 10.30 pm, we reached our destination.

At the position of assembly, which was at the junction between the Guillemont – Combles road (known officially as Mount Street) and the sunken road leading to Ginchy, we found things in a state of considerable confusion. The battalion we had come to relieve had apparently thought it unnecessary to await our arrival, and consequently there was no one to allot the few shallow trenches that were available. A sort of general scramble was going on, each officer being naturally anxious to get his own men under cover, before the daylight of the morning should reveal them to the enemy.

Luckily, the enemy was now quiet, and before it was light enough to see, the troops were disposed more or less in their 'jumping-off' positions, where they were to wait some forty hours or more for 'Zero'– the moment of attack.

During the night a wounded Saxon crept into the trench close by me and I sent him to the rear.

9 September 1916 [In Trenches, facing Ginchy]

We spent yesterday in getting ready for the attack, and this morning (Saturday), between eight and nine o'clock, our artillery began to bombard the German lines.[4]

My adjutant went sick with trench fever and had to be sent down. In his place I have appointed young Jourdain[5] – a boy of 18½ – who seems to be possessed of wisdom far beyond his years.

My headquarters are in a trench which runs alongside the sunken road, and which was German until a few days ago. There is a hole in the side (marked in pencil with the name of a German soldier) – about 4 feet square by 8 feet deep, which serves as a sleeping-place for two or three at a time. The first German trench is some 300 yards in front; and has been reported as only lightly held. We shall know more about this tomorrow.

On our left front, some 750 yards away, is the village of Ginchy: on the right is Leuze Wood (universally known among our people as Lousy Wood).

10 September 1916 [Happy Valley]

It is over. After a wait of forty-two hours, the leading Companies of the Brigade went over the parapet yesterday afternoon at forty-seven minutes past four o'clock.

The scheduled moment of 'Zero' as a matter of fact was two minutes earlier, but at the last moment, orders came to postpone the assault two minutes, to give time for a final intensive bombardment of the German lines.

The pre-arranged plan was that the 6th Royal Irish Regiment on the

71

right and the 8th Royal Munster Fusiliers on the left should lead the attack for the 47th Brigade, in four waves, at distances of 50 paces, and that they should be followed at 15 paces by two more waves, composed of the 6th Connaught Rangers, with one Company of the 7th Leinster Regiment and two of the 11th Hampshire (Pioneers). The 168th Brigade was to be on our right.

The 48th Brigade – which like ourselves belongs to the Irish Division – was on our immediate left, and moved forward at 4.45, having presumably failed to hear of the postponement.

The leading wave of the 47th Brigade, as I have said, left the trench at 4.47. It was immediately mowed down, as it crossed the parapet, by a terrific machine-gun and rifle fire, directed from the trench in front and from numerous fortified shell-holes. The succeeding waves suffered similarly.

Then, Captains Steuart and Bain, who commanded C and D Companies of the Connaught Rangers, observing a check, got out of the trench and started to rush their men forward: but they had only gone a few yards when both fell wounded.

On the right, there being no suitable jumping-off trench, it had been arranged that the Leinster and Hampshire parties, which were under my command for the day, should cross the open to their starting point. But before they were able to reach it, all the officers but one of the latter battalion had been hit, in addition to many of the rank and file. The officer commanding the Hampshire Companies had already been wounded by a sniper earlier in the day.

The trench in front of us, hidden and believed innocuous, which had in consequence been more or less ignored in the preliminary artillery programme, had perhaps for this very reason, developed as the enemy's main resistance.

This, in fact, being believed to be the easy section of the attack, had been allotted to the tired and battered 47th Brigade. Such are the surprises of war! Supplemented by machine-gun nests in shell-holes, the trench was found by the few who reached close enough to see into it, to be a veritable hornets' nest. Moreover, it had escaped our bombardment altogether, or nearly so.

While the battle was in progress one of our aeroplanes, after flying overhead, dropped a map reporting the enemy in force there, but the news came too late to be of value. To the left of the Brigade, where heavy opposition had been expected and provided for, comparatively little was encountered. The artillery had done its work well, and the infantry was able to push forward and enter Ginchy.

In the meantime, the jumping-off trench soon became packed with the returned attacking troops and their wounded. The former were disordered and obviously shaken. Indeed, it was more than ever apparent they were in no condition for battle of this strenuous order.

One of the first sights I saw was poor Steuart being carried back on a stretcher. A few minutes before I had been talking and laughing with him and as I stopped to speak to him now, his face wore the same cheery expression. I had known him only two days, but had formed the very highest opinion of his character, and since our first meeting, had counted much on his help during the trying times that were before us. He was full of life and spirits and daring – the acme of the perfect soldier. But such men are rare: they often die young; and this, I fear, is to be his fate. The bullet that hit him penetrated his hip, and glancing upwards, is reported to have touched a vital part. He lay some hours in the trench, until his turn came, and the firing had quieted down sufficiently to send him away, never once by word or gesture betraying the pain he must have been enduring.

Later during the afternoon, another of my officers – Seppings Wright[6] – was killed in the trench by shrapnel. I came upon his body during one of my rounds, and helped to lift him – he was a big and heavy man – into a shell-hole, beside the place where he had fallen. He had been in charge of the machine-guns.

Heavy shelling continued throughout the rest of the day and during the night – a lurid night of countless rockets and star-shells from the enemy, who was nervous; a night of wild bursts of machine-gun and rifle fire, delaying our relief by the 4th Grenadier Guards.

Then, after three practically sleepless nights under shell-fire most of the time, we marched back to Carnoy Craters. Here we are bivouacked, and I have just had a good sleep on the ground, under the canopy of a transport wagon.

The scene was very weird as we picked our way back this morning, through the waste of shell-holes with their mournful contents, accompanied by our wounded, and preceded by a stretcher on which lay the body of Colonel Curzon[7] who had commanded the Royal Irish, and who dined opposite me with the Brigadier four nights ago – on the night I joined this Brigade. I found myself following immediately behind his body.

During the three days, my casualties have amounted to 92 (9 officers and 83 other ranks), out of the 16 officers and 250 other ranks with which I started, bringing the total casualties of the battalion for the past nine days, to 23 officers and 407 NCOs and men. Of the latter, 63 are missing; 54 were killed, and others have since died. Thanks to my splendid doctor – Knight, a Newfoundlander – we got away all the wounded.[8]

Later – This afternoon we marched to 'Happy Valley', where we are bivouacked.

*   *   *

73

13 September 1916 [Corbie]

The battalion is resting at Vaux, a pretty little village on the Somme, about a mile from Corbie, where I have seized a few minutes at the Town Major's office to write to you.

My days are spent in reorganising the battalion, which, as you may imagine, is not an easy task, since practically all the old officers, including the Adjutant, have become casualties. The boy Jourdain is still acting Adjutant and is doing it marvellously well, in spite of his extreme youth.

16 September 1916 [Vaux-sur-Somme]

The Guards were in action yesterday, and my old battalion has once again suffered badly. Guy Baring and all four Company Commanders have been killed.[9]

As we came away from the Ginchy attack the other day, I passed the battalion, which was bivouacked near us in Happy Valley. They were then 'next for it'. I stopped for lunch. The young officers crowded round me afterwards to hear my news, joking and laughing about it all, and asking what it was like 'up there'. Poor little Dilbéroglue, who commanded one of the Companies, clung to the boy next to him, and pretended to shiver with fear at the prospect of what was before him. And the Fates have taken his joke seriously, for today he is dead. He was a very competent young officer.

I shall write to Geoffrey Feilding – I feel sure you would have me do this – and ask him if through this action the Guards Division is short of officers, to consider me available in any capacity.

This afternoon I had a call from Major Willie Redmond[10] – brother of John Redmond and Member for Waterford – such a simple nice fellow. This (16th Irish) Division, on the Staff of which he is, is very evidently the apple of his eye. He congratulated me, both on arrival and departure, though whether upon having been appointed to command a battalion in the Division, or upon having come unscathed out of the recent fighting, he did not indicate.

17 September 1916 [Vaux-sur-Somme]

We received the melancholy news last night that Steuart had just died of his wounds. He is the greatest possible loss. He was a magnificent smiling type of officer, and I never saw grander courage than he displayed both before and after receiving his wound. I have told you how patiently he waited to be taken away, and I now add that the manner in which – without any sign of annoyance – he endured for several hours the heavy shelling, was remarkable to see. He makes the fifth of my officers that has died as the result of that day.

11.30 am. – I have just had a call from General Hickie, my new Divisional Commander.[11] It was the first time I had seen him. He seemed very pleased and proud of his Division. He asked why I was wearing only a Major's crowns. I said I had only authority for that. He then told me at once to put up a Lieut.-Colonel's badges; so, from today, I may ask you to address my letters by that rank!

You have absolutely nothing to worry about now. I shall, for a time at any rate, be in the safest of places.

19 September 1916 [Huppy]

We left Vaux yesterday morning, and after marching a few miles, 'embussed' (as the army language has it). Then, after 5½ hours on wheels, we finished with a short march, which brought us here to Huppy where we billeted for the night, and from where I write.

I forgot to tell you that the battalion has a band of drums and fifes, and Irish bagpipes.

22 September 1916 [Fontainehouck]

We are in Belgium. We got to this place about seven o'clock last evening, after a 3 mile march from Bailleul, the detraining station. We are in very comfortable billets, well behind the line, and it is a nice sunny day: so all looks rosy.

23 September 1916 [Fontainehouck]

The change in things generally is most gratifying. The battalion has made wonderful strides during the last few days, and everything is getting shipshape now.

25 September 1916 [Locre]

It is like living in a new world to be among these Irishmen, so great is the contrast between their national characteristics and those of the men I have come from. Unlike some Irish battalions, this one is composed practically entirely of Irishmen. They are, I should imagine, difficult to drive, but easy to lead. They are intensely religious, loyal to their officers, and they are an exceedingly satisfactory body of men to deal with. As yet, they have comparatively little training.[12]

They are easily made happy. Perhaps they are easily depressed. Perhaps, too, like many others who are not Irish, they are better when things are going well than badly. Most of the officers are Irish, though not all, and I feel the sincerest gratitude for the generous and open-hearted manner in which they received me, and the zeal with which they have supported me.

The losses of the Guards between Ginchy and Lesboeufs on the 15th appear to have been very heavy, and I keep hearing daily of the loss of friends. Pike Pease was killed that day.[13] Do you remember him? I saw him, for the last time, I think, last November, at the hospital at Merville.

He was a typical specimen of the clean English boy; with a fine brain and a promising career before him, and he was only nineteen.,

Claude Bartholomew, too. I saw a good deal of him during the days I was at Morlancourt, his camp being a few yards only from my billet. He was a great little soldier. He was as you know on the Stock Exchange before the war. He was full of resource and ingenuity, and a master in the tactical handling of machine-guns, of which he commanded a Company. One of the last times I saw him was on the day we first heard of Roumania's entry into the war. He had looked in at the 1st Battalion Head-quarters' mess, where I was sitting alone. He took the line that the war must now be over in six months. 'How damnable,' he said, 'to think that peace must come so soon, yet it is a moral certainty that, after surviving so many months of it, you and I will both be dead in a fortnight.'

That was three weeks ago, on the eve of the attack. He is a great loss and will be difficult to replace.

This morning the battalion was inspected by General Plumer, who commands the 2nd Army, to which we now belong. He was in Matabeleland when I was there, in the rebellion of 1896.[14]

26 September 1916 [Locre]

Today I have been to reconnoitre the trenches, or rather breastworks, which we are to take over. They cross the swampy ground below the Wytschaete Ridge, which, crowned by the ruins of the Hospice and a red pile of brick, frowns down upon them. Some 5 miles to the left stands the skeleton, of Ypres, where the ruined Cathedral can be seen from our trenches, towering into the sky.

All was very quiet.

The line will be wet and nasty in winter, but today the sun was shining, and the whole country seemed smiling. The silence was quite extra-ordinary. There was no shelling. Moreover, trees are standing, and many of the buildings are only slightly damaged. The fields are green and coloured with wild flowers and today I saw two cows grazing not so very far behind the firing-line. As I walked along the communication trench, two cackling cock-pheasants flew overhead.

After the Somme it seems like coming from Hell to the Thames Valley in summer-time; and they say it has always been like this lately. Is it bad to say, 'long may it continue so'?

After breakfast at the Convent this morning, I was taken to see the room, full of silent girls – mostly refugees from Ypres, where the lace is made. Though so close to the firing line (about 7,000 yards), the atmo-sphere was the same as that, for example, of the Convent in Kensington Square;– the same well-swept, polished floors; the same clean-looking, sweet-faced nuns, moving quietly and quickly about their business.

They told me that the Germans spent ten days in the Convent and behaved well, but never paid for anything. In the village they seem to have looted considerably.

27 September 1916 [In Front of Wytschaete]

We have come up and are holding the front line, and I write from my headquarters in a farmhouse on the Kemmel–Vierstraat road (known officially as 'York House'), some fifteen hundred yards behind the fire-trench, part ruined, yet commodious and comfortable.

The signallers, runners, and my headquarter officers live and sleep in sandbag shelters in what used to be the garden. It is as quiet as Gordon Place. Substitute an occasional rifle-shot or a burst of machine-gun fire for the traffic in Church Street, and you have it.

On my way up I saw a German observation balloon that had broken loose and was drifting, half hidden by the clouds. Our anti-aircraft guns were shooting vivaciously; and it soon began to drop, looking more bedraggled each minute as the shrapnel hit it and the gas leaked out. The wind was blowing in our direction, and the balloon was sinking towards the ground our side of the line, therefore there did not seem much point in pounding it; but I suppose the rare temptation of a steady target is over-mastering.

Then aeroplanes hove into sight from all quarters, like vultures round a dying mule, and circling round, peppered the balloon with their Lewis guns. Suddenly, it took fire. Burning like a huge candle from the upper end, it fell out of my sight, leaving behind it a column of smoke.

Lest you may think this inhuman and brutal behaviour on the part of our 'Archies' and airmen, I am sure it is safe to say that the occupants of the balloon had long since made themselves safe, reaching the ground with the aid of their parachutes.[15]

27 September 1916 [Wytschaete]

My dearest Joan,

My battalion is in the trenches as I write, and my Headquarters are in a battered farmhouse just behind. On my way up this afternoon, I saw a German observation balloon brought down in flames by our guns. I think we are beating the Germans now, but I expect Mother will already have told you that.

How splendid of you to have made £5 at Auntie Agnes' bazaar. My General called on me the other day and told me to immediately wear a Lt. Colonel's rank badges; so I am now a Colonel, though I have not been gazetted yet.

You must frame a photo of Mother and yourself and the others for me by your 'passe-partout'.

In one of the villages in which we were billeted on our way up, I stayed in a farmhouse belonging to a very old – the dearest old – woman. She had a little granddaughter, about a year and a quarter old, whom she was very proud of. She said when she was 3 months old she could say the 'Hail Mary'. She was the dearest little girl, and used to walk into my room whenever the grandmother wasn't looking and steal my spurs or anything else shiny she could see. The grandmother told me that when she spoke of me, it was always as 'Monsieur le Cure'. She evidently thought I was the priest.

Your loving Daddy.

30 September 1916 [In front of Wytschaete]

I have an orderly named Lavender, who shadows me wherever I go, and when I say that he shadows me I mean it literally. I find from experience that I have only to call quietly 'Corporal Lavender', and I immediately get his reply in a deep Irish brogue, 'Here, sorr'. No matter where I may chance to be, he is always there. He is a splendid type of Irishman, tall in stature, gentle in manner, and always solemn. Indeed, he never smiles. He has an eye which misses nothing; a memory that rarely fails him, and altogether, he inspires much confidence.

Being always with me, he is bound sometimes to overhear things which are not for general knowledge, and I remarked to him upon this fact the other day. To which I got the following reply: 'When I was in the Royal Irish Constabulary, sorr, I was taught three things – to keep my eyes and my ears open, and my mouth shut.'

Like all Irishmen he is a bit of a politician, and as we pass along the communication trenches on our way to or from the front line, we sometimes discuss the politics of his native land. A few days ago the subject was the relative aims of the Nationalists and the Sinn Feiners, and I asked his views. Said he: 'The Nationalists aim at getting independence by constitutional, the Sinn Feiners by unconstitutional, means':– which, after all, is about as concise a way of putting it as he could have chosen.[16]

1 October 1916 [In front of Wytschaete]

This evening a German aeroplane was brought down opposite us, in flames. It fell like a stone, leaving a vertical column of smoke behind it.

This place is as bad as any I have seen – even on this front – for rats. I can walk out any night, at any time, and by switching on a torch, count on seeing several at once. Even during the day they run about, almost as though man were non-existent. The fact is, they have come to be accepted so much as part and parcel of the war that their presence is generally ignored, and they enjoy an immunity that must be very gratifying to them.

The other night I was waiting in the fire-trench for the return of an officer's patrol from examining the German wire. The patrol had been gone a long time, and I was beginning to feel some apprehension regarding its fate, when a huge rat ran along the parapet. Instead of trying to kill it, the men in the trench started calling 'puss, puss':– which will show you the terms we are on with the rats!

9 October 1916 [Siege Farm]

Fresh officers have been joining almost daily, and I now have thirty-eight, including a regular Major of twenty years service, who is attached for instruction. And next week two more Captains are expected, including the Nationalist member of Parliament, Stephen Gwynn[17] – who seems very popular with everybody. So you will understand that I am well occupied. Indeed, I look forward to the trenches for a rest.

We had a battalion concert tonight, when considerable talent came to the surface. An officer named Holloway[18] was responsible for the programme:– a very clever professional, who was at the Gaiety, I think, when the war broke out.

12 October 1916 [La Clytte]

Today I took my mare – the best I have ridden since I came to France, inherited from poor Lenox-Conyngham, the late Colonel of this battalion – and rode into Ypres. I have long yearned to see the city. But what a scene of desolation – truly a city of the dead; a ghostly solitude. Not a sound unless that of a gun or bursting shell: not a soul to be seen in the long streets of ruins, except rarely, here and there, an English sentry, or a party of English soldiers, with rifle, pick and shovel, marching to or from the trenches: not a man, woman or child of the nation that built and owns the city. It is indeed a tragic sight.

15 October 1916 [In front of Wytschaete]

During my rounds this afternoon, I met poor Parke (who until a few days ago was acting as my second in command) being carried along the communication trench known as Watling Street, on a stretcher.

He had just been killed by a direct hit from a chance shell. He was forty-seven years old, and I was just trying to get him a rest behind the line;– which, added to the fact that he was only recently married and had just returned from spending a short leave with his wife, makes it all the sadder. He was brother to the Parke who was with Stanley in 'Darkest Africa'. He was a cheery fellow, and I shall miss him very much.

17 October 1916 [In front of Wytschaete]

I feel, though I have written many letters, that I have told you really very little about the battalion I am commanding. But now that I have got to know it, and to be proud of it, I think I must try and give you some idea of the people I am with, and the atmosphere I live in.

First of all then, I find both officers and men magnificent – plucky and patient, keen and cheerful. Since I came here I have introduced gradually many innovations – notions I learnt from the Guards. I have tightened up the discipline a lot. Inferior men might have resented it; yet I have not once encountered from any rank anything but the most loyal and wholehearted co-operation. I have heard it said, that there is no such thing as a 'bounder' in Scotland, and I think I have learnt here that the same may be said of Ireland. The result is that the officers' messes of the Division, though they include many 'diamonds in the rough', are pleasant places to live – full of goodwill and good cheer. Among my lot I have a successful trainer of racehorses, an MFH, an actor, a barrister, a squireen or two, a ranker from the Grenadiers, a banker; a quartermaster from the 9th Lancers, a doctor from Newfoundland;– members, in short, of many professions; a lot of boys too young to have professions:– and a Nationalist MP is coming![19]

This morning one of my corporals killed a German and wounded another in No Man's Land. The latter crawled back towards his line and as he neared it, three of his friends came out after him. My men then acted in a manner which would perhaps nowadays be regarded as quixotic, so relaxed – thanks to our opponents – have the rules of this game of war become.

They did not shoot.

26 October 1916 [Butterfly Farm, in Brigade Reserve]
Stephen Gwynn arrived today. He has just been in to lunch. He is the very antithesis of the Irish politician as popularly represented by the Tory school. He is old for a Company Commander – fifty-two. All the more sporting therefore, to have come out in that capacity, especially since he seems to have had a hard tussle with the War Office Authorities before they would consent to send him.[20]

31 October 1916 [In front of Wytschaete]
At last, after seven days, M.'s[21] long description has come, and I know something of the new baby I have never seen.

I had a delicious letter from J[22] on the subject, in which she said that so far she had only seen Pru with her eyes shut. The whole letter radiated with the spirit of the 'Little Mother'.

How war alters one's preconceived ideas. You know the sort of impression one is apt to get in England of the Irish Nationalist MP. Well, ours here – you should see him – a refined, polished, brave gentleman; adored by his Company, which he commanded before, earlier in the war. Knee-deep in mud and slush; enthusiastically doing the duty of a boy of twenty. I have seldom met a man who, on first acquaintance, took my fancy more. Have you ever read his books, which I am told are very beautiful? My only fear is that the exaction of the trenches during the winter months may prove too much for him[23].

7 November 1916 [Curragh Camp]

My darling Joan,

I have two letters to thank you for. We came away from the trenches yesterday and while there I had very little time for writing. One of my men – Hughes[24] by name – has just won the VC, and we are going to celebrate it by an entertainment to be held one evening this week. One of the officers is a very clever singer and actor and he is writing a musical play for it.[25]

What a lovely baby Prunella sounds from your description. I am simply pining to see her. I hope she will keep her blue eyes – I mean that they won't change colour: then I shall have four daughters, all completely different.

Your loving Daddy.

7 November 1916 [Curragh Camp]

I enclose two newspaper cuttings. They quote what were probably the last writings of Kettle, a talented Nationalist Member of Parliament, who belonged to this Brigade and was killed at Ginchy on September 9. I think his ode to his child is very fine.[26]

From the Weekly Irish Times, November, 1916.

LIEUTENANT KETTLE AND CONCILIATION

Mrs. Kettle has asked us to publish the following copy of a note which her husband, the late Lieutenant T. M. Kettle, wrote for publication, a few days before his death in action:

'Had I lived, I had meant to call my next book on the relations of Ireland and England, "The Two Fools: A Tragedy of Errors". It has needed all the folly of England and all the folly of Ireland to produce the situation, in which our unhappy country is now involved. I have mixed much with Englishmen and Protestant Ulstermen, and I know that there is no real or abiding reason for the gulfs, saltier than the sea, that now dismember the natural alliance of both of them with us Irish Nationalists. It needs only a Fiat lux, of a kind very easily compassed, to replace the unnatural by the natural.

In the name, and by the seal, of the blood given in the last two years, I ask for Colonial Home Rule for Ireland, a thing essential in itself, and essential as a prologue to the reconstruction of the Empire. Ulster will agree.'

TO MY DAUGHTER BETTY – THE GIFT OF LOVE
(These are the last verses written by the late Lieutenant Kettle – a few days before his death in action at Ginchy.)

In wiser days, my darling rosebud, blown
To beauty proud as was your mother's prime

In that desired, delayed, incredible time
You'll ask why I abandoned you, my own,
And the dear breast that was your baby's throne.
To dice with death, and, oh! they'll give you rhyme
And reason; one will call the thing sublime,
And one decry it in a knowing tone.
So here, while the mad guns curse overhead,
And tired men sigh, with mud for couch and floor,
Know that we fools, now with the foolish dead,
Died not for Flag, nor King, nor Emperor,
But for a dream, born in a herdsman's shed
And for the secret Scripture of the poor.

T. M. Kettle

In the Field before Guillemont, Somme, September 4, 1916.

9 November 1916 [Curragh Camp]

Today we have a plethora of Generals and Staff Officers. It has often struck me as extraordinary, seeing the pain which is caused to some Generals by seeing the least spot of dirt about the camp or personnel of a tired trench worn battalion of infantry, that the same Generals should be so blind to similar defects in their own entourage, where there is no possible excuse for such laxity. Yet, so far as my experience goes, there is generally an uncouthness which it would be difficult to match.

Indeed, if I ever meet one of my men on the road, unshaved, or with flowing hair, or otherwise unmilitary, I immediately conclude that he is 'detached' from the battalion, and employed on some Staff job: and I am hardly ever mistaken.

13 November 1916 [Curragh Camp]

Bar accidents, it is arranged that I go on leave on the 23rd (in ten days). I have had over seven months of it this time, with only seven days at home, and though I could not possibly be better in health, I feel I may be getting stale.

We return to the trenches tomorrow.

17 November 1916 [In front of Wytschaete]

The Staff Captain rang me up this morning to say that a Divisional car is going to Boulogne on the 21st, and would I like to go by that? However, I have decided to stick to my original plan, and not to go till the battalion is out of the trenches.

It is freezing hard, and the breastworks are frozen-stiff.

RCF goes on leave 23 November–7 December 1916. He visits his family at Gordon Place, Kensington and is able to see his fourth baby daughter, Prunella, for the first time.

8 December 1916 [Facing Messines – Cooker Farm]

I learnt to my surprise that the Brigade had moved during my absence, and that the battalion, which was due to return to the trenches today had been ordered up three days before its time, into a new sector, nearly a mile to the right of where it had been before.

13 December 1916 [Curragh Camp]

Sleet has been falling continuously and the men are wet through. We came out of the trenches last night, and I took off my clothes for the first time since I said 'goodbye' to you last Thursday (the 7th), at Charing Cross.

I have been busy arranging details; visited by the Divisional General; also by Filson Young of the 'Daily Mail' and Philip Gibbs[27] of the 'Daily Chronicle' – War Correspondents.

14 December 1916 [Curragh Camp]

I have for many weeks past been working to get some good Company Sergeant-Majors out from home. One in particular I have been trying for – a Sergeant-Major McGrath, reputed to have been the best at Kinsale. His Commanding Officer very kindly agreed to send him to me, although he wrote that he regretted parting with him. McGrath arrived the day after I returned from leave, and within half an hour of his reaching the fire-trench, was lying dead, a heavy trench-mortar bomb having fallen upon him, killing him and two others, and wounding two more. Now, is not that a case of hard luck 'chasing' a man, when you consider how long others of us last? I never even saw him alive.

I visited the fire-trench just after the bomb had fallen. It had dropped into the trench, and the sight was not a pleasant one. It was moreover aggravated by the figure of one of the dead, who had been blown out of the trench on to the parapet, and was silhouetted grotesquely against the darkening sky.

But what I saw was inspiring, nevertheless. The sentries stood like statues. At the spot where the bomb had burst – within 40 yards of the Germans – officers and men were already hard at work in the rain, quietly repairing the damage done to our trench, and clearing away the remains of the dead; all – to outward appearance – oblivious to the possibility of further trouble from the trench-mortar, trained upon this special bit of trench, that had fired the fatal round.

What wonderful people are our infantry. And what a joy it is to be with them. When I am here, I feel – well, I can hardly describe it. I feel, if it were possible, that one should never go away from them; and nobody who has not seen them can ever understand.

According to the present routine, we stay in the front line eight days and nights; then go out for the same period. Each Company spends four days and four nights in the fire-trench before being relieved. The men are practically without rest. They are wet through much of the time. They are shelled and trench-mortared. They may not be hit, but they are kept in a perpetual state of unrest and strain. They work all night and every night, and a good part of each day, digging and filling sandbags, and repairing the breaches in the breastworks;– that is when they are not on sentry. The temperature is icy. They have not even a blanket. The last two days it has been snowing. They cannot move more than a few feet from their posts: therefore, except when they are actually digging, they cannot keep themselves warm by exercise; and, when they try to sleep, they freeze. At present, they are getting a tablespoon of rum to console them, once in three days.

Think of these things, and compare them with what are considered serious hardships in normal life! Yet these men play their part uncom-plainingly. Freezing, or snowing, or drenching rain; always, smothered with mud; you may ask any one of them, any moment of the day or night, 'Are you cold?', or 'Are you wet?' – and, you will get but one answer. The Irishman will reply – always with a smile – 'Not too cold, sir', or 'Not too wet, sir'. It makes me feel sick. It makes me think I never want to see the British Isles again so long as the war lasts. It makes one feel ashamed, for those Irishmen; and also of those fellow-countrymen of our own, earning huge wages, yet, forever clamouring for more; striking, or threatening to strike; while the country is engaged upon this murderous struggle.

Why, we ask here, has not the whole nation, civil as well as military, been conscripted? The curious thing is that all seem so much more contented here than the people at home. The poor Tommy, shivering in the trenches, is happier than the beast who makes capital out of the war. Everybody laughs at everything, here. It is the only way.

17 December 1916 (Sunday) [Curragh Camp]

It occurred to me that it would be a nice idea to celebrate the battalion's period in Divisional Reserve by a special Church Parade: so, this morning, we marched with the drums and pipes to the village church of Locre, where High Mass was sung. Three priests officiated. Soldiers, accompanied by a soldier organist, composed the choir; and the battalion bugles sounded the 'General Salute' during the Elevation. All was very impressive, and consid-ering that they are only out of the trenches for a few days rest, the smart and soldierly appearance of the men was very remarkable. But there is never any difficulty in getting a good Irish battalion to turn out well to go to Mass.

20 December 1916 [Curragh Camp]

My darling Joan,

Thank you for your letter. It is freezing cold here and today it has been snowing. We go back to the trenches this afternoon for eight days. I am afraid the men will be very cold. You must remember what they are going through for you, and pray for them. I am sure you do that, and also that they benefit very much from your prayers. They do it very cheerfully and very bravely.

Your loving Daddy.

Christmas Day 1916 [Facing Messines, Cooker Farm]

No letter today, but the post has, I know, been hung up by the gale.

Though this is Christmas Day, things have not been as quiet as they might have been, and though we have not suffered, I fancy the battalion on our right has done so to some extent. In fact, as I passed along their fire-trench, I saw them at work; digging out some poor fellows who had been buried by a trench-mortar bomb.

This morning I was first visited by the Brigadier, who went on to wish the men in the fire-trench 'as happy a Christmas as possible under the circumstances'. Then the Divisional Commander came, accompanied by his ADC, who was carrying round the General's visiting book for signature. This contained many interesting names. I also had several other visitors.

When I had finished with my callers, I went out with my little .45 gun to see if I could kill a pheasant. I got one, which we had for lunch. My servant Glover acts keeper on these occasions. I need scarcely say that I cannot spare time for shooting pheasants, and today was my first attempt, but the other officers go out, especially one – a stout Dublin lawyer in private life, who is a very good shot. He went out yesterday, and before starting, consulted Glover, who at once brightened up and said: 'If you want a couple of birds for your Christmas dinner, sir, I can put you on to a certainty, if you don't get shot yourself.' He took him and they got two.

Today, Glover took me to the same place. But it turned out to be no spot to linger in – a medley of unhealthily new shell-holes, under full view of the Germans. Certainly a good place for pheasants: but imagine what courts-martial there would be if a casualty took place under such circumstances. I have now put that locality out of bounds, pheasants or no pheasants.

The Chaplain came up and said Mass for the men this morning. I was prevented from going at the last moment, by the Divisional Commander's visit, but it must have been an impressive sight. The men manning the fire-trench of course could not attend, but it was not a case of driving the rest;– rather indeed of keeping them away. The intensity of their religion is something quite remarkable, and I had under-estimated it.

The Service was held in the open – not more than 500 yards from the German line, in a depression in the ground below the skeleton buildings known as Shamus Farm: though the place is concealed from the enemy by an intervening ridge, promiscuous bits do come over, and I debated for some time whether to allow it. In the end, expecting perhaps a hundred men, I consented. But though, like most soldiers, they will shirk fatigues if they get the chance, these men will not shirk what they consider to be their religious duties, and about 300 turned up.

However, with the exception of German shrapnel which burst harmlessly about a hundred yards away during the Service, all went well, though I imagine Stephen Gwynn, who was the senior officer present, was given some food for thought.

In the evening I went round and wished the men scarcely a Merry Christmas, but good luck in the New Year, and may they never have to spend another Christmas in the front line. This meant much repetition on my part, passing from one fire-bay to another, but I was amply rewarded. It is a treat to hear these men open out, and their manners are always perfect.

I have a good many recruits just now. Some of them went into the line for the first time last night. I visited them at their posts soon after they had reached the fire-trench, and asked them how they liked it. They are just boys feeling their way. They wore a rather bewildered look. This evening I asked them again. They were already becoming veterans.

They are all going to have their Christmas dinner on the 30th, after we get out.

26 December 1916 [Wytschaete Ridge, Cooker Farm]

Every little section of trench here, as elsewhere, is known and labelled by some fancy name, and one of the very worst bits of the fire-trench is called 'Happier Moments'. He must have been an optimist who thought of that.

As I came out along the communication trench this evening after dark, I was spluttered with mud twice by trench-mortar bombs. These things make a horrible noise and mess when they land, but are so big and come so slowly that if you spot them in the air you can generally dodge them, and for this reason the men affect not to mind them much. I, on the other hand, admit that I do not share this feeling of confidence. Frankly, I respect trench-mortar bombs.[28]

After dark I went round the line and found the men cheery as usual. For one of the recruits – a boy – it had been his first experience, his baptism of fire. He had picked up a splinter of shrapnel in his bay, which he was treasuring as a souvenir, and showed me delightedly like a child would a new toy.

When times are quiet, as at present, things which are comparatively insignificant gather importance. A case of 'trench feet', for example, will provoke far more correspondence and censure than a heavy casualty list, which provokes none at all.

28 December 1916 [Derry Huts, near Dranoutre]

Do you remember the silly letters that used to appear in the newspapers – I think it was last year – about linnets and pheasants in Norfolk having had their ear-drums broken by the percussion caused by mythical distant battles in the North Sea? Yesterday, while the bombardment was at its height, a robin was hopping playfully about, from sandbag to sandbag, within 10 feet of me: a blackbird was doing the same a few feet further away; and a cat was stalking between the two; all three unconcerned among their infernal surroundings!

30 December 1916 [Derry Huts]

Today, the battalion being out of the trenches, we celebrated Christmas in a sort of way; that is to say, the men had turkey and plum-pudding, and French beer for dinner, and a holiday from 'fatigues'.

I hope they enjoyed it. The extras – over and above those contributed by friends at home (whose presents had been very liberal) – cost the battalion funds about £90. But when I went round and saw the dinners I must confess I was disappointed. Our surroundings do not lend themselves to this kind of entertainment; and as to appliances – tables, plates, cutlery, etc.– well, we have none. The turkeys had to be cut into shreds and dished up in the mess tins. The beer had to be ladled out of buckets later, into the same mess-tins; out of which also the plum-pudding was taken, the men sitting herded about on the floors of the dark huts. It was indeed most unlike a Christmas dinner, but it was the best possible under the circumstances. The Chaplain came over in the early morning and said Mass and gave Communion.

They are a curious crowd. They will report sick pretty readily when they are in Divisional Reserve, and there are drills and fatigues to be done: but when in the line, I do not think the average is more than one or two per day for the whole battalion. It seems to be a matter of honour with them:– and where Mass is concerned, they are never too tired to attend. Their devotion is quite amazing.

Although well within range of the daily shell-fire there is a woman with a baby living in the farm where I and my headquarter officers mess. There have, during the past few days, been some heavy bombardments, and there is a hole through the roof of the hut in which I live, made by shrapnel.

Still, the woman with the baby clings to her home: I wonder at these women with their babies. They must be possessed of boundless faith. There seems to be a sort of fatalism about them, and, as a matter of fact, they seldom get injured.

31 December 1916 (Midnight) [Derry Huts]

It is midnight. As I write all the 'heavies' we possess are loosing off their New Year's 'Joy' to the Germans, making my hut vibrate. The men in their huts are cheering and singing 'Old Lang Syne'.

NOTES

1. Brigadier-General G Pereira (1865–1923); joined Grenadier Guards, 1884; took part in the relief of the legations at Peking, 1900, where he was wounded; DSO 1900; as military attaché with the Japanese army, he witnessed the Manchurian campaign, 1905; OC 4/RWF, June 1915; GOC 47th Brigade, January 1916–November 1917; known as 'Old Hoppy' on account of his lameness; his brother was Major-General Cecil 'Pinto' Pereira, GOC 2nd Division.
2. The CO was Lieutenant-Colonel JSM Lenox-Conyngham (1861–1916). Having retired in 1912, he was recalled in 1914, when his long pre-war service with the Connaught Rangers was recognised and he was given command of the newly formed 6th Battalion. Despite coming from a prominent Ulster Protestant family, he was highly regarded by his largely Catholic and nationalist battalion. He was killed leading his men into the action on 3 September 1916. His second-in-command, Major MIM Campbell MC (1880–1916) was wounded and died the following day. Campbell had only recently returned to the front after being wounded in 1915.
3. At the Battle of Guillemont, the 47th Brigade (comprising 6/Connaught Rangers, 7/Leinsters, 6/Royal Irish, 8/Royal Munsters) suffered losses of 1,147 out of 2,400 men committed to the battle.
4. This attack on Ginchy, on 9 September 1916, was not the first. The 7th Division had captured the village on 3 September, but lost it soon afterwards. Successive assaults were made by other units, including the 16th (Irish) Division, in the days following.
5. 2nd Lieutenant FWS Jourdain, possibly a relation of Lieutenant-Colonel HFN Jourdain, who later had temporary command of the 6/Connaughts.
6. Lieutenant SWS Wright; son of HCS Wright, artist and war correspondent; 1/Connaught Rangers, att. 6/Connaughts; killed in action, 9 September 1916, two weeks after arriving at the front.
7. Lieutenant-Colonel FEP Curzon (1859–1916); grandson of 1st Earl Howe; served Egyptian campaign, 1898; Boer War, 1900–2; OC 6/Royal Irish, 1907; killed in action, 9 September 1916.
8. The total casualties of the 16th (Irish) Division from 1–10 September 1916 were 240 officers and 4,090 other ranks – nearly half of those committed to the battle.
9. The attack on Lesboeufs was part of the larger Battle of Flers-Courcelette, 15–22 September 1916. The 1/Coldstream, together with 3/Grenadiers, were in the van of the attack on Lesboeufs. The 1/Coldstream War Diary reports that the battalion attacked with seventeen officers and 690 OR and came out with three officers and 221 OR. The majority of officers became casualties immediately and the ensuing chaos was compounded by staff errors within the Guards Division. In addition to the loss of Guy Baring, those killed included, T/Captains Jackson, Lawrence, Woods, and Lieutenants Dilbéroglue, Grissell, Maynard and Pease; see PRO WO95/1219; also Harold Macmillan, *Winds of Change 1914–1939,* Macmillan, 1966, pp. 85–91.

10. Major WHK Redmond MP (1861–1916); sat as a Nationalist MP from 1883 until the date of his death. His brother, John Redmond MP, was the leader of the Irish Parliamentary Party. 'Willie' was a firebrand in his early political career, but later became widely respected, and indeed friendly with many political opponents. He believed he was fighting for a free Ireland, within the Empire; see Terence Denman, *A Lonely Grave. The Life and Death of William Redmond*, Irish Academic Press, 1995.

11. Major-General Sir William Hickie (1865–1950); Boer War, 1900–2; DAQMG, 8th Division 1903–6; Brigadier-General 1914; Hickie was a popular and energetic commander. The 16th (Irish) Division had been raised and trained by 66-year-old Lieutenant-General Parsons, but as a Catholic and a younger man, Hickie was deemed more suitable in 1916 to command the division on the Western Front; Esmonde Robertson, draft typescript, 'John Redmond and General Parsons', Parsons Papers, Liddell Hart Archives, KCL.

12. The number of Irishmen in the battalion was to change as the war progressed – see Patrick Callan, 'Recruiting for the British Army in Ireland during the First World War, *Irish Sword*, Vol. XVII, no. 66, 1987. Also Nicholas Perry, 'Maintaining Regimental Identity in the Great War: the Case of the Irish Infantry Regiments', *Stand To!*, April 1998.

13. Lieutenant RH Pike Pease (1897–1916); son of Herbert Pike Pease MP, Assistant Postmaster-General. Another of RCF's contemporaries from the 3/Coldstream to be killed on 15 September 1916 was Major GE 'Little Man' Vaughan MC (1880–1915).

14. The Matabele rebellion took place in modern day Zimbabwe. Plumer was charged with raising a Relief Force to secure Bulawayo.

15. This incident on 27 September 1916 refers to the German balloon reported to have broken away from its mooring near Bapaume, and which drifted north towards Ypres. 'A British pilot of No. 40 Squadron was about to shoot it down, when he saw its observer, hanging from the rigging, waving a large handkerchief. He held his fire. The balloon was about 1200 ft from the ground, when a de Havilland pilot of No. 29 Squadron came from the opposite side, and before realising the position, shot the balloon down in flames'; HA Jones, *The War in the Air, Vol. II*, OUP, 1928, pp. 294–5.

16. Moderate nationalist opinion (at this stage, the prevalent force) was represented by John Redmond's Irish National Party. Broadly, Redmond wanted to achieve a self-governing Ireland, within the Empire. His supporters were prepared to fight 'Prussian militarism' as an autonomous nation (modelled on Canada, Australia or South Africa), while Sinn Fein totally rejected the idea of Empire and demanded a complete break from Britain; see 'The Great War and national identity, 1914–16', in Thomas Hennessey's, *Dividing Ireland – World War I and Partition*, Routledge, 1998.

17. Captain Stephen Gwynn MP (1864–1950); grandson of William Smith O'Brien; educated St Columba's College, Ireland, and Brasenose College, Oxford; schoolmaster and journalist in London; although a Protestant, he became Nationalist MP (Redmond's Irish Party) for Galway City 1906, until the collapse of the party in 1918; served in ranks with Leinster Regiment, January–April 1915; April 1915, commissioned 6/Connaughts, promoted Captain, July 1915; temporary transfer to 11/Royal Dublin Fusiliers, July 1916; returned to 6/Connaughts; relinquished commission, June 1917; 'Special List' until 1919; wrote numerous books and biographies after the war; see service record, WO339/26731, PRO, including interesting correspondence with Lloyd George.

18. Second Lieutenant Stanley Augustus Holloway (1890–1982), later famous comedy actor and singer; commissioned December 1915 into 4/Connaughts, on account of his pre-war service as a Private in the London Rifle Brigade; saw action during the 1916 Easter Rising; attached 6/Connaughts, July 1916, where he remained until the Armistice; his London stage musical debut was not until 1919 in *Kissing Time*. Prior to 1914 he had trained as an opera singer and had toured South America in a variety troupe. Leslie Henson signed him for a juvenile lead at the Gaiety, just as war broke out; Roy Walding to Editor, 6 December 2000.

19. Stephen Gwynn MP served with the 6/Connaughts, but he was not the only sitting Nationalist MP to serve in the 16th (Irish) Division. The others were, Willie Redmond, William Archer Redmond (son of John), Daniel Sheehan, JL Esmonde and Tom Kettle (killed in action, 9 September 1916); for the role of the Irish National Party in recruiting, see Thomas P Dooley, *Irishmen or English Soldiers?*, Liverpool University Press, 1995.

20. Stephen Gwynn had originally come out to the Front as a Company Commander with the 6/Connaughts in December 1915. After the crisis of the Easter Rising in 1916, he returned home on parliamentary duty in May 1916. After hearing of the heavy Irish officer casualties in September 1916, he wrote to Lloyd George, requesting to be sent back to the 6/Connaughts at the Front; Gwynn to LG, 11 October 1916, PRO WO339/26731.

21. 'M' refers to Monica Stapleton-Bretherton.

22. 'J' is Joan Feilding, eldest daughter and correspondent with RCF.

23. There had been intense pressure for the 16th (Irish) Division to offer commissions to Nationalist MPs, to boost recruiting in Ireland. However, the average age of those prominent MPs who joined the Division was very high, and Gwynn, Redmond and Kettle, all over 50, suffered ill health at the Front; see Terence Denman, *Ireland's Unknown Soldiers – The 16th (Irish) Division in the Great War*, Irish Academic Press, 1992, pp. 46–8.

24. Private Thomas Hughes (1885–1942); apprentice jockey from Co. Monaghan. During the Battle of Guillemont, Hughes was wounded, returned to action and single-handedly overcame a machine-gun post. Wounded again, he still managed to bring back three prisoners; the division's second VC at Guillemont was won by Lieutenant J Holland; see Myles Dungan, *Irish Voices from the Great War*, Irish Academic Press, 1995, pp. 136.

25. RCF persuaded Holloway to organise the show. It was Stanley Holloway's first production and was titled *Wear That Ribbon*. The show featured talent from among the Connaught Rangers and was a blueprint for further successful army shows; see Roy Walding, *An Arm of Iron*, THE, 1996, pp. 12–16.

26. T/Lieutenant Thomas M Kettle (1880–1916); noted writer, poet, barrister and MP for East Tyrone, 1906. He opposed the Boer War, but supported the Empire cause in the Great War, defending the independence of Belgium, a 'small' country, similar to Ireland. He was commissioned to purchase arms in Belgium in 1914 for the Catholic 'Irish Volunteers'. After the 1916 Easter Rising, which he dubbed 'The Sinn Fein Nightmare', he volunteered for service in 9/Royal Dublin Fusiliers. He was killed in action 9 September 1916. He is remembered for his essay, 'The Ways of War' (1917), and 'Battle Songs for the Irish Brigades' (1915).

27. Philip (later Sir Philip) Gibbs (1877–1962); entered journalism, 1902; successively literary editor of the *Daily Mail*, the *Daily Chronicle* and the

Tribune; prodigious author and probably the most capable and well informed of the war correspondents.

28. German trench-mortar bombs came in three different sizes: 76mm, 175mm and 245mm; known variously as 'minnies', 'rum jars' or 'flying pigs'.

WAR LETTERS TO A WIFE

PART II : 1917

SERVICE WITH THE CONNAUGHT RANGERS

1st Battalion (1 January onwards)

1 January 1917 [Derry Huts, near Dranoutre]
We heard Mass again this New Year's morning; our third Sunday in three days! The first was our Christmas Day; the second was yesterday, the real Sunday, when Monseigneur Ryan[1] from Tipperary, preached; the third was today.

5 January 1917 [Facing Messines – Wytschaete Ridge]
You may perhaps think it strange that already I begin to feel myself again, but so it is. There is unquestionably some health producing quality in the effluvia of a trench and the 'frowstiness' of a dug-out which is not to be found outside, and after the war, I quite expect to see 'Trench' cures, just as there are now 'Open Air' cures!

Night of 7–8 January 1917 [Facing Messines – Wytschaete]
I wonder if I have enough energy left tonight. It is nearly 2 am, and it has been a heavy day. The enemy declared war upon the battalion this morning, at the unearthly hour of 4.15, when he opened an intense bombardment.

The enemy's artillery set upon the skeleton buildings known as Shamus Farm, which soon burst into flames. The buildings contained, in addition to large reserves of ammunition, a quantity of inflammable stores – smoke candles and smoke bombs – to which the fire at once spread. In the old farmyard too, outside the flaming buildings, piled up against the walls, were boxes containing 5,000 Mills grenades, as well as several hundred Stokes mortar bombs.

I venture to think that most people under the circumstances would have considered their duty sufficiently fulfilled in getting their men clear of the threatened buildings, but that was not Sergeant Casey's way. Immediately, and without orders, there being no officer present, this splendid NCO set himself to save the ammunition. Under fierce fire, with the assistance of his men, he succeeded in shifting all that was in direct danger. While he was doing so, at least twenty shells fell within a radius of 20 yards about the place. Then, for an hour or more, he continued to fight the flames. In the end, the buildings were demolished, but the ammunition was saved.

The casualties for the day have been remarkably light, that is to say fifteen, though these include five or six dead, one of whom was an excellent officer, Lieut. George Haire.

I will go and sleep a bit now.

P. S. (January 8). I must reopen my letter to tell you of a sight I saw yesterday.

One of our aeroplanes flew overhead, very low, engaged upon reconnaissance work. I looked up and saw a German aeroplane swoop down upon our man. Then there was a fusillade of machine-gun fire between the two. Then our man's petrol tank was hit and took fire, and the machine became a long streak of streaming flame, making for home, and earth. Every second I thought it must collapse. It seemed impossible that either pilot or observer could be alive, or that the engine could be working. But the rush through the air kept the flames from the canvas, and the aeroplane flew on. It was an inspiring sight; a magnificent fight between man and death, in which the man won – for the time being.

After a long slanting flight, the aeroplane came to ground, a mile or more behind our line. I sent an officer to the spot. Though I could have sworn the occupants were dead, they were not. The aeroplane was a crumpled, shapeless mass, the fire having engulfed it the moment it settled, but both were alive, though one was so severely burned that he is not likely to recover.[2]

9 January 1917 [Facing Messines – Wytschaete Ridge]

The whole place is a sea of mud and misery, but I must not grumble at the mud. It saves many thousands of lives by localising the shell-bursts, and by muffling those very nasty German trench-mortar bombs. 'The more dirt the less hurt' – as I think Jorrocks said on one occasion, though speaking of a different subject.

The officers and men stand these poundings like heroes, as they truly are.

10 January 1917 [Facing Messines – Wytschaete Ridge]

A fairly quiet day. In the evening, while I was in the fire-trench, I saw three enemy aeroplanes dash across to one of our 'sausage' balloons and set it alight. The occupants of the balloon, which had burned out before it reached the ground, came down by their parachutes.

It was dashingly done, I must admit, and the Germans were back behind their lines almost before our anti-aircraft people had realised what they were at, though I think one of them was winged.

*   *   *

14 January 1917 (Sunday) [Curragh Camp, Locre]

We came out of the trenches last night. I could not describe them if I tried, but they are more wretched-looking than any I have seen since I came to the war.

The most imaginative mind could not conceive a picture of the frail and battered wall of shredded sandbags without actually seeing it, nor the heroic manner in which the men who hold it, face its dangers and discomforts;– the mud and the slush and the snow; often knee-deep, and deeper still, in water; the foulest of weather; four days and nights without moving from one spot; pounded incessantly with what the soldiers call 'rum jars' – great canisters of high-explosive, fired from wooden mortars, making monstrous explosions; and in addition, often going through an hour or two during the day or night of intense bombardment.

From the front line, after eight days, the battalion goes into Brigade Reserve. Even from there, the men go up to the front line most nights on working parties and are pounded again. Then eight days in the front line once more. Then eight days here, in Divisional Reserve, where at least we are free from shell-fire.

The Brigadier goes home on three weeks leave on the 18th; a unique event for him.

17 January 1917 [Curragh Camp, Locre]

We woke up to find the ground white with snow, and it has been snowing mildly all day. I dined with Stephen Gwynn in a private room at the Locre Convent. He had a party comprising, amongst others, Major Willie Redmond, Bishop Cleary of Auckland, New Zealand, General Powell, CRA in the Ulster Division (in peace-time a master of fox-hounds in Co. Cork), Smiley (MP for Antrim)[3] – also of the Ulster Division, and Father Brown, who used to be Chaplain to the 1st Irish Guards, and was wounded on September 15 last year, on the Somme.

Afterwards, I walked part of the way home with Willie Redmond. He is a charming fellow, with a gentle and very taking manner.[4]

26 January 1917 [Derry Huts, near Dranoutre]

We were suddenly and unexpectedly relieved today. I was not sorry. The weather has been and is 'arctic', with a biting east wind, and the strain in the front line is considerable. Probably, the enemy gets it worse, since the wind catches him in the back, where – if his breastworks are anything like ours – there is little in the way of parados to screen him. The breastworks are in a horrible state, frozen hard as stone, the ground is white with snow, and the garrison stands four days and nights at a time, in the paralysing cold, without exercise, numbed, trench-mortared, and shelled.

*   *   *

28 January 1917 (Sunday) [Derry Huts, near Dranoutre]

This evening I rode 5 miles to Corps Headquarters at Bailleul, to dine with the Corps Commander, General Hamilton Gordon.[5] Many Generals present, including the GOC Ulster Division (General Nugent).[6]

1 February 1917 [Facing Spanbroekmolen, Fort Victoria]

The enemy tried again to raid the battalion this morning. At 5.15 he opened a sudden and fierce bombardment with artillery and trench-mortars on the front line and wire, and twenty minutes later the raiders came over the snow, camouflaged in white overalls and head-covers.

The Lewis gun protecting the point which they made for had been put out of action during the bombardment, but the team manned the parapet with their rifles, and two more Lewis guns were brought up, with the result that the Germans were soon put to flight, leaving seven or eight white figures dead in No Man's Land. We shall get these in, or some of them, tonight.

4 February 1917 [Wisques]

We got in another German body after the moon had dropped early yesterday morning. It was dressed only in a thin cellular vest and drawers, besides the tunic and trousers, and was without a shirt. Imagine the cruelty of it this bitter weather, with the thermometer, as it is, registering thirty degrees of frost!

We are burying this man together with one of his comrades in a corner of our own cemetery in Kemmel, and I have given orders for a notice-board to be shown on the parapet, telling the enemy that we have done so; though I am not sure that such a departure from present-day methods will be approved of if it becomes known.

The two dead men are Saxons, and therefore probably RC, so I have also arranged for our Chaplain to read the burial service over them.[7]

RCF is sent on a battalion commander's Course at Wisques and Cassel (2nd Army HQ) for five days.

11 February 1917 [Kemmel Shelters]

I returned to the battalion last evening, and found that the enemy had been shelling my battalion in Camp. It is in Divisional Reserve – training in a 'safe' place. Four have been killed and nine wounded, and the huts so badly smashed that two Companies have had to be moved elsewhere.

14 February, 1917 [Kemmel Shelters]

My darling Joan,

I am writing you each a letter on official buff forms (as they call them) because I am running short of paper.

Will you tell Mother that I got a beautiful German revolver the other day as my share of the booty, for our collection at Gordon Place.[8] I also have some other things.

I was so glad to hear that poor little Pru has got through her operation all right.

We are just leaving for the trenches again.

Your loving Daddy.

15 February 1917 [Facing Spanbroekmolen]

Here we are in the trenches again. This morning, in daylight, a German came running across No Man's Land with his hands up, and was shot by his own people just as he reached our wire. We shall get his body in tonight.

Ivan Garvey,[9] who commands the Company holding the line at the point where it happened, says that three of his men immediately came rushing along the trench to tell him, and that when he went to the spot he found the platoon gazing over the parapet at the dead German. Some of them wanted to go and fetch him in then and there, but Garvey naturally did not allow that.

16 February 1917 [Facing Spanbroekmolen]

During the night we got in the German whom I spoke of in my last letter – shot through the back by his own side.

He deserved his fate, of course. But how fed up he must have been to do as he did. He was a fine fellow physically; about twenty years of age; and will be buried tomorrow in a corner of the cemetery. His pocket was stuffed with picture postcards of and from ladies, and photographs of himself and his family.

18 February 1917 ['Doctor's House', Kemmel]

It is late at night, and at half-past three tomorrow morning, we set off on a rather desperate enterprise.

The intention is to raid the enemy at three points in daylight, in a fog, or failing a fog, under cover of a smoke cloud, <u>without</u> preliminary bombardment. The weather so far has been entirely and persistently inappropriate to our purpose. Tonight it seems that we may have the conditions we have wished for.

I am not entirely satisfied with the arrangements. First, Roche, the Trench-Mortar Officer, in whom I have complete faith, was sent away on a fortnight's course – much against his own will as well as mine – before the cutting of the enemy's wire, which had been entrusted to the medium mortars; and without him I do not quite trust the rest, either to make the necessary gaps, or to keep them open.

Secondly, I have lost two of the principal officers whom I had detailed for the raid – both leaders of assaulting parties; one wounded; the other away on an officer's course (the curse, often, of us Battalion Commanders, since we have no option in the matter, and are obliged to send away officers when called for). I have applied for this officer back again, and have been refused him. Consequently, though the raid has been well practised over a replica of the German trench which I have had prepared behind our line, the training of these two important adjuncts has been thrown away.

Finally, a one minute's intense lightning Stokes[10] mortar bombardment which I asked for at Zero has been vetoed, Pereira's view being that this would alarm the Germans in the front line and bring them to their posts. It would doubtless bring _him_ to _his_ post, but he is apt to forget, I think, that all men are not like himself.

However, for better or worse, we tackle the job tomorrow morning, and all preparations having been completed in so far as is feasible under the circumstances. We have been having a game of Bridge; and now I am off for a few hours sleep before starting.

20 February 1917 ['Doctor's House', Kemmel]

With my Headquarters officers, I reached Shamus Farm at about 4 o'clock yesterday morning, in a dense fog. The men of the raiding parties were already filing in and out of the ruins, loading up with Mills grenades, smoke bombs and all the other paraphernalia necessary for the undertaking. The green oval patches were being stripped from their sleeves, and everything by which the battalion might be identified, such as letters, regimental numerals, and cap badges, were being collected and put away in sandbags.

Each man, as he completed these preliminaries, passed silently into the communication trench leading to the firing line, where all was absolutely still – uncannily so.

Michael Sweetman[11] was with me. He had persisted in coming, and I had given way, though I feel that perhaps I should have refused him, seeing that he is only attached to the battalion and had no duty to perform; and I am devoutly thankful to say that no harm has come of it.

At seven o'clock I passed along the fire-trench, where the raiders were now waiting for the moment of Zero. Most were cheerfully tucking green miniature Irish flags into their caps or buttonholes, and all seemed full of confidence.

At 7.15 the three parties, comprising 9 officers and 190 other ranks, without any preparatory bombardment, scaled the parapet, and made a wild dash across No Man's Land. At the same moment our artillery opened, according to programme, and put a box barrage round the selected section of the enemy trench.

The centre party reached the German wire, but found it uncut, having – perhaps owing to the fog – missed the gap. 2nd Lieut. Williamson, second

97

in command of the party, was killed as he neared the wire, and 2nd Lieut. Kent, commanding, was wounded in the arm but continued firing with his revolver at the enemy, holding up his wounded arm with his free hand. When he had fired off his six rounds he lay down and reloaded. J. White, a private, then stood up and bombed the enemy in the trench. This party found a covering group lying out in front of the German wire, which fell back into the trench as our men approached.

The right party had no casualties till it reached the wire. Then 2nd Lieut. Bradshaw, second in command, was wounded, and a minute or two later was hit again and killed. 2nd Lieut. Cardwell, commanding the party, was also wounded severely by a stick bomb, which blew away the calf of his leg. His men then threw all the bombs they were carrying across the wire into the German trench, after which, seeing that the party on their left was retiring, and having lost both their officers, they fell back.

The first wave of the left party started off well under 2nd Lieut. Cummins, a very gallant young officer whom I had put in command in place of the original commander. Then Sergeant Hackett was almost immediately killed. The party met with heavy opposition, and some of the men behind them faltering, Captain Garvey, who was in charge of the assaulting parties, ran out across No Man's Land to rally them. He fell wounded, and Lieut. T. Hughes, commanding the left support, ran forward to help rally the waverers. Private John Collins did the same. This man acted with great dash, rushing recklessly towards the German trench, shouting 'Come on the Connaughts' – a cry which some of the enemy took up. Sergeant Purcell and Privates Twohig and Elwin also did their best to encourage the others, the latter standing up and firing with his rifle at the Germans, who now began freely to expose themselves, until he fell, shot through the neck.

Hughes showed great gallantry, again and again exposing himself; then, recognising that the raid had failed, he fell back, and with the aid of Cummins and two privates – King and Healy, carried Garvey back to the shelter of our trench.

In the meantime, the enemy had been retaliating violently upon our front line and communication trench with high explosive and shrapnel, as was to be expected.

After some two hours, the firing on both sides died away, and by 9.30 all was quiet. An incident then took place which I think was as remarkable as any that this most unchivalrous of wars can have yet produced.

Our dead and many of the wounded still lay out in No Man's Land, and when the fog lifted, the German trench became clearly visible. As I stood in the middle of the fire-trench a man came running to me and reported that the enemy had allowed what he called 'an armistice', for the purpose of collecting the wounded who were lying in front of the right extremity of the section.

I hurried along the trench and found that this was literally true. Already parties of men were out dressing the wounded and carrying them back to our line. One of my officers and a German were bending together over a wounded man alongside the enemy wire. The Germans, in considerable numbers, were lolling over and even sitting upon their parapet, watching the proceedings. My own men were doing the same. As the stretcher-bearers started to move the dead, the enemy called out, 'leave the dead alone', but no notice was taken of this.

I asked how this extraordinary state of affairs had originated. I was told that the Germans had called out in English, 'Send out your stretcher men', and that a number of volunteers had immediately climbed over the parapet.

I noticed Private Collins. He is one of the 'wild men' of the battalion. He was sauntering about with a pipe in his mouth, wearing a bomber's waistcoat, the pockets bulging with bombs. This was obviously out of order under the circumstances, and was only asking for trouble; in fact the Germans, I had been told, when they issued their invitation to the stretcher-bearers had stipulated (rather naturally) that the latter should come unarmed.

I told Collins to put down his bombs, which he did rather sheepishly, as though he had suddenly remembered for the first time that he had them on. Then, after a parting warning, I moved off towards the left section of the trench, to see how things were faring there.

The 'armistice' had spread, and the scene, if possible, was more remarkable than that which I had left. The distance between the enemy's trench and ours is considerably less here than on the right, being not more than 40 yards at the narrowest point.

I found numerous Germans – almost shoulder to shoulder – leaning over their parapet, exposed from the waist up: on our side it was the same. All were watching the stretcher-bearers at work in No Man's Land. A German officer was walking excitedly up and down along the top of his parapet, shouting in perfect English to my men to 'get their heads down or he would open fire', at the same time gesticulating vigorously with his arm.

The whole proceeding was of course highly irregular, and the last of our wounded and dead having by this time been recovered, I ordered the men below the parapet. A second or two later, every head on both sides had disappeared: both the German trench and ours had become normal, and the war had restarted.[12]

I thought to myself, 'These people cannot always be so bad as they are painted'. Then I proceeded to take stock. The enemy had exacted payment for his generosity. The officer I had seen near the German wire was missing, as were one or two others.

There may be something to be said in the case of the officer. He had foolishly neglected to remove his revolver (or rather revolvers, since he had two) before going out, and having looked into the enemy's trench, was perhaps fair game. At the same time, by what subterfuge he and the others were inveigled into becoming prisoners, I do not know, and shall not know till the war is over; if then.[13]

20 February 1917 (Night).

I fly to you when I am in trouble, and I am feeling very sick at heart tonight. Ivan Garvey – the ideal Company Commander – the bravest, the cheeriest, the most loyal and perfect of men, was reported a few hours ago to be dead of his wounds. How readily he undertook the work when I first proposed it to him.

As I passed the Aid Post yesterday, on my way back from the line, I went in, and found him asleep under morphia, so did not get a chance to speak to him. Nobody thought he would die then.

My God! If the people at home could actually see with their eyes this massacring of the cream of our race, what a terrible shock it would be to them. But we must see it through. All are agreed upon that.

Nine of my best officers went over yesterday. Three of these are left today. And, in addition, one more of my Company Commanders (Fitzgerald) is gone, as the result of this enterprise. He was wounded while cutting the gaps through our own wire, preparatory to the raid, so severely that he too may die.[14]

But all this is not unusual. It is the toll to be expected from a raid when it is unsuccessful, and indeed often when it is successful: and the success or failure of a raid is largely a matter of chance.

This afternoon, I was present at the burial of some of those killed, including two of my most promising young officers. That is the tragedy of the war. The best are taken. The second best are often left in the safe places.

General Pereira came and saw me this morning, and stayed some time. He was more kind and consoling than I can say.

Private Elwin, too, has died.

22 February 1917 [Kemmel]

My dearest Joan,

Thank you for your letter. We are leaving the trenches today and shall be away from them for the usual number of days. I send four German postcards. Choose the one you like best and give the others to Anita, Peggy and Pru. We found them on a dead German.

I think I know which postcard you will choose. The postcards have just been returned to me by the Brigade to whom I sent them first, so that they might see if they contain any news of military importance.

Your loving Daddy.

*   *   *

26 February 1917 [Curragh Camp]

There is a sequel to the affair of the 19th. It has been suggested that the so-called 'armistice' constituted a breach of the order which forbids fraternisation. The incident unfortunately occurred right on the top of a memorandum dealing with the subject.

As a matter of fact I had not seen this memorandum, which arrived when I was away from the battalion. God knows whether I should have acted differently had I done so. Anyway, a Court of Enquiry is to be convened, to decide whether we did fraternise or not, and orders still more stringent have been issued.

In future, if fifty of our wounded are lying in No Man's Land, they are (as before) to remain there till dark, when we may get them in if we can; but no assistance, tacit or otherwise, is to be accepted from the enemy. Ruthlessness is to be the order of the day. Frightfulness is to be our watchword. Sportsmanship, chivalry, pity – all the qualities which Englishmen used to pride themselves in possessing – are to be scrapped.

In short, our methods henceforth are to be strictly Prussian; those very methods which we claim to be fighting this war to abolish.

And all because the enemy took toll for his generosity the other day.

27 February 1917 [Curragh Camp]

I have written to you much of the staying powers of the men. You cannot dig trenches in this locality because you get drowned out. So you bank up sandbags and stand behind them. And the enemy flattens these every day or two with his 'rum jars'; and we do the same to his.

'Rum jar' is the soldier's name for the German canister, which is their simplest form of heavy trench-mortar bomb. Picture a cylindrical oil-drum, 15 inches long and about 11 inches in diameter, flat at both ends, and filled with high explosive. That is the 'rum jar'. In the dark, if you spot it coming, you can just distinguish it in the air, by the fizzling of the fuse.

But it arrives silently, and is not easy to detect, until it lands with a mighty bang. If one happens to hit a man or a collection of men, it blows them to bits. And these things come in hundreds, and are a perpetual menace to the men in the front line, day and night.

I will tell you two stories which may amuse you.

A certain very charming and gallant General, who sometimes visits us, is fond of making little speeches to any group of men he may find drilling, or in the huts when we are out of the line. He also – very properly – likes to take an opportunity to shake hands with any man who has been rewarded or mentioned for having performed a gallant action: and he has a way on such occasions of turning suddenly to the senior officer present and asking, 'What were the details of the act for which this man was recommended?'

Among so many stirring events, that is not always easy to recall at a moment's notice, especially when some period has elapsed since the recommendation was made.

Some little time ago, I was told to put forward the name of an NCO or man for a certain foreign decoration. It so happened at the moment that there was no 'specific act' outstanding. However, I decided to give the chance to the Lewis gunners, who I thought had not been recognised as well as they might have been.

Immediately, one of the Company Commanders who happened to be in the room, said to me: 'Why not put forward Sergeant R_____? He has done excellent work ever since the battalion came to France, and has got nothing.'

This was very true, and no other man being forthcoming, I asked, 'What is the specific act?' The Company Commander said: 'Well, I don't quite know about that'. I said: 'Think it over, and if you can recommend Sergeant R_____ for a specific act, I shall be glad to put his name forward'.

The Company Commander went away, and later in the evening I received his recommendation, couched in the glowing style which is required if these efforts are to be successful. I sent it forward, and, not long afterwards, Sergeant R was awarded the Military Medal – a better decoration than that for which he had been recommended. Incidentally, Sergeant R had received what he richly deserved, though perhaps would never have had but for the circumstances I have mentioned.

Weeks passed. I went away on a course. Many exciting incidents intervened, and I confess that the nature of Sergeant R_____'s 'specific act' had entirely escaped my memory, when the General arrived on the scene, while Sergeant R_____'s company was at exercise.

He first made the men a little speech. Then, having finished, he turned to me and asked: 'Is there anyone in this Company who has received any decoration lately?'

I said: 'Yes, sir, Sergeant R_____ has received the Military Medal'. He went on: 'What was the act for which Sergeant R_____ received the Military Medal?' As I have said, the literary effusion which had secured the well merited award had gone completely out of my head. I looked towards the Company Commander. He, too, for a moment, was nonplussed. Then he butted boldly forward, and in glowing language described how one night when the enemy had demolished part of our breastwork Sergeant R had collected six bombers and without any orders had taken up a position in the battered breach, etc., etc., etc.

The General then called Sergeant R_____ out in front of the Company, and shaking him by the hand said: 'I am glad to have this opportunity of congratulating Sergeant R_____ for his gallant act, when in the middle of a heavy trench-mortar bombardment he collected six bombers, etc., etc.'; then, turning to the Company Commander, he asked: 'And what were the names of the six bombers? I should like to congratulate them, too'.

This time the Company Commander really was defeated. But the most amusing part of the episode was the look of modest surprise which mounted into the face of Sergeant R_____ as he heard his 'specific act' recounted. He stood like a stolid block, his eyebrows rising higher and higher, while the Company gazed in amazement at their hero.

I fancy the General, who is very wide awake, saw through it: but he was far too wise to show the fact.

There are many funny stories about these men when they first joined the army. It was a common thing for a man to call an officer 'Your honour', and one who wished to be particularly respectful is said on a certain occasion to have addressed the Colonel as 'Your Reverence'.

3 March 1917 [Derry Huts, near Dranoutre]

The Battalion Commanders were sent for this morning, to meet General Plumer, the Second (i.e. my) Army Commander, at Brigade Headquarters. We went in one by one, and had a tête-à-tête conversation with him.

When my turn came, I found only Colonel Monck-Mason[15] (temporarily commanding the Brigade during the Brigadier's absence) and the Army Commander in the room. The latter was very friendly, and very human. That is one of his many admirable qualities. He takes the trouble to know even his Battalion Commanders, and for this and other reasons has earned great confidence among the troops of his army.[16]

After shaking hands, he referred to the raid of February 19. He expressed the opinion that there should have been a preliminary bombardment by artillery, and asked me why this had not been done. Obviously, I could not enter into explanations, but he quickly turned to Colonel Monck-Mason, who replied that the trenches were too close together for that.

'Then', said the General, 'you should have had a trench-mortar bombardment'. Then he turned to me and said: 'I know all about your having asked for a Stokes mortar bombardment. General Pereira has told me'.

I felt I could see General Pereira telling him this, and explaining that it was he who had refused it; blaming himself, in fact, for the failure of the raid. Now, that is just Pereira all over, and I repeat it that you may know the man, and understand why every officer and soldier of his Brigade swears by him. As one of my brother COs once said to me: 'You know if he trusts you, that he will defend you, and that no one will be allowed to belittle you except across his mangled corpse'. And the feeling in regard to Plumer among the fighting troops is much the same.

We came here yesterday, into Brigade Reserve, to find that the enemy had been shelling the place with high explosives and gas – the latter still hangs heavily on the ground. One shell hit the house where my headquarters are, but the family (mother, baby and all) still cling on.

(Midnight) – I have just got my leave.

RCF goes on leave for twenty-one days.

28 March 1917 [Mont des Cats]

On returning from leave, I found the battalion quite changed by the arrival of eighteen new officers, and temporarily commanded by Colonel Jourdain,[17] a regular officer of the Connaught Rangers.

5 April 1917 [Butterfly Farm, near Locre]

Tomorrow, I shall have completed exactly seven months in the command of this battalion. The glamour and romance of the war die away after a time, and only the reek of it remains. One's life is dictated by a sense of duty, which is the one and only incentive. It is only latterly I have felt like this. Until recently, the life interested and held me, and I shall always look back upon 1915 and 1916 as a time of extraordinary happiness.

6 April 1917 (Good Friday) ['Turnerstown Left', Vierstraat Sector]

My headquarters are very cramped, and I have been obliged to leave several officers behind. Michael Sweetman is still here, and went round the trenches with me today. He always goes with me on my rounds. He is a very faithful friend, besides being – as 'M' would say – very calm, cool and collected on all occasions, and the more I see of him the more I am struck with his rare selflessness.

9 April 1917 ['Turnerstown Left']

Yesterday (Easter Sunday) was a heavenly day of sunshine – the finest we have had this year.

Moreover, it was so quiet and peaceful that Michael and I, after going round the lines, sat out in the open and read the papers. There was a good deal of aerial activity, and as we lolled about, the aeroplanes pooped away overhead with their Lewis guns, and the 'Archies' spoke from below. During the night following there was but little gunning over our lines, though for some hours in the morning there were the sounds of what seemed like a big battle far away to the right.

The enemy has knocked over the last outstanding fragment of Ypres Cathedral. When I looked yesterday from the fire-trench for this great landmark, it had gone.

10 April 1917 ['Turnerstown Left']

The firing on our right which I spoke of yesterday was of course the huge battle raging on the Vimy Ridge, of which I then knew nothing.

The enemy certainly seems to be catching it on all sides, hot and strong. What a mess he has made of the diplomatic side of the war! To have brought in the USA – quite unnecessarily;– what a blunder from his point of view. Surely, the nation must have gone mad! I think most of us here are sorry that America has come in. We feel we are capable of finishing the job, and we would prefer to do so by ourselves.[18]

Snow and cold strong wind again today. Will spring ever come?

11 April 1917 [Rossignol Estaminet, near Kemmel]

This morning, we three Colonels – Michael, Jourdain and I – were reconnoitring some trenches. A good deal of shelling was going on – some much too close to be pleasant. One shell fell within a few feet of us, in Watling Street, nearly bagging the lot, and covering us with earth. Michael was in the middle and caught the greater part. He was grazed by a bulky thing, which looked to me like a big piece of shell, so I enquired anxiously if he was hurt: but he picked himself up and muttered, 'Thank God, it's only a brick!'

13 April 1917 [Rossignol Estaminet, near Kemmel]

Before we came up to the trenches the other day we were practising open fighting, according to a new method of organisation, whereby the men are divided up and classified under different categories – Lewis gunners, bombers, rifle grenadiers, riflemen, etc.[19]

The Army Commander inspected them, and before his arrival the function of each man in the attack was carefully impressed upon him. It was explained to the riflemen, for example, that, if asked, they were to reply that they were riflemen; the bombers that they were bombers, and so on.

So pat, in fact, had one man of the battalion got his answer on his lips, that when the General asked him unexpectedly, 'Are you a Catholic?', he replied, 'I am a Rifleman, sir'.

15 April 1917 [Rossignol Estaminet, near Kemmel]

This morning (Sunday) the Chaplain has been going round the Companies, which are scattered, saying Mass, and speaking to the men about your miniature crucifixes.

He explained all about these;– how you had arranged to have them blessed by the Pope, specially for this battalion; how Cardinal Bourne[20] had brought them from Rome; and how, next Sunday, when we shall be back behind the trenches, we are to have a Parade Mass, when they will be distributed. And he said many nice things about you.

17 April 1917 ['Turnerstown Left']

Last night we captured two big Prussian Grenadiers (unwounded) on our wire. They were brought to my dugout at 2 am, looking frightened –

with their hands still outstretched in the orthodox manner of the surrendered prisoner who desires to show that he is not armed; coated with
mud; one bleeding from a tear from the wire; but neither seeming too
unhappy.

If one only knew German this would be the proper time to extract
information. They are too scared to lie much. Later, when they find out
how kindly is the British soldier, they become sly and independent.

22 April 1917 (Sunday) [Birr Barracks, Locre]

The ceremony of presenting your crucifixes was performed this
morning. All of the battalion that was available – between 600 and 700 –
marched in sunshine to the Parish Church of Locre, led by the regimental
pipes and drums. When we reached the gates we found the Divisional
band awaiting us, which, as the drums stopped, struck up and played the
battalion into church. A crowd of soldiers and civilians were watching,
and overhead, high up in the sky, a German aeroplane was passing, at
which the 'Archies' were potting wildly.

Inside, the church was packed. The Divisional Commander and the
Brigadier were there, and with myself, had seats in the chancel. Lined up,
facing one another along each side of the chancel, was a Guard of Honour
of sixteen, with fixed bayonets, which presented arms at the Elevation,
while the buglers sounded the General Salute. The Divisional band stood
in the doorway of the church, and played at intervals.

The priest (Father O'Connell), from the pulpit, gave an address, in
which he described your happy idea. He spoke about you and also myself,
and commended the 'spirit' of the battalion. He said that today's Mass
was to be 'for Mrs. Feilding's intention', and asked everyone present to
pray specially for you – that all might go well with you. So you have had
a church full of soldiers – there must have been nearly a thousand
altogether – straight from the battle line – praying for you this day. I
wonder if any other woman has had the same experience.[21]

When Mass was over, the priest asked all but the two Generals and the
Connaught Rangers to leave the church, and he then presented the
crucifixes; first to the Generals; then to the Guard of Honour; then to the
officers and men of the battalion, all of whom kissed them as they received
them, and have, I believe, since hung them round their necks.

One of my non-Catholic Company Commanders asked if he might take
a crucifix.[22] He told me, later, that it was the most impressive ceremony he
had ever seen: and I may admit that the devout reverence of these soldiers,
as they filed up towards the altar, affected me too, very deeply.

2 May 1917 [Birr Barracks, Locre]

The battalion has twice played football lately against battalions of the
Carson (36th) Division, and I am sorry to say got beaten both times. On the

second occasion there was a big crowd of soldier spectators – certainly 2,000 or 3,000.

When I arrived, the sight of the crowd, I confess, made me anxious. A hostile aeroplane overhead with wireless apparatus; a German battery behind; a sudden hurricane bombardment with shrapnel; and considerable damage might have followed. And I was the senior officer present.

But to stop a match in process of being cleanly fought before a sporting audience between the two great opposing factions of Ireland, in a spirit of friendliness which, so far as I am aware, seems unattainable on Ireland's native soil, was a serious matter; and I decided to let the game go on.

During the game a wag on the Ulster side was heard to say: 'I wonder if we shall get into trouble for fraternising with the enemy!'

Michael is leaving me, and though I am naturally glad that he has got a good job, I shall be most sorry to lose him. His military training and knowledge of military affairs have been invaluable to me.

4 May 1917 [Birr Barracks, Locre]

The Padre came to me this morning, and said that there were still about fifty men or more in the battalion who have not yet had your crosses, and were longing for them. It seems that on the Sunday when they were distributed, every one who could possibly claim to be a Connaught Ranger – any men in fact who are detached from the battalion – heard of what was on, and went to church.

I rode into Bailleul the other day, and met Willie Redmond. He was with another Nationalist Member of Parliament – Captain Esmonde.[23] The latter looks about nineteen. Redmond said that everybody in the House of Commons is determined now to have an Irish settlement, and he seems confident that Ireland is going to get Home Rule at last.[24]

5 May 1917 [Birr Barracks]

Again a glorious summer day. After breakfast I walked round the Nuns' garden. It was the first time I had been there. In one corner is a shrine to The Blessed Virgin – a sort of miniature Grotto of Lourdes. In front of this is a flower-bed, in the centre of which – planted over and surrounded by flowers – is the grave of a Canadian private soldier, beautifully cared for by the Nuns, with his name and number on a polished brass plate, fixed to a cross which marks the head.

Should it be my fate not to survive this war, I cannot imagine a more pleasant resting-place, and, if I get the opportunity, I shall mention this to the Reverend Mother.

6 May 1917 (Sunday) [Butterfly Farm, near Locre]

Last evening we came into Brigade Reserve, relieving the same battalion that we relieved two nights before the attack on Ginchy.

It is disgusting to think of the successes the Germans are having with their submarines. What a lot those cranks have to answer for who opposed and defeated the Channel Tunnel idea so long ago!

8 May 1917 [Butterfly Farm]

The German artillery continues to be very aggressive, shelling our back areas, roads, and billets, at intervals during the nights. These bombardments have, of course, levied their toll in killed and wounded men, and also in horses. (Michael and I, during a walk yesterday, came upon ten horses, killed by one shell.)

Last night, the Germans got a bit of their own back. At 8.45, by prearranged order, practically every gun and howitzer in the 2nd Army opened fire simultaneously, and continued at top blast for exactly five minutes, bombarding their back areas, roads and billets.

It was an impressive sight to watch the hundreds – perhaps thousands – of guns in action together, flashing intermittently in the darkness. And each time the enemy ventured to retaliate upon any area, he got a double dose.

From eleven o'clock until five minutes past, the operation was repeated. After that the enemy was as quiet as a mouse for the rest of the night.

15 May 1917 [Kemmel Shelters]

The very fact of my being here must cause you intense anxiety, but there is nothing you can do to deter the enemy from any villainy he may contemplate. And I continue writing to you of all the dangers of the war, remembering that you once said that if I hid anything you would know it, and only imagine worse things than were really happening.

The last few weeks there has been rather an epidemic of crime in the battalion, on a small scale; insubordination among a few men, who are marched in front of me time after time, and who seem equally impervious to leniency and the severest kind of discipline. I have sent some for court-martial and they have received heavy sentences, which, however, the General has commuted to Field Punishment. The result is that instead of having got rid of these men they remain with the battalion, and are a constant source of trouble and annoyance.[25]

I fully appreciate the General's difficulties. During these times a certain kind of scrimshanker, scenting danger ahead, is apt to commit some crime, hoping thereby to get imprisonment, and so be removed from the firing line. Others will achieve the same object, more safely, by going sick, and they are often taken, on reaching home, for heroes instead of what they really are. In the case of the former, the Authorities are fully alive to the trick. Consequently, there is a tendency to commute all sentences of imprisonment – which for obvious reasons are served away from the line – to Field Punishment,[26] which is served in it. But, in the latter case, the punishment falls so flat that the hardened offender cares nothing for it.

In 1915 a different method was followed. Sentences of imprisonment were deferred until the end of the war, and this method had a double advantage. First, the bad soldier had a sort of sword of Damocles ever poised above his head, and secondly, the better man, whose trouble had come from some momentary lapse (an ever-present possibility in war, as in peace), had a chance of atoning for his delinquency, and often, by good behaviour or a gallant act on the battlefield, he earned a complete reprieve.

Apart from the few troublesome ones I have mentioned – perhaps half a dozen – the battalion is in first-rate form and very cheerful, and the work it is doing here is being well and rapidly carried out, and is receiving much praise.

18 May 1917 [Coulomby]

This morning (my birthday) we moved on again by foot, doing 15 miles – a trying march, since the day was hot and the men were heavily loaded up. They came along splendidly, nevertheless, with the drums leading, and finished in the evening with plenty of swing at Coulomby, where many officers and men of other battalions of the Brigade stood by the road, watching them pass.

All along the route numerous inhabitants (who are not so blasé about British soldiers as they are nearer the line) turned out to have a look at the battalion. Bevies of children ran alongside, and an old Frenchman – evidently a veteran of the Franco-Prussian War – had all his medals ready, and held them up behind his cottage window, at the same time drawing his hand across his throat in signification of his sentiments towards his country's enemies.

20 May 1917 [Coulomby]

The rest is already beginning to work marvels with the men, and although we have so far had only two days of it, the cheered-up look and the renewed freshness in the battalion is surprising to see.

We had a football match this afternoon, and won it: and this morning (Sunday) we had Church Parade in an orchard. I must say I felt very proud of the battalion. The men had all groomed themselves up like new pins. The mud of the trenches had entirely disappeared. The brass was polished: the leather about the drums was well pipe-clayed: even the cookers and water-carts, the harness, chains, and limbers, were shining and resplendent. The spirit is there: of that there is no doubt; and it is wonderful.

One of my Companies has produced an enormous green flag with a yellow Irish harp upon it, which the men carry about with them on the march, and fly outside their billets. It has not got the Crown, and therefore would be ranked by some people as 'Sinn Fein', I feel sure. But it does not seem to make any difference to their loyalty and devotion. How times have changed!

24 May 1917 [Coulomby]

I have not written during the last two or three days. We have been training, and this keeps me out from early morning until late afternoon, after which I have the usual routine work to do, and then am tempted to ride out and explore this glorious part of the country, and enjoy the spring scenery. You will understand what a pleasant contrast our present surroundings are, to the ear-splitting, war torn zone from which we have come.

On Tuesday, I marched the battalion to Lumbres, where we spent the day on the banks of the brook, in the same field where Lord Cavan inspected the then newly-formed 2nd Guards Brigade in September, 1915, just before Loos. I think everyone enjoyed the outing.

The other day I went to St. Omer, where I lunched with GHQ Staff, and afterwards was shown a very interesting exhibition, which Colonel Foulkes (who has control of these eccentricities of modern warfare) had kindly arranged, of the latest and most horrible ways of killing our enemies. It was an instructive afternoon, and there is no doubt that we are already miles ahead of the Germans at their own game. But I cannot go into details, as you will understand.

At the rate we are going I think the enemy ought to be beaten very soon.

26 May 1917 [Coulomby]

Today we had a big practice day over prepared ground, and the Army Commander (General Plumer), the Corps Commander, and other Generals came to see us perform.

Tomorrow (Sunday) I have arranged a battalion day; platoon and section competitions in the morning, and in the afternoon sports:– a nice, free from the war day for men and officers, in fact. We have put up jumps, as the programme includes horse jumping (in which I am going to compete). And all the Brigade has been invited.

But Courts-Martial and Generals' Conferences are intervening, and everything promises to be spoilt. It may turn out all right, but it doesn't look hopeful at the moment (11.30 pm).

27 May 1917 (Sunday) [Coulomby]

This morning at eight o'clock one of the Padres said Mass in the orchard. He also preached a short sermon, in the course of which he exhorted the men to join in the singing of the hymns. He told them that they ought not to be ashamed of the men on either side hearing them, however badly they did it, and assured us that God didn't mind at all whether we sang in tune or not, so long as we sang.

Then he burst out: 'I don't say you're so bad. Anyway, you're miles ahead of the Munsters! I'm simply fed up with the Munsters . . . at any rate so far as singing is concerned!'

In the afternoon we had our sports after all, and many people came. The weather was perfect, and all was a huge success. Moreover, we managed to get some English stout and gave each man a free drink, which gave great satisfaction to all.

29 May 1917 [Arques]

We moved at half-past six this morning, and after a 15 mile march, halted here, where we are billeted for the night. We have two more days marching in front of us before we reach the line.

It has been a fine day for marching. Each time the drums struck up, and each time they stopped, a wild Irish yell went up; and, as 'Brian Boru'[27] was played, that cry which marks certain bars in this spirited tune was rendered in a style that would have brought either tears or laughter to your eyes, could you have heard it.

1 June 1917 [Clare Camp, 2 miles N. of Bailleul]

As we marched yesterday into Bailleul we passed refugees – women, children, and others, the women pushing perambulators with their babies and other belongings. They were leaving the place.

Furniture vans were loading up in front of some of the houses, and in Locre, which is of course very much nearer the line, though I have not yet revisited the hospitable Convent there, I hear that the children have already been sent away.

On the other hand, many sturdy inhabitants remain, and in my wanderings today I saw a sight which struck me as pathetic. It was that of a <u>very</u> old man and a tiny boy of three or four, crouched together in a flimsy dugout which the old man had made alongside his still more flimsy cottage.

We reached camp in the afternoon, after a 15-mile march, and found that the enemy had been shelling there.

This evening I went with Goode – one of my Company Commanders – to the top of Kemmel Hill, and from one of the artillery observation posts that have been burrowed into the hill watched a fierce bombardment of the German trenches.

P.S. Goode's Company marched in front yesterday, and consequently he rode beside me. He is an excellent officer, and comes out frequently with ideas. Now and again he makes a very sage remark. In the course of the day we passed a fat major of the sort one sees behind the line with plenty of decorations, evidently the happy occupant of some 'fat and cushy' job. Goode remarked: 'I'll bet the only time <u>he</u> gets the wind up is when he thinks the war is going to end'.

Cruel, but possibly true. How many are there like that? I wonder.

8 June 1917 [Rossignol Wood]

After a bombardment without equal in history, we attacked the Germans yesterday morning at ten minutes past three, and took the Messines–Wytschaete Ridge.

Our Brigade was allotted what was expected to be the most formidable task of the day – the capture of Wytschaete Village, which has been held by the enemy since 1914.

The village tops the crest of the Messines Ridge, and the breastworks, which we have occupied since we came from the Somme, last September, run across the swampy fields to the west of and below it, with the hospice (or convent) – represented by a heap of bricks – standing out prominently against the skyline, beyond the Petit Bois.

Now, the whole ridge and much beyond it is ours, and I am writing this letter sitting in the open in a wood, which the day before yesterday, would not have been a healthy thing to do.

It was during the night of June 2 that we came up to the trenches to take our part in the battle. The day had been chiefly occupied with conferences – with my officers, with the Brigadier, and the Divisional General. At noon, Major Keating – a Connaught Ranger officer, now commanding Tanks – had sent his car for me, and after giving me lunch had shown me his Squadron, comprising the latest super-tanks as well as old veterans that had fought on the Somme. All were well 'camouflaged', awaiting the order to advance to the attack.[28]

At 9.30 pm, we left for the trenches. A good deal of shelling was going on, and we had six wounded and a sergeant killed on the way up. When I reached my Headquarters to be, I found that the enemy had been shelling there. In fact, so hot had the CO of the outgoing battalion found it, that he had just moved out.

On June 3, I was visited by the Brigadier and many others, and spent a busy day, preparing details and writing orders for a trench raid, which, suddenly and unexpectedly, I had been called upon to make the following night. Our artillery bombarded the German trenches very heavily all that day, the enemy replying wildly and everywhere, on our front line and the back areas. Our artillery and trench-mortar batteries had full-dress and magnificent rehearsals of intense barrage, under Divisional, Corps and Army arrangements. The latest refinements of chemical warfare were a feature of the day; incendiary oil shells; thermit – a mixture of aluminium powder and magnetic oxide of iron, which, on the bursting of the shell, combine, producing a temperature high enough to melt steel, and descend in a glittering cascade of white-hot molten metal on to anybody or anything that happens to be below; gas from projectors; flying-pigs (i.e. bombs from the 9.45 inch trench-mortars, otherwise known as Duchesses); footballs (the big spherical bombs attached to 2-inch steel rods which are fired from the medium trench-mortars); and guns and howitzers of all descriptions and calibres.

Presently, at Battalion Headquarters, two heavy shells dropped within a few yards of us. Then a third seemed to fall in the doorway where I was standing. Immediately, all was darkness. The shelter was choked with a cloud of dust and debris. From a corner came a wail: 'Mother of God, I'm kilt entoirely'. I wondered how many really were killed, and when the dust had cleared away, felt around to see. The shell had fallen on a big dump of trench-mortar ammunition about 30 yards along the trench, and exploded it. There was a hole 50 feet wide and 20 feet deep.

The damage, otherwise, was slight. Two men had been killed outside, and two slightly wounded in the doorway. As for myself, I got the blast and the dust, broken by the turn in the trench, but otherwise full in the face, and everything looked scarlet. It was a nasty feeling at first. I heard the doctor whispering, and wondered if I was permanently blinded. For the rest of that day I could not open my eyes. My head ached.

At 10.30 on the night of June 4, I launched my raid – 250 officers and men under Captain Tuite. The objective was the third line of the enemy's trenches, in Wytschaete Wood. Tuite was to advance behind a creeping artillery barrage and was given twelve minutes to reach his final objective. The guns were then to form a 'box' barrage until the raiders got home again. He was allowed forty-five minutes in which to do the whole business.[29]

The raid was skilfully led and was entirely successful.

These affairs sometimes seem to go off better when done on the spur of the moment than after long fussy preparation. About sixty Germans were killed and seven prisoners were brought back, including an acting officer wearing the iron cross. The raiders returned in rags, their clothing torn to shreds by the enemy's wire, and today, after four more days of fighting, their clothes are in no better condition, as you can imagine.

We lost three officers – two killed, and one blinded for life I am afraid, by a bullet which penetrated his eye. There were about forty casualties among the men, mostly slight.[30]

I was up most of the night. In the early morning (about 3.45) the enemy once more started shelling my Headquarters with heavy shell – 8-inch and over.

The ultimate result of this bombardment was a big mess, but little material damage. One of the three principal shelters ('Harley House' – the one in which I had received my shaking two days before) was however, flattened, and Murphy – one of the regimental police who was on sentry duty – was killed. Another man, also, was buried, but was gallantly recovered, after an hour and a half, badly wounded but still alive, by the pioneer corporal (Coleman), while the shells were still falling. Poor Murphy had a photograph of his children in his pocket – a delightful looking family.

After midnight (June 5–6) we were relieved from the actual front line by the 6th Royal Irish Regiment. It was the beginning of the great battle. The troops were massed during this night for the coming attack, and the process was a slow one.

During the night, a lance-corporal of mine, who had been reported missing on the night of the raid – Fielding by name – was found in No Man's Land, by another regiment, and brought in. He had been lying there twenty-four hours with six wounds. His finders were greatly impressed by his stoic behaviour.

That evening (June 6) we tea'd in the open, about half a mile behind the fire-trench, our artillery shooting hard over our heads all the time, but eliciting no reply from the enemy. The Brigadier called and congratulated us on the success of the raid. He was in the best of form, and indeed everybody was very cheerful and full of confidence.

The 6th Connaught Rangers were to be broken up for the battle in order to provide 'mopping up' and carrying parties for the attacking battalions, thus leaving me personally with very little to do, and after dinner I moved to my Battle Headquarters – a deep mined dug-out in Rossignol Wood, above which I am now writing this letter.

Yesterday morning (the great day) I got up and went out at three o'clock. The exact moment of the assault is known by us as 'Zero'; by the French as 'l'heure H'.

I climbed on to the bank of the communication trench, known as Rossignol Avenue, and waited. Dawn had not yet broken. The night was very still. Our artillery was lobbing over an occasional shell; the enemy – oblivious of the doom descending upon him – was leisurely putting back gas shells, which burst in and around my wood with little dull pops, adding to the smell but doing no injury.

The minute hand of my watch crept on to the fatal moment. Then followed a 'tableau' so sudden and dramatic that I cannot hope to describe it. Out of the silence and the darkness, along the front, twenty mines – some of them having waited two years and more for this occasion – containing hundreds of tons of high explosive, almost simultaneously, and with a roar to wake the dead, burst into the sky in great sheets of flame, developing into mountainous clouds of dust and earth and stones and trees.[31]

For some seconds the earth trembled and swayed. Then the guns and howitzers in their thousands spoke: the machine-gun barrage opened; and the infantry on a 10 mile front left the trenches and advanced behind the barrage against the enemy.

Once the battle was launched, all was oblivion. No news came through for several hours: there was just the roar of the artillery.

The extent of our advance you will have learnt from the newspapers, and I hope you and all the world will have learnt also that the South Irish Division and the Ulster Division went forward side by side;– that they opened the battle.[32]

The Staff work yesterday was perfect. What a contrast to the time of Loos! We were inundated with paper beforehand on this occasion, so much so that it became a saying: 'If ink will win this war we certainly shall win it'; but no contingency, so far as I know, was unforeseen, and within six hours of the first assault parties were already at work, making roads across the mutilated zone and even laying water-pipes. All objectives had been reached punctually to scheduled time.

There was nothing to keep me any longer at the telephone, and I went forward to study results. German prisoners were carrying back the wounded. Already our Field Artillery was on the move forward – a stirring sight which always fascinates me.

Then over No Man's Land. As we stepped out there, my orderly, O'Rourke, remarked: 'This is the first time for two years that anyone has had the privilege of walking over this ground in daylight, sir'. We visited some of the mine craters made at the Zero hour, and huge indeed they are. Then we explored Petit Bois and Wytschaete Wood – blown into space by our fire and non-existent – the scene of our raid of the night of June 4. We found the bodies of an officer and a man of ours, missing since that night, which I have since had fetched out and buried among many of their comrades.

Our Tanks were now advancing – a dozen or more of them – going forward to take part in the capture of the fifth and sixth objectives. Their duty is to reduce local opposition, when it is encountered, and there they were, lumbering along, picking their way through the honeycomb of shell-holes and craters, getting into difficulties, getting out again, sometimes defeated, but generally in the end winning their way through this area of devastation, where nothing has been left alive, not even a blade of grass.

I cannot hope to describe to you all the details of a battle on this scale. The outstanding feature, I think, was the astounding smallness of our casualties. The contrast in this respect with Loos and the Somme was most remarkable. Scarcely any dead were to be seen. The German dead had been mostly buried by the shell-fire.

But, as is always the way, we lost some of our best. A single shell and a small one at that, knocked out twelve, killing three outright and wounding nine – two of the latter mortally. Among the victims of this shell were Major Stannus,[33] commanding the 7th Leinsters, and his Adjutant (Acton), and Roche,[34] the Brigade trench-mortar officer. I passed the last-named in my wanderings, lying by a dead private on the fire-step. He was, I think, one of the wittiest 'raconteurs' I have ever met, and as brave and ready a soldier as I have ever seen. As Brigade trench-mortar officer he was a genius. In conversation he was remarkable. I lifted the sandbag which some one had thrown over his face. It was discoloured by the explosion of the shell that had killed him, but otherwise was quite untouched, and it wore the same slight smile that in life used to precede and follow his wonderful sallies. In peace-time he was a barrister.

Willie Redmond also is dead. Aged fifty-four, he asked to be allowed to go over with his regiment. He should not have been there at all. His duties latterly were far from the fighting line. But, as I say, he asked and was allowed to go – on the condition that he came back directly the first objective was reached; and Fate has decreed that he should come back on a stretcher.[35]

How one's ideas change! And how war makes one loathe the party politics that condone and even approve when his opponents revile such a man as this! I classify him with Stephen Gwynn and Harrison[36] – all three men, Irish Nationalists, too, whom you and I, in our Tory schooling, have been brought up to regard as anathema! What effect will his death have in Ireland? I wonder. Will he be a saint or a traitor? I hope and pray it may teach all – North as well as South – something of the larger side of their duty to the Empire.

P.S. My men found a dead German machine-gunner chained to his gun. This is authentic. We have the gun, and the fact is vouched for by my men who took the gun, and is confirmed by their officer, who saw it. I do not understand the meaning of this:– whether it was done under orders, or was a voluntary act on the part of the gunner to ensure his sticking to his gun. If the latter, it is a thing to be admired greatly.

As always seems to be my fate on these occasions, I was reported seriously wounded!

The following extract is from captured correspondence:

> Today the 7th, the alarm was given. Terrible drum fire was heard all during the night. A terrible firing has driven us under cover. To the right and left of me, my friends are all drenched with blood. A drum fire which no-one could ever describe. I pray the Lord will get me out of this sap. I swear to it I will be the next. While I am writing, he still gives us power and loves us. My trousers and tunic are drenched in blood, all from my poor mates. I have prayed to God, He might save me, not for my sake, but for my poor parents. I feel as if I could cry out, my thoughts are all the time with them.[37]
>
> The slaughtering takes place behind Comines,[38] which place the English have taken. I have already done twelve months on the Western Front; have been through hard fighting, but never such slaughter.

10 June 1917 [Kemmel Shelters]

I see from the papers that the battle of the 7th is considered to have been the most successful of the war to date.

116

Of course, I could not even hint this to you, but, while we were behind, 'resting' – so-called, we were in reality practising the attack over fascinating dummy representations of the Petit Bois, etc., and the German trenches beyond the Wytschaete–Messines Ridge. Nothing was left to chance. We even had a large-scale model, covering about an acre, which represented, to scale, Wytschaete, the woods, and the villages beyond. This latter, which I believe was made by the engineers, was a triumph of skill. It looked like a huge toy village, and would have delighted the children.

Willie Redmond is buried in the nuns' garden, on almost the very spot I had chosen for myself.[39]

A large number of the men of the battalion are now the proud possessors of wrist watches – trophies of war.

12 June 1917 [Kemmel Shelters]

We are still where we have been the last three days, and are sending large working parties up towards the new front line, day and night.

Mrs. Glover, apparently, has had a row with her mother-in-law and the neighbours in Yorkshire. Glover says it is because she speaks with a London and not a Yorkshire accent. Also, he says, a girl whom he used to court is making mischief. He has insisted on my reading a 'stinker' he has received from this girl.

It begins – 'Private Glover' . . . and ends 'Yours Respectively'. Perhaps she meant to say 'Yours Retro-spectively'!

I went up to the forward area this afternoon, and what I saw made me more proud than ever before, if possible, of being British. Roads, water-pipes, and railways are advancing across the wilderness, and all is being done under shell-fire.

You see little locomotives puffing where a few days ago no man could show himself and live. I rode most of the way, and my mare – for the first time – annoyed me. She shied at the guns, and the locomotives, and the lorries, and worked herself, and me, into such a lather, that in the end I left her and took to my feet. I have since made amends to her with sugar.

I picked up Brett[40], who was the Company Commander on duty, and we explored together the ruins of Wytschaete. You can just distinguish where the roads were. You can recognise what was the chief outstanding feature – the church – only by tracing its position from the map. It should be in the middle of the square. But you cannot recognise the square. All is dust and rubble. We visited the famous Hospice, which caps the ridge, and used to be the most prominent landmark during the long months when we occupied the breastworks in the swamp below.

The only structures that have resisted our bombardments are the steel and concrete emplacements built by the enemy among the foundations of the village, several of which have withstood the racket fairly well; and if the garrisons had stood their ground they could have given a lot of trouble.

I found a YMCA man in one of these emplacements. He had actually established a forward canteen in it, and had a few packets of cigarettes and other things to sell to the troops. Brett took me to this hole. He explained that the man who occupied it was an 'ex-parson'. I asked him what he meant by an ex-parson. He said: 'Oh, he gave up his "see" to come out here' – (which showed how much Brett knew about ecclesiastical matters!).

It turned out that this fine sportsman was a Nonconformist minister!

14 June 1917 [Oultersteene]
Yesterday, we marched back here – to safety – in grilling heat. What with their box respirators with extensions, steel helmets, PH gas helmets, rifles, ammunition, packs, etc., there is little doubt but that the infantry soldier is getting overloaded for marching. His equipment grows as the inventions for killing grow.

Already, he must carry between 70 lbs and 80 lbs. And after a long bout of inactivity in the trenches (I refer only to the lack of exercise), you can well understand that he is not in condition for weight-carrying.

The Corps Commander (General Hamilton Gordon) met us by the way, and called me to his side while the battalion marched by. He has a very lugubrious face, and looked so melancholy that he might have lost a battle instead of having won one.

I am sleeping and messing in a spotless cottage. The Companies are very scattered – I should think well over a mile apart, from extreme to extreme. Many of the men are bivouacked in the open, or under their ground-sheets, as the weather is beautiful. After the fighting they were in rags from the German wire, and as all identification marks had been removed prior to the raid of June 4, much patching up and sewing on has been necessary.

Did you see that poor Stephen Gwynn went to speak to his constituents at Castlegar, accompanied only by a local newspaper correspondent, and that they refused to hear him? He was mobbed, in fact, by the young bloods of the place, who stoned him. One went so far as to throw a rotten egg in his face from a range of a yard.[41]

I venture to think that the same lad who did that foul thing would be like a lamb if we had him here;– or perhaps like a lion. I am quite sure he would not have felt even inclined to do as he did. No body of troops could be more amenable or better mannered and behaved, under all conditions, or more faithful and patient than the Irishmen in France. Yet, were they in Ireland, I feel pretty certain that some of them would be liable to emulate the hero of Gwynn's political meeting.[42]

They are truly an extraordinary and inexplicable race. They will do anything they are asked to do, even to the death. But they become like mules if they think they are being driven. And that is a fact which we English as a nation have not yet appreciated.

Again, why, after committing the most atrocious crimes in Ireland, are they often allowed to go scot-free? That is another mistake. They do not resent punishment, even of the severest kind, when they know they have earned it, as I have found here. However, there it is. Ireland will always be Ireland and politically, they do not themselves know what they want. And, God knows, we do not.

28 June 1917 [Bollezeele, near Zeggers Cappel]

To show you how shifting is the officer population of a present-day battalion, I may remark that today, though I have about forty officers, I am the only one who was present at the battle at Ginchy last September.

30 June 1917 [Bollezeele]

I am getting rather bitten with agriculture. No wonder these peasants get rich; or, if they do not, there must be something radically wrong with the whole system of land tenure in this country.

They are the most industrious and the thriftiest people I have ever seen, and though during this time of war the work is done entirely by women, children, old men, wounded men, and men hopelessly unfit for active soldiering – with a few soldiers (very few) released temporarily for the purpose.

In the farm where I am billeted there is a farm-hand – a girl of about eighteen. She sleeps on the straw, on the floor of a stable. She is up, bursting with life and spirits, each morning at five o'clock; and she works, at top pressure, without ceasing, till dark. Then she returns to her straw. She is slim, but has the strength of an average man. She handles the farm horses with a single rein, and by word of mouth. Apparently, she neither eats nor drinks.

It is the 'manure' season. That is to say, it is the time of year when they carry out the loathsome liquid accumulation of the past twelve months and spread it over the fields, and so wrapped up is this girl in the work, that you would think she revelled in it.

She moves always at the double – whether through the chicken run, whence every bird flies scared and panic-stricken at her wild approach, or through the manure heap (for she never goes round it). Each time I pass her she looks up with full face and a cheery grin. I don't suppose she ever washes, and she must reek of manure, but she fascinates me because of her extraordinary vitality.

3 July 1917 [No. 10 Stationary Hospital, St. Omer]

Today I should be one of a party with General Plumer, making a presentation of the bell of Wytschaete Church (which has been dug out of the ruins), to the King of the Belgians; but, instead, I am in bed in the hospital at St. Omer, enduring the torments of the damned each time I am obliged to make the smallest movement.

Briefly, I turned a somersault with my mare over the sandbag wall at the Royal Munster Sports yesterday, at Zeggers Cappel, straining or tearing some muscles in my back, and breaking a bone or two in my left hand. The last I remember was crawling away from the course, and the soldiers clapping as I picked myself up from the ground. They are always like that.

I came here in an ambulance – 19 miles – and arrived after eleven o'clock, last night. I am glad I have had the experience. I think I understand now in a small degree how the wounded must suffer when they are carried back over the bumpy roads.

RCF suffers a broken hand and fractured rib.[43] *He is sent back to England on 11 July, on sick leave. During his absence, the 6/Connaught Rangers are temporarily commanded by Lieutenant-Colonel JD Mather.*

The battalion – part of Hubert Gough's Fifth Army – spends the rest of July training for the Ypres offensive. The 16th (Irish) Division is to attack Langemarck, alongside the 36th (Ulster) Division, on 14 August. The Rangers are in action for the two weeks before, supporting other units and suffering 250 casualties. The attack by the exhausted Irish divisions is a disaster and recriminations follow.[44]

The 16th (Irish) Division is moved to the Third Army, Arras sector, on 25 August. They are still in this area when RCF returns to France, medically fit, on 18 September 1917.

20 September 1917 [Croisilles–Ecoust Railway Cutting]

We had a fair crossing on the 18th, and as the train did not leave until the next morning, I put up for the night at the Louvre Hotel, in Boulogne.

On the train yesterday afternoon, we saw that old familiar sight, the line of observation balloons, indicating our line, and later passed through the shattered town familiarised to you and me by our visit to the Grafton Galleries (Arras).

At Boisleux-aux-Monts I met Esmonde, the Irish MP, who had come by the same train, and whom I had not seen since that day when he was introduced to me in the street at Bailleul, by Willie Redmond. As neither of us found anybody or any conveyance to meet us, we had a long and interesting talk about Ireland, and he told me many things about the history of that unhappy country.

Apparently, it is quite untrue to say that Ireland never was a nation, as the scoffers maintain. There were four kingdoms – Ulster, Leinster, Munster and Connaught, and a head King ruling all. And when the English claim that the King of Ireland invited Strongbow over, they misstate the case. It was one of the four minor kings who did that, and he was in rebellion at the time!

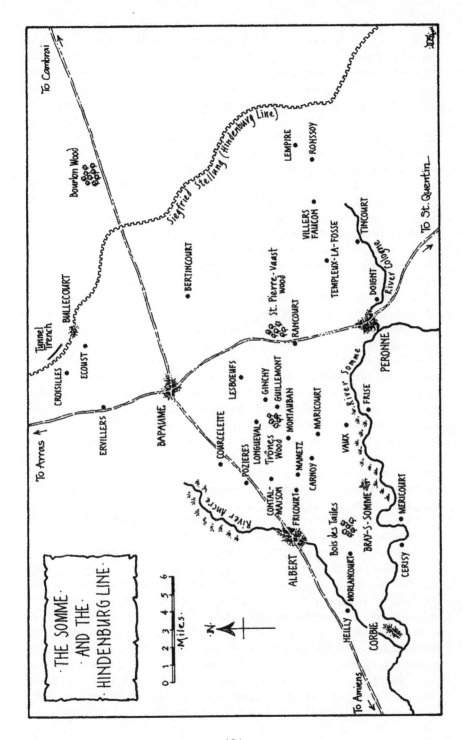

THE SOMME AND THE HINDENBURG LINE.

However, I am straying. I spent the night, in the ruined village of Ervillers. To reach this place I had motored 6 miles, through country which has been reduced to the primeval condition of the African veldt. The newspapers did not exaggerate. The Germans in their retreat – as the Swazis[45] would have done – did their work thoroughly. They left nothing living – not even the apple trees, and nothing standing that had been built by man. For miles and miles in every direction, the eye meets nothing but rank grass and weed. The villages, though many of them have never seen a shell-burst, are levelled with the plain; all but the churches, whose sites are revealed today by cones of rubble. The avenues of trees which lined the roads are sawn off just above the ground and lie prone. Each cross-road is marked by a yawning mine crater, which our people are busily filling in. The desolation, reaching far and wide, would be more ghastly, had one not become accustomed to such sights.[46]

Pereira is Acting Divisional Commander during General Hickie's absence on leave, and has visited me. He gave me a warm welcome back to the Brigade.

This evening I have been round the front line with Crofton, acting second in command. It is, in part, that famous line called after one of the most famous German Generals (Hindenburg) – an impregnable line, prepared at his leisure and without embarrassment, miles behind his then front line, and so strong that he believed no troops in the world could reach it. Yet our troops managed to do so, and to capture it (or part of it) last spring, and its former glory is represented today by the 'Mebus',[47] that is to say the formidable reinforced concrete emplacements, yards thick and massive as the foundations of a great cathedral, and by a tunnelled trench, safe, you would think, from the heaviest shell. Some of these Mebus are shattered by our fire, and their steel skeletons, torn and twisted, stick out of the lacerated earth, like huge decayed teeth; but many are intact, or nearly so, and to have conquered these latter reflects great glory on the troops that did it.

I found the battalion in support for eight days, of which three have expired. We go next into the front line for eight days; then out for sixteen.

My Headquarters are in a comfortable set of dug-outs in a railway cutting, and the trenches are good. I am at present writing in my sleeping dug-out. The roof is of curved corrugated steel sheeting (known as a 'big Elephant' or cupola), covered with sandbags and sods. The floor is boarded and looks like a Pompeian mosaic, since the boards are pieces sawn from what once was the sign board of an inn or shop, salved from the ruins nearby. There is a fireplace with a white enamelled tile floor and a cast-iron grate, burning wood; all, both fireplace and wood, collected from the said ruins. The fender is beaten out of old biscuit tins; the bed – a canvas stretcher – took half an hour to make. And the table on which I write has been made to my order by the pioneer corporal – also from salvage.

The battalion had a bad time in the fighting at Passchendaele while I was away – after July 31, for four or five days, and again on August 16. Many good men are gone, including one of my two orderly room sergeants, who was killed by a shell. The weather and the Fates fought against them, but though the casualties have been heavy, the battalion has come out well.

The following extract is from a letter written by a German officer (regiment unknown), from the VI Corps Intelligence Summary:

> If it were not for the men who have been spared me on this fierce day, and who are lying around me and looking timidly at me, I should shed hot and bitter tears over the terrors that have menaced me during these hours. On the morning of September 18th, the dug-out, containing seventeen men, was shot to pieces over our heads. I am the only one who withstood the maddening bombardment of three days and still survives. You cannot imagine the frightful mental torments I have undergone in those few hours. After crawling out through the bleeding remnants of my comrades and the smoke and debris, and wandering and fleeing in the midst of the raging artillery fire in search of a refuge, I am now awaiting death at any moment.
>
> You do not know what Flanders means. Flanders means endless endurance. Flanders means blood and scraps of human bodies. Flanders means heroic courage and faithfulness, even unto death.

22 September 1917 [Croisilles–Ecoust Railway Cutting]

Yesterday morning, at 4.30, I was woken by a heavy trench-mortar bombardment, and got up to see what it was. All along the German line was the usual firework display;– coloured rockets and golden rain, soaring up and tumbling down.

At intervals, throughout today, the enemy has been pouring an almost continuous stream of heavy shells into the ruins of Croisilles and Ecoust – the villages on either side of us. From my observation post I watched for a time through my glasses a German soldier leisurely walking along a trail behind his lines. He was about 6,000 yards away and out of rifle shot, and as the artillery apparently did not consider him a worthy target, he still remains unconscious of the interest he aroused in me. How often, I wonder, am I an object of similar interest to the people with spy-glasses over there?

24 September 1917 [Croisilles–Ecoust Railway Cutting]

The whole of this morning and part of the afternoon I spent going round the trenches. I have over a mile of frontage to look after, which is quite an exceptionally long stretch, and it takes four or five hours to visit all the posts.

The scene is that of some of the fiercest fighting of this year's spring: you do not have to go far for proof of that. Indeed, the fire-trench itself is more or less a graveyard. In one part, particularly, it is lined with tin discs with numbers on them, indicating where soldiers have been buried in the parapet; and, wherever you dig, you are liable to come upon these poor remains. It is not even necessary to dig, for they outcrop in places.[48]

We are top-dog here, so far at any rate as position goes, and altogether better off than we have been since I first took over the command of this battalion. Our line is a patchwork meandering one:– here, a piece of the famous German 'pièce de résistance', with all its concrete and tunnelling; there, one of the sunken roads, so common in these parts, turned into a defence.

1 October 1917 [Croisilles–Ecoust Railway Cutting]

We do not resent visitors, but I think we are apt to regard them something like trespassers. That is because we get so few. The popularity of the infantry seems to vary with the section of line which it is holding. At Wytschaete, which was a boisterous place, we were left severely alone. Here, our privacy is frequently invaded. Perhaps it is a coincidence, but Red tabs of high degree are a common sight in the trenches here. Even Corps Commanders come to see us. They go into our forward saps, and so peaceful do they find their surroundings, that they pull out maps, and exposing themselves freely, identify the outstanding landmarks.

Then they pass on their way, and, perhaps a quarter of an hour later, the sentry group occupying the sap gets shelled. In self-defence we have put up a notice or two, worded as follows:

'Visitors are requested not to show themselves, as by doing so they may give away our positions to the enemy. We live here. You don't.'

We have visits here, in fact from all kinds of strangers, and they do not always have the civility to report themselves at Battalion Headquarters before going through the trenches. They might, quite logically, be arrested as spies, and they are sometimes. And it serves them right.

The other day I came upon a stranger. I asked him who he was. He said he was an officer of the Siege Artillery.[49] Now, we do not see much of the Siege Artillery in the Front Line. They shoot off the map, from behind, and seem to scorn forward observation. One of their majors called upon me not long ago. I asked him if he would like some targets, explaining that the battalion observers were very alert, and could probably put him on to some good ones.

He said: 'Oh, it doesn't matter, thank you'. That is the Siege Artillery way – and it is not encouraging to the infantry.

So I gave the officer in the trench a few hints on manners. I said: 'We know the Field Artillery well (the 18-pounders). Their officers are always with us. But your people we do not know. Indeed, all that our men know of you is that they occasionally get one of your shells in the small of the back.'

Which was perhaps rude, but perfectly true.

4 October 1917 [Dysart Camp, near Ervillers]

I started off at 8.15 this morning to visit the scenes of our fighting during September, last year, returning in the evening; and it has been a wonderfully interesting though a melancholy day.

The notorious villages – Guillemont and Ginchy – are conspicuous by their absence. I can truthfully say that I have never seen a whole brick in the former place, and the latter – which I had not seen before except from a trench – is much the same. I stumbled through the shell-holes this time in broad daylight, and even so lost my position on the map more than once. I thought of that horrible night of September 7 – so short a time after I had taken over the command of this battalion, or rather the remnant of it, and it no longer surprised me that the guide had lost his way on that occasion.

I rode past Ligny-Thilloy, Flers, Longueval, and the dead stumps alternating with soldiers' graves which represent the ill-starred Delville Wood (Devil's Wood, as the men called it) and High Wood.

Miles of devastation and deserted ruined villages and shell-holes – all now grown over with weed and grass. Not a living creature but the magpies, which flit silently about the waste. The ground is just as it was left, thickly littered with the debris of battle. Rifles, with the bayonets fixed, lie as they were dropped; limbers smashed and half buried by shell-fire; perforated shrapnel helmets – German and British; equipment, boots, ammunition, stretchers, derelict aeroplanes, and tanks; in fact all the accoutrements of war; with here and there a reminder of the pre-war peace days, in the shape of a shredded threshing-machine or the big sugar refinery of Guillemont – the latter riddled and torn, the steel-work tangled and twisted like crumpled paper.

A land of poisoned wells (the Germans saw to this) with the labels nailed up by our sanitary people marking them. A land whose loneliness is so great that it is almost frightening. A land of wooden crosses, which you can count dotted about, each indicating a soldier's grave, and the spot where he fell.

After several miles of this I came upon the first living human beings, parties of the Salvage Corps, working forwards from the old battle line, gathering up all that is worth saving of the relics I have mentioned. These are mostly of coloured men, who have come from all parts of the world. The first party I saw was composed of Burmans from Mandalay, and dressed as they were, with woollen Balaclava helmets pulled down over their heads and shoulders, cringing from the wet and cold, they looked like the ghosts of the dead.

Further back, I came upon the work of the Graves Registration Unit, which, behind the Salvage men, follows the Army forward. Its job is to 'prospect' for the dead, and so skilful have its members become at detecting the position of a buried soldier, that their 'cuttings' seldom draw blank. Indeed, this is not surprising, for, no matter where they look, they are almost certain to find what they are searching for. Then they dig up the decomposed fragments, to see if they can identify them, which they seldom do; after which they re-bury them, marking the spot with the universal wooden cross.[50]

I rode on to Montauban, of which I saw so much when I was with the Entrenching Battalion. The famous figure of the Virgin, which stood by the church, and which survived all the bombardments of last year, though all around Her was destroyed, had been blown down by the wind, and, as the head was missing, I suppose somebody must have taken it for a souvenir. The shattered remains lay upon the ground. She was much gilded and painted, and was made of cheap terracotta, hollow inside.

I then wandered through one of our cemeteries at Guillemont, and saw Raymond Asquith's[51] grave, and those of one or two Coldstreamers I knew. And above another single grave I read the names of between sixty and seventy NCOs and men of the Rifle Brigade.

Finally, outside what used to be the village of Guillemont, I looked for the only landmark that remains – the old French pre-war cemetery. There is a great tombstone there, covering the family vault, of the people who owned the sugar refinery. This presents a most extraordinary sight. It is strong, being of massive stone. Consequently, on account of the protection which it afforded from shell-fire, the Germans had used it as a dug-out; and, when they left it, some of our signallers had evidently taken over the tenancy. It is unoccupied by living men today, though the floor is still strewn with army forms. A stove is fitted in one corner, with a tin chimney to conduct the smoke outside. In one of the bricked recesses of the vault lies a coffin, undisturbed. The other recesses have been used as soldiers' beds, and, as a second coffin occupied a recess which was evidently required as a bedroom, the coffin has been pulled out, and lies on the floor:– and further, shameful to relate, the zinc lining of this coffin has been torn open, exposing a woman's face and body. Amid such sur-roundings, the occupants of this gruesome dug-out appear to have eaten and worked and slept for many months.

From here I was able to locate my old trench by the Ginchy sunken road, and though all is now fallen in and grown over, I succeeded in re-tracing our positions of September 9.

I advanced across No Man's Land and made for my objective of that day.

I explored the site of Ginchy, and came across a little group of Guards' graves, including several of my old battalion. I found Jackson,

Dilbéroglue, Pike Pease, and Scott, lying side by side in the order I have named; little 'Bunny' Pease with his steel hat lying on his grave – a custom which has been largely followed by our troops on the Somme, in imitation of the French habit of hanging the soldier's cap upon the cross over his grave. One away from Pease was Walters'[52] – a machine-gun officer of the Irish Guards – a splendid type of boy, whom I knew well.

My present sniping officer arrived when I was at home. He is very young, and very keen, and very talkative. He spits out whatever comes into his mind. For a few days, while we were in the line, I had to put him in command of a Company, as the Company Commander was away on leave. He did it very well, and displayed, in a marked degree, what is known in military parlance as the 'offensive spirit'.

When I inspected his section of the line I was struck by his audacity, and began in my mind to compare my nerve with his. However, one morning, as he and I were talking together in the trench – whizz – a German shell skimmed close over our heads. It took him unawares. He clutched hold of my arm as one of our children might have done.

8 October 1917 [Dysart Camp, near Ervillers]

It is an interesting bit of line that the Division is holding, and the opportunities are excellent for watching the enemy at his little daily avocations. From one of the front line observation posts, the other day, I saw three Germans in the course of a quarter of an hour, casually sauntering along their trench at a point where it had been blown in by a shell, and unconsciously exposing themselves from their knees upwards. With my glasses I could see them so clearly that I could have counted their buttons.

That was when we first went up. But such scenes are daily becoming rarer, since our snipers have got to work. The battalion snipers are very good just at present, and the sniping from both sides is active. It is very necessary, but what a callous business it is. I have to order others to do it, but I cannot say I like the idea.[53]

The section of front line which I hold is, as I have told you, more or less of a graveyard. Many soldiers lie buried in the parapet, and in some cases their feet project into the trench. The positions are marked, where known. We come across others, unmarked, as we dig. On such occasions the men put up little notices, some of which combine with the tragedy of it all a certain amount of pathetic and unintended humour. As you may imagine, the names of the dead are generally undiscoverable. On one board is written: 'In loving memory of an unknown British soldier'. On another (in this case the man's paybook was found on his body and therefore his name is known) the following words appear in chalk: 'Sleep on, Beloved Brother; take thy Gentle Rest'. In another case somebody has contented himself by just writing piously in chalk on the sole of a projecting foot:

'R.I.P'. Over another grave, the Head of Christ has been carved with a jack-knife on a piece of the chalk through which the trench is dug. It is embellished with hair and a fine halo drawn in purple indelible pencil.[54]

If you saw it all you wouldn't know whether to laugh or cry.

12 October 1917 [Dysart Camp]

We are getting a lot of leave for the men at present, which is splendid:– sixteen a day. They are cleaned up and fitted with good clothes before they leave, so that they do not arrive at Victoria covered with the mud of the trenches. Each man, too, has to have a certificate that he is free from vermin; so I hope they arrive sufficiently pure and spick and span, though I am sure they cannot give half so much satisfaction in the streets of London as they would if they arrived muddy.

13 October 1917 [Dysart Camp]

My darling Joan,

I have been meaning to write to you for a long time. The sun has come out today, but yesterday was awful, and my camp is a sea of mud. Yesterday, I rode through one of the flattened villages near here. The church was represented by a mound of stones and dirt. Beside it, a great crucifix still stands undamaged. One sees that so often in France nowadays.

I have built myself a little hut in which I burn wood. A week ago it was a small ruined stable, but I had the walls patched up and a roof put on, and a fire-place made. I should so much like to show it to you. I am even having a little garden made outside, to grow vegetables in, though I don't suppose I shall be here to eat them. It was a garden before the war and there are still a few Michaelmas daisies and gooseberry bushes to show where the garden was, though bricks from the ruins and bits of timber and even a child's cot lie about in it, and there are several huge shell-holes made, I expect, by our great 15 inch howitzers.

Your loving Daddy.

14 October 1917 (Sunday) [Dysart Camp]

Today is Sunday, and the battalion has been having Sports. Lance-Corporal Pierpoint played clown. I have known him for a year or so, but only as a bombing corporal – and a good one, too. Today he showed himself off in a new capacity – that of contortionist, a spineless man, and a buffoon of a high order, which it seems was one of various callings which he followed before the war.

He boxed today, arriving in the ring with a back somersault. He walked about during the sports on his hands, with his legs twisted under his elbows. He tied himself in knots, placing his head between his legs and one leg round his neck, like Anita[55] used to do when she was a baby. His antics were most ludicrous and most extraordinary.

Amongst other faculties which he possesses is one which is invaluable in the trenches. It is that of being able to judge exactly where a trench-mortar bomb is going to fall. His friends in his platoon collect around him when the German 'rum jars' are flying about, and he advises them what to do to dodge each one as he sees it coming through the air. He signals with his arms whether to move to the right or left along the trench, or to stand still.

He was certainly the feature at the Sports today. 'By the Holy St Patrick, look at that', I heard a man call out, as he watched Pierpoint keeping goal in the football match for the Company championship.

17 October 1917 [Dysart Camp]

Yesterday, I travelled far from here and again visited the scenes of the fighting of last autumn. I explored the ground where we fought on September 9, and was able this time to trace out all the old trenches, both ours and the Germans'. A baby's shattered perambulator lies in a shell-hole just in front of our jumping off trench.[56]

You will remember what a terrific fire we encountered when we attacked at this place. I have ever since been curious to know where that fire came from, and how so powerful a concentration of machine-guns could have completely escaped our artillery. Now I know. A well concealed and winding trench, branching into two, and worked in conjunction with nests of shell-holes adapted as machine-gun positions. That is what we ran into, and it was a hopeless task we undertook that day. Indeed, after we had been relieved by the 4th Grenadiers, it continued to hold up the whole advance for four days. I walked over a dead German still lying in the German trench, and I daresay there were many others, but the ground is so overgrown with weed that such sights are hidden from the eye.

Combles is a weird, uncanny sight. It was a large village – almost a town – but our army has advanced far beyond it, and its ruins are deserted. The only living creatures I saw were a white cat, crouching among the bricks, and a wandering soldier. I went on through Morval, Lesboeufs (where the three Coldstream battalions attacked in line), Gueudecourt, Beaulencourt and Bapaume.

All the villages are so wrecked, and the roads through them so broken up with shell-holes and blocked with fallen trees and ruins, that it is difficult and sometimes impossible to pick one's way along them on horseback.

18 October 1917 [Croisilles–Ecoust Railway Cutting]

We took over the Front Line today.

A successful raid was made on the Tunnel Trench, two days ago, by the 7th Leinsters. They employed a ruse, which was certainly a brain-wave on the part of somebody.

On October 11, a thousand gas bombs were fired from 'projectors' – 500 at 8 pm, and 500 at midnight. Judging from intercepted enemy telephone conversations, these did considerable execution.

In parentheses, I may explain that the projector is a kind of mortar.[57] In appearance, it is a short stumpy steel cylinder, about 9 or 10 inches in diameter and perhaps a couple of feet long. Five hundred or a thousand of these are planted in the ground, with their muzzles pointed upwards. All are directed upon the same chosen spot in the enemy's lines. Each is charged with a gas-container, or bomb. The projectors are fired simultaneously, by electricity, and then the gas-containers soar upwards, making, in their collective flight, a rushing sound, as of a mighty wind. They burst as they reach the ground.

The raid was made on the early morning of October 16. It was preluded by a repetition of the projector bombardment of the 11th, but on this occasion, the containers held no poison gas.

Immediately upon the discharge of the projectors, the raiders dashed into the German trench. Some of them went down into the tunnel: Major Holbrow, a Sapper officer, was among the latter. He took a tape-measure with him, and made measurements. The garrison was found wearing respirators.

The sight of our men raiding in the middle of a gas cloud, without respirators, puzzled the enemy. Indeed, it was quite a time before the prisoners could be persuaded that there was no gas.

When, at last, they realised how they had been had, they became quite indignant.

20 October 1917 [Croisilles–Ecoust Railway Cutting]

The day before yesterday we had a visit from the Mayor of Wexford[58] and a friend of his – a red hot Sinn Feiner, from Dublin. They had come to Belgium to visit Willie Redmond's grave, and had got passes to come on to the Irish Division.

They were to have gone up into the firing line, but a relief was in progress, so they were not taken further than Battalion Headquarters. It was the first time I had ever seen a civilian in or near the trenches, and their black coats created great interest amongst all ranks.

Yesterday, from one of the battalion observation posts, I saw six Germans, in twenty minutes, through a telescope. They were well out of rifle range, but I could plainly watch all their movements, which were somehow interesting. There is an unaccountable fascination in watching your enemy in his leisure moments.

21 October 1917 [Croisilles–Ecoust Railway Cutting]

My young sniping officer tells me he had a shot this morning, but his would-be victim signalled a 'miss', raising and lowering a stick above the parapet. I have known them do this before with a shovel. Our enemy evidently has some humour in spite of what people say.

Life in London must be getting more and more deadly. I fear it is becoming daily, more and more, a struggle for existence. I hope you do not have to stand in the queues to get your sugar and tea, and I pray that you are not starving yourself.

23 October 1917 [Croisilles–Ecoust Railway Cutting]
Yesterday, with the doctor, I visited the 2nd Suffolks on our right. We were sniped at vigorously by machine-gun fire as we crossed the Bullecourt–Ecoust road, on the way home. It is an exposed spot, and must be a source of a good deal of amusement to the enemy.

27 October 1917 [Croisilles–Ecoust Railway Cutting]
Last night I got orders to go back this morning to Dysart Camp, to meet Cardinal Bourne, who is in France on a visit to the Army.

I arrived before the General and the 'super-padres', and seeing a small group of officers, and among them a priest not in uniform, I asked him if he had come over with the Cardinal. He replied that he had, so I asked him if Monseigneur Jackman had come over too. He said: 'I am he'. He asked to be remembered to you. I thanked him for arranging the crucifixes from Rome, and he pulled out a larger one from his pocket and gave it to me.

Afterwards, I had a talk with the Cardinal, who also gave a short address to those of the troops who are resting. Then I returned to the line, lunching with the Leinsters on the way.

I rode, both ways, with Colonel Roche-Kelly,[59] who commands the 6th Royal Irish. It was a muddy ride, and was enlivened by the enemy, who was shelling the valley through which we had to pass. Willie Redmond was in Roche-Kelly's battalion, and I asked him to tell me how he came to go over the top on June 7 at Wytschaete.

He said that the Divisional Commander had kept Redmond back from Guillemont and Ginchy because he thought he was too old (as he certainly was); he said poor Redmond worried about this. To make matters worse, he kept getting anonymous letters from Ireland, accusing him of staying behind because he was afraid. (Can you believe that such beasts exist?) But, in spite of repeated appeals, the GOC would not swerve in his decision. I know that Redmond, during this period, was wont to ask his friends if they thought the men ever felt that he was holding back.

Well, when the attack on Wytschaete came, he implored so insistently, that the General at last gave way, and said he might go – on the understanding that he returned immediately the first objective was reached, and reported to Divisional Headquarters how the battle was progressing.

Roche-Kelly says that when Redmond arrived at his Battalion

Headquarters, and said he had the General's permission, he at first tried to keep him with him; but no, he wanted to go with his Company:– so, thinking that the first Company to go over (as Redmond's happened to be) would have the easiest time, he allowed him to go as a sort of 'liaison' officer.

He was hit in the hand or wrist immediately he crossed the parapet, but continued, and was hit a second time in the leg as he reached the German wire. Neither were serious wounds, but, as the General had said, Redmond was too old for the game, and he died when they got him to the dressing station.

Two nights ago Roche-Kelly's battalion, on my immediate left, caught two German prisoners going the unexpected way. They had escaped from a French prisoner-of-war camp, and though dressed in German uniform, were trying to make their way through our lines, back to their own.

This, I may say, is an almost impossible thing to do. Besides being extremely dangerous, the adventurer runs the imminent risk of being shot or bayoneted, not only by our people, but by his own.

Therefore, I regard these men as sportsmen. One was very sore at being caught. He said he had been fifteen years in the Army and wanted to go on fighting. The other was a lesser kind of man, and did not carry it off with the same bravado.

I have spoken more than once of the excellent opportunities we have here of observing the habits of our enemies. Any day we can watch them. Many do not get the opportunity of displaying themselves more than once or twice, but there is one sentry who has his 'exemption' card, so to speak. He stands by the Mebu known as 'Neptune', and except when he is being relieved, we see no movement. He is an exemplary sentry. Unconsciously, he shows his steel helmet – no more – and that rarely stirs.

He is not allowed to be shot at, because that would spoil the picture.

30 October 1917 [Croisilles–Ecoust Railway Cutting]

The variations and vagaries of war are very peculiar. My present acting second in command is TA Dillon, aged twenty-two. By the fortune of war he is acting second in command; while I have some forty other officers, including lieutenants and 2nd Lieutenants – some of them almost brilliant – aged thirty, more or less.

The battalion was never in better form than it is at present. In addition to a good lot of officers, I have many excellent NCOs – mostly old Regulars, who have been joining in large numbers during the last few months.

Acting upon orders, we fired over some leaflets today, to our enemies across the way, telling them in the choicest German about the fate of their Zeppelins which attempted to raid London a few days ago. I rather fancy a note was added, in English, to the effect that Otto Weiss – a German

NCO with an iron cross, whom we got on our wire three nights ago – has received a Christian burial. I am now wondering if this latter will be regarded as 'fraternising' with the enemy?

4 November 1917 (Sunday) [Dysart Camp, near Ervillers]

We were relieved the night before last, after holding the front line for sixteen days. Yesterday and today (Sunday) have been devoted to hair-cutting, baths, and overhauling of clothing and equipment.

Father Wrafter,[60] who has been out with the Division since it first came to France, came up with the relieving battalion, and while we were waiting for the completion of the relief – a tedious process which always takes an hour or two, he talked and told stories.

We discussed the origin of various expressions much in vogue here. Nobody seems to know where the word 'Boche' comes from. 'Alliman', which was largely used by the men in 1915, and is the sole inscription (in pencil) on many a wooden cross, is a corruption of the French word, but Father Wrafter says that many of the men used it, thinking it meant 'Ally-man' – or a man who belonged to the Allies!

'Jerry' (or Gerry), which is the word nearly all our men use when referring to the people opposite (the word 'Fritz' is hardly ever used now), is, so Father Wrafter says, contracted from 'German'.[61]

It was All Saints' Day, and a priest was saying Mass in a dug-out when the shelling started. After the fourth shell, Mass then being over, I dispersed the crowd as a precautionary measure. Then came the real 'hate' – the 8.2 inch shells, which make a huge and hideous hole in the ground.

To switch off to the front line. How brave – before the war – we should have thought a man who sat looking through a periscope, with no protection over his head beyond the 'tin-hat', immobile, while high explosive was being dropped around him. That is what our sentries do. The last morning the battalion was up, while I was doing my rounds, I was standing with one of the Company Commanders beside a sentry, trying to make out what some object was in No Man's Land – a heap of tangled wire or something of that kind;– when a faint 'swish' sounded above, and with a sudden bang, there exploded a few yards away a 'granatenwerfer', or aerial dart, or pine-apple, or whatever you like to call it;– one of those triangular fish-tailed things, with a body like a prickly pear.

Our interest in the heap of wire quite suddenly vanishes. We wait for 'the next', which we know will follow shortly. Strictly, it is my duty to move away. It is the sentry's duty to continue looking through the periscope. But I cannot leave him like that. Therefore I hang about until the second bomb crashes. Then I say a word or two to the sentry and pass along on my rounds. I give you that by way of a glimpse into the life of the trenches.

Last night I went to the Divisional cinema, which is in a restored barn among the ruins of Ervillers. Charlie Chaplin was there, figuratively, and at his best. I confess I am getting to appreciate him; and if you could see how the soldiers love him you would like him too. When his image appears upon the screen, they welcome it with such shouts of approval that it might be the living Charlie. The men all flock to these shows, and hundreds are turned away nightly.[62]

6 November 1917 [Dysart Camp, near Ervillers]

I got your letter today, describing the air-raid, which interested me enormously and filled me with pride to think of you all joking at the bottom of the kitchen stairs.[63]

I cannot tell you how much I admire the way in which you have handled this problem, forcing the children to look upon air-raids as a game. It is splendid. The others will inevitably take their cue from you. Had you been a man you would have made an ideal soldier. Above all, I admire the way in which you have never woken the children till, in your opinion, the danger has become imminent. You are becoming a veteran now, and I have every faith in your leadership, and that it will carry you and the household through.

I am glad to think you are all praying for us. We have a tame lot opposite, but one never knows how they may develop.

10 November 1917 [Dysart Camp, Ervillers]

The Italians, like the Russians, are going to let us down. I have always felt that this war would end in a duel between ourselves and the Germans, and it looks more and more like it every day. We shall certainly win.

The weather continues to be horrible, and we have been training and shivering all the morning. As we marched back to camp we passed a woman, walking with a French soldier. She was the first woman I had seen since September 19 (nearly two months ago), and in the case of the majority of the battalion, the gap has been considerably longer; so you may imagine what interest she aroused. She had no doubt come to have a look at her ruined home, or perhaps to dig up treasures which she had buried before she left it.

Spit and polish is the order of the day, and I am all for it – in reason. But when the men have just come out, after sixteen days in the line, where they have been squeezed up in muddy dug-outs in the daytime, and stand to all night, I think it is a bit thick when high-placed officers, who do not share their dangers and discomforts, and scarcely ever go into the firing line, kick up Hell's delight because the bayonet scabbards are not polished! Yet such is the kind of thing we have to put up with from our friends behind the front.[64]

Personally, I prefer the attentions of our enemies. These are at least logical, and so think all on the front line. Although, during the sixteen days and nights the battalion has been up, the breastworks have been collapsed by the rains to say nothing of German shells and trench-mortars; though our patrols have nightly explored No Man's Land and the German wire, not a word is said about that. Not a remark. Not a comment. It is <u>polished</u> bayonet scabbards that they want. The real business we are here for is not even referred to. Can you believe it?

25 November 1917 [Croisilles–Ecoust Railway Cutting]

I have not written to you much lately, and now that you have read the papers you will know why.

Although we have not been in the centre of the picture (the main objective having been Cambrai), and the business upon which we have been engaged has been a side-show, it has been none the less absorbing for the individuals concerned.[65]

We have fought and won a success which was a very heroic affair. Many officers and men of this battalion distinguished themselves greatly, having in fact done as good a thing as I have seen up to the present. Nevertheless, other things have happened which I will tell you about some other day, and, though they are washed out now, the pleasure of the success is washed out too, to a large extent, by the loss of my Brigadier (General George Pereira), who has left us, and who, after a few misunderstandings at the beginning of our acquaintanceship, had become a very dear friend to me, as he had to every officer and man of the Brigade. He is about fifty-three, but has got to look like an old man. He is, I think, the most loyal and faithful and brave and unselfish man I have ever met, and I feel a great personal loss in his departure.[66]

To tell you the story. I have of course known for long of these impending operations, but I think you will agree that even you could not have guessed this from my letters. I have been obliged to keep my own counsel, without confiding even in my Adjutant or the Company Commanders.

We came up to the front line on the 18th, having for a few days previously practised the attack over a prepared replica of the German trenches which were to be our objective. This naturally suggested to all ranks what was before them, and, the whole battalion flocked to Confession the last evening, the 17th, in the patched-up barn at Ervillers which serves as a church when we are resting.

No one who has not seen it can ever realise the intense devotion of these Irish soldiers who have come to fight in France. What they are like in their own homes in peacetime I do not know, but here in the war, it is very impressive to see them. For hours that evening the priests were engaged, the men crowding up silently, passing one by one to the canvas Confessionals in the far corners of the old ruin, which was dimly lighted by a candle or two for the occasion.

The following morning (Sunday) all went to non-fasting Communion, since it was late in the day, this being allowed by the Church before going into action. They are getting used to non-fasting Communion now, though many of them in the earlier days could not get over the idea that they were committing a sin by doing so.[67]

During the night a German came over and surrendered himself. He said that three of his comrades had started with him, but our Lewis gunners had got on to them, and they did not reach their destination. Of course, the Lewis gunners could not know, in the dark, what these people were coming for.

Unfortunately, the one man who did arrive reached our line just alongside the point of contact with the battalion on our left. He crept over the parapet at a spot where there happens to be what is known in military language as a latrine (pronounced by the men latter-reen). One of my men was in occupation at the time, and seeing a figure appear on the skyline, said, ' 'Ere, 'ands up and wait till I've finished'. The German, not understanding, and frightened, dropped hastily behind the parapet, and crept along to the first post of the next battalion, a few yards away.

It was thus that the Connaught Rangers failed to obtain the credit of this catch, from which the Intelligence Department claims to have extracted some very useful information.

The German trench opposed to us was the famous Hindenburg line. It is a very elaborate work. The surface trench is wide and deep, and at intervals of about 25 yards, stairways descend from the parapet side to a heavily-timbered tunnel. Let into the wall of the tunnel at the foot of each stairway were heavy charges of high explosive, connected by wires with an electric battery one or two kilometres behind the German line, and intended to blow up the tunnel if it should ever fall into our hands. On the surface, at intervals along the trench, are 'Mebus' ('Pillboxes', as the newspapers call them) – those massive emplacements or shelters of concrete which I have already described, reinforced with steel, the interiors of which are practically impervious to shell-fire, though the exteriors have been in almost every case reduced to a mangled skeleton of twisted steel.[68]

This roughly describes the position we were to attack, on a frontage of 350 yards, at 6.20 o'clock on the morning of November 20. My orders were to assault with two Companies, which were to advance on the extreme right of the Division, and as the Brigade on my right was to take no part in the action, it meant that I was to attack with my right flank 'in the air'.

It was very edifying to watch the officers and men preparing for the attack – all optimistic, full of confidence, and cheery:– a little more silent than usual perhaps, during dinner the night before, though Brett,[69] commanding the right assaulting Company, celebrated the occasion by getting up a lot of oysters of which he very generously sent me a liberal share.

At about 2 am, the assaulting Companies began to get into position, and by an hour before Zero, each man was in his appointed place, ready for battle. My Battle Headquarters were in a mined dug-out which had been allotted to me in one of the main communication trenches known as Queen's Lane, some 250 yards behind the firing-line.

My orders to the right Company, which was formed up in Martin Road – a sunken road in front of the fire-trench, and which had only some 75 yards to go to the nearest objective – had been to start at two minutes after Zero, so as to give our guns time to lift. The danger on these occasions, if they start too soon, is that the men in the impetuous rush forward may run into our own barrage – a thing, unfortunately, that often happens.

The left Company, which had further to go, had instructions to start a minute earlier. The concentrated artillery was to play upon the German trench for four minutes, commencing at Zero, and then to lift, and I calculated that by the time-table I had given them, the assaulting Companies would reach the objective as soon as it was safe to do so.

As a precautionary measure, I had had the direction of the objective marked out with tape the night before, having learned, from previous experience, the difficulty of keeping direction in the dark.

Absolutely to the tick, I watched the men scaling the ladders and scrambling over the parapet. The signallers under their Sergeant (Rogers), struggling with the coils of telephone wire that was to keep me in touch with the assaulting troops, once they had established themselves in the German trench. Those are sights that are very inspiring, and which engrave themselves upon the memory.

I had not time to get back to my proper Headquarters, so remained at the head of the communication trench, where there was an advanced signal station with a telephone. By this time the usual inferno had worked up to its full fury. The semi-darkness of the early morning was illuminated by the bursts of the shells, trench-mortar bombs, smoke bombs, and the flares and excited SOS rockets of the enemy. The air vibrated with the hurricane of our machine-gun barrage whistling from behind, and that of the enemy from the front.

I decided to control the attack from the forward telephone, but no sooner had I made up my mind to do so, than the wounded began to stream back. Prisoners also began to arrive, still holding up their hands and muttering 'Kamerade': so that soon the dug-out was so packed with bleeding men that it was impossible to function, and I decided to go to my proper Headquarters, where at least I should find room to breathe.

At this moment poor Brett came stumbling back, crimson with blood, having been shot through the face, bringing further confirmation of the news which I had already had from him by runner, that the enemy was furiously counter-attacking our exposed right flank. I left him with Barron, the Intelligence Officer, and made for Queen's Lane. Then the messages began to arrive, thick and fast.

I will now stop for the present, and finish in another letter.

27 November 1917 [Dysart Camp, near Ervillers]

We were relieved in the line last night, and have come back to Dysart Camp. I will continue where I left off, at the moment when I had reached my Battle Headquarters. I was inundated with messages.

Our smoke barrage had deceived the Germans and led them to believe, as had been intended, that gas was being sent over, so that when our men reached their objective they were found wearing gas masks. They appeared to be in a very dazed condition. There were a few sentries in the saps, and a number of men grouped in the tunnel entrances, who were shot or bayoneted.

Immediately the trench had been occupied, the two Mebus, known as 'Jove' and 'Mars', were approached from behind, according to plan, both surrendering after slight resistance. Simultaneously, a sentry was posted at each tunnel entrance, and parties provided with wirecutters to cut the electric wires leading to the mines at the foot of each stairway were sent into the tunnel to clear it of the enemy. This operation was so skilfully and so quickly carried out that not a single mine exploded.

The left Company Commander (Tuite)[70] established his Headquarters in the Mebu 'Mars', in which, in the meantime, the signallers were installing a telephone. The right Company Commander began to make similar arrangements in 'Jove', he having himself led the party which stormed that Mebu and shot at least one of the garrison with his revolver. The tunnel was cleared, and up to 7.30 am, 121 prisoners had been counted and sent to the rear. Further captures subsequently increased this number to 152.

At about 7.10 am, the enemy began to counter-attack our right flank, which he was quick to spot was in the air. These counter-attacks were repeated over and over again, the fighting becoming very furious, and continuing almost hand to hand for some hours. You will appreciate its severity when I tell you that the Commander and twenty-six out of twenty-eight other ranks of the right flank platoon became casualties. The officers and men fought with the most heroic determination in spite of a failing supply of bombs, supplementing the limited supply which they had carried over with them, with German bombs which they picked up in the trench.

At a critical moment, one of the men, Private K White, rushed close up to a traverse from behind which the enemy was bombing, and actually catching some of their bombs in the air, threw them back before they had exploded.

After the first hour the right Company Commander, Brett, was wounded and with their bomb supplies exhausted, the survivors began slowly to fall back upon the Mebu 'Mars'. Continuing to hold the enemy in check by Lewis gun and rifle fire, and yielding their ground inch by inch, leaving a trail of dead behind them, they withdrew.

At 9.45 am, Captain Tuite, then commanding both front Companies, was reported severely wounded; but in spite of this most serious loss, the remainder stuck it and held their own at 'Mars'. Thirty-five lay dead, and 105 had been wounded.

A little after one o'clock I was able to leave the telephone, and crossed No Man's Land to the captured trench. I took one of my orderlies, Private Moran, with me. We made a safe crossing and found that a firm defensive flank had been established at 'Mars'.[71] The enemy was apparently exhausted for the moment, but was still shelling furiously.

It was the end, for the time being, of a fine piece of work. The advance to the attack across No Man's Land had been carried out precisely as rehearsed and according to programme, and the subsequent defence of the exposed right flank had been beyond praise.

As it is late, I will continue in another letter.

28 November 1917 [Dysart Camp, near Ervillers]

In yesterday's letter, I had just reached the captured Tunnel Trench, after a safe crossing of No Man's Land, with my orderly, Private Moran. I talked to the men as I passed along the line, and found them in good spirits, and confident in the knowledge of the splendid part they had played that morning.

The familiar scene of desolation confronted me. Each time I see this kind of thing I think it is worse than the last time, and on this occasion, so churned up was the surface, that there was little left to indicate where the trench had been. It was just a sea of overlapping craters of huge dimensions – a dismal chaos of fresh-turned earth. Some of the German dead still wore gas masks.

On my return journey I explored the tunnel. Half-way down a stairway I came upon three wounded Connaught Rangers. These I promised to send for, and then went down into the tunnel. It was littered with German clothing and equipment. Here and there lay a dead man, and a living German sat, smoking a cigarette, while he nursed a dying comrade.

I followed the tunnel for some distance. The same description applies. At the foot of one of the stairways lay a dead officer. At the first alarm, they told me, he had challenged the entry of the storming party, and the young Connaught Ranger officer in charge had thrown down a bomb which had wounded him mortally. Another officer lay dying, his servant attending him. The officer died next morning, when the servant – a delicate-looking, square-headed youth in spectacles – was sent back, a prisoner.

I left the tunnel, and climbed again to the surface. The enemy shell-fire had increased. I chanced it and crossed what had been No Man's Land earlier in the day, and as I dropped into the old front line, I breathed freely once more.

It is late and I will finish tomorrow.

29 November 1917 [Dysart Camp, near Ervillers]

My last letter ends the story of November 20. Among the loot, we collected some fine suits of steel body-armour,[72] a specimen of which I have sent you; numerous letters (of no value); a machine-gun or two; 'granatenwerfers' (aerial dart-throwers); a big trench-mortar, with a pile of shells beside it; also photographs taken from the ground and from the air: and finally, maps.

The maps show not only all the enemy's private arrangements behind his line, but our own as well, our trenches in many instances being actually described by the names under which we know them! This, I must say, interests me very much. It means either that they have secured some of our secret trench maps, or else have extracted the information from prisoners. It is well known that they have all sorts of dodges. The most stoic and loyal of prisoners may be bamboozled into giving away information. For example, the enemy will dress up an English-speaking German as an English soldier and put him among the prisoners – who think he is one of themselves – to pick up snatches of conversation. As before, Wytschaete my own Headquarters were well marked out in their true position.

The Germans were still occupying the tunnel underneath our right flank, so, after a consultation with Norman, who was now commanding the front line, arrangements were made to storm and recapture the Mebu 'Jove' at one o'clock that day, and to block the tunnel.

This, however, was vetoed by the Higher Command, who presumably thought that the battalion had had enough.

On the 22nd, smoke was issuing from the tunnel entrance, 40 yards from my right flank, indicating that the enemy was still beneath us. So a party, under Norman, went and dropped a charge of high-explosive down the stairway, which must at least have disconcerted the occupants of the tunnel.

The same evening, after dark, we were relieved and went into support in Railway Reserve. The 7th Leinsters, under Colonel Buckley,[73] were put in to retake 'Jove', which they did very thoroughly.

I visited the place an hour or two afterwards. Many of my own dead lay around the Mebu and on the parapet of the trench near by, their positions proving how devotedly they had fought. One of them was locked in grips with a dead German. Among them were many enemy dead, both those that my men had killed on the 20th, and sometimes lying on the top of them, were the bayoneted corpses of the second fight.

We recovered all our dead and buried them in a little 'war' cemetery behind the embankment near what used to be Croisilles Railway Station, and not a single living man remained in the hands of the enemy.

*   *   *

30 November 1917 [Dysart Camp, near Ervillers]

I have done my best to describe this battalion's part in the capture of the famous Hindenburg Tunnel trench. I have told you the things which I have thought would interest you. But, of course, there are many incidents in a battle of this kind which are impossible to set down, and it would bore you if I attempted it.

I am sending home a German bayonet and scabbard; also a sort of backhanded and rather pathetic souvenir – a Connaught Ranger's shoulder-strap. The Mebu 'Jove', which we captured on the 20th, passed back temporarily to the enemy the same day. During the time it remained in their hands they cut the identifications from our dead.

When the Mebu came back to us on the night of the 23rd, this shoulder-strap was recovered from a dead German.

I think the enemy must be short of shoe-leather. As I passed along the recaptured piece of trench on the 25th, I noticed the body of a young officer of the Royal Irish Regiment, who had been killed while on a wiring party. The enemy had stripped him of his boots.

8 December 1917 [Tincourt]

Further details of the fight of November 20 continue to appear. I enclose a letter written by Lance-Corporal Parle to his platoon commander. He was a Lewis gunner and a stout fellow, as you will see from the letter.

They got real fighting mad that day, and Roche-Kelly told me that several days after we had been relieved, he found the body of one of my men lying far inside the enemy lines, with six dead Germans around it.

FRANCE, Saturday, Nov. 24/11/17.

' DEAR MR. RUSSELL,

I hope you got out of the Battle Safe. But my object in writing this letter is to let you know where to get the Lewis gun, as I know you will be uneasy about it. this is the story. I only had 4 men in the Section going in to battle on Tuesday morning so first Whelan got Shell Shock, then when Coy asked for reinforcements I done my leven best to get what of the Section that was left over nomans land But McFaddin got killed, Cloyne got wounded and Trogers got burried. So there was no one left only myself. I had Still about 100 yards to go to where A Coy was. I tryed to take 4 magazings with the gun as I knew the gun was no good without them But a Shell hit near where I was and I got one bit in my back and one in the left leg, so that done it. So I took the gun back with me. I could not see any of the Connaughts to give it to. I left it with the Leinsters. I don't know the number of the gun as L/C Lynch had my gun so I must have had Lynch's.

If there is any more which you wish to know about the gun it will give me the greatest Joy to tell you my address is 3835 L/C Parle, 6 Conn. Rangers, No. 2 General Hospital, Qnag. Section B.E.F. France.

I expect to be with the Connaughts in a few weeks as my wounds are not very bad.

I remain your humbel servent,
V. PARLE.'

9 December 1917 [Tincourt]

I am getting an old soldier now, and I never count on anything for more than a few hours ahead – leastways when it is something nice. How severe will be the 'Sunday sickness' when, after the war, we have to settle down to the monotony of knowing to a certainty where we are going to be, so far ahead as even the following week! I shall be restless, I know, – perhaps even when I come on leave, and you must make full allowance for any sort of mood I may develop. The tedium of home life after this is bound to produce reaction, just as the old pre-war Sundays used to do after a hard week in the City. Don't misunderstand my use of the word 'tedium'. God knows how we all long for it sometimes!

Yesterday, the four Battalion Commanders of the Brigade rode out with the new Brigadier (Gregorie),[74] to reconnoitre the back areas of the line. It was a nasty day. We visited the Divisional General, who has been ill, but is nearly well again.

P.S. In the old churchyard, close by the hut from which I write, two German soldiers, killed in the Franco-Prussian War, lie buried. Over them their compatriots have, during their recent occupation of this village, put up an expensive granite tombstone – 'to our comrades of 1870–1'.

In the German graveyards which I have seen lately, many of the crosses are of elaborate stonework. But there do not seem to be the thousands of graves which our cemeteries represent with their wooden crosses. Can it be that we are not doing them as much damage as we think, or that they have other cemeteries, on a larger scale, further back?[75]

10 December 1917 [Tincourt]

The Divisional General called this morning. He was full of praise and told me that when we left Ervillers on Sunday, December 2, we were destined for Bourlon Wood, but were switched off, to come to this area.

Thus, though all ranks were nerved up and ready for the worst that might happen – we were spared what was at that time probably the most damnable spot on God's earth; a veritable hell; so drenched with gas that the troops holding it had practically to live in their box respirators;– a salient so sharp and so shelled that it was untenable.

Indeed, it has since been evacuated, as you have no doubt learnt from the newspapers.

12 December 1917 [Ronssoy]

We came up into support yesterday. We are in one of a group of large villages which, judging from the ruins, and from the foundations, gates and gardens (which in many cases are all that is left), must before the war have been prosperous sugar manufacturing centres. There are plenty of modern mansions of a rather pretentious kind.

I sleep in a mined dug-out, 40 feet below the surface, which is comfortable and safe, but, strange to say, cold. When I emerge into the open to visit my platoons – a job that takes several hours since they are very scattered – I have to dodge the shells, and I got well sprinkled yesterday, almost immediately after my arrival, by one which crashed into a garden wall less than the width of the road from where I was walking.

Across the way, some of my officers and men are living in the cellar of the ancient Château – a ruin surrounded by a moat, which before the war must have been quite an imposing building. It is pitiful to see it now: no form or semblance of its former glory, but the great double stone staircase, leading to where once the front door stood, has so far escaped complete obliteration.

The cellar with its stone walls and arched roofs suggests Guy Fawkes and the dungeons of the Tower of London, and it makes a fair dugout, though owing to the shell shattered condition of the building above it, it is necessary to crawl on hands and knees to get into it.

When I visited it yesterday, I found that a German shell had just killed a battery Sergeant-Major near the doorway.

15 December 1917 [Ronssoy]

The Brigadier has just rung up to say that the Major-General will not allow two CO's away at the same time, and as Roche-Kelly was the first for leave, he has been allowed to go. This is as it should be, but it is rather a blow. Still, if I am not home for Christmas, I shall hope to be there a few days later, but I feel I cannot ask the children to postpone their Christmas tree.

The line we are holding is different to any I have seen before. A ridge obscures the approach, and the only indication that you are nearing the front is a barricade of wire, which has been thrown across the road to prevent accidents.

There is a story that, before this barrier was erected, the doctor of one of the battalions which preceded us, having returned with a mess-cart full of provisions, failed to recognise his bearings, and entered the enemy's domain.

The enemy kept everything but the mess-cart and the driver, whom they sent back with a note to the English Colonel. 'Thank you very much,' the note said, 'for all the good things you have sent us. They will be most useful.'

Then the note added, 'So will the doctor, when he gets sober.'

16 December 1917 [Ronssoy]

I was wandering about the ruins of this village this morning, looking for cellars into which to put my men in case of bombardment, when we passed the old peace-time cemetery. It is a shocking sight. Practically every grave has been opened by the enemy; why, I cannot guess. Can it have been to look for supposed hidden treasure, or just wanton insult and desecration?

In one case the great stone slab covering a deep vault has been dropped on to three coffins which lie on the floor below, smashing them, and overturning two, which lie upon their sides, so that the crumbling contents are dribbling out. Into another vault a silvered crucifix has been thrown and lies broken at the bottom. What can the enemy think is the good of all this? What result can he expect from it but the creation in the minds of the French of a furious desire for vengeance?

A new second in command has come to me today – Major R M. Raynsford,[76] of the Leinster Regiment.

P.S. One of my Company Commanders has just come in to say that he has had a direct hit on one of his platoons – a casual shell.

18 December 1917 [Tombois Farm to Island Traverse, Lempire]

We are in the front line again, having come up last night, and I think we are safer by the change.

We woke up yesterday to find snow upon the ground. This silenced the guns, on both sides, for a bit, and thus has its advantages. You see, the sweep of the discharge, when snow is on the ground, gives away the position of batteries to the aerial photographers. So the gunners restrain themselves until they have got their white sheets spread out. Last winter our people had such perfect photographs of the German positions that it was a case of 'embarras de richesses'. The counter-batteries had so many targets to choose from that they scarcely knew which to pick out first.

When I wrote last – two nights ago – we had just had what had been described to me as a direct hit on one of the platoons in their billet. As a matter of fact, the shell had fallen in the road, just outside the door. It was an unlucky one, and nine times out of ten would have done no damage. It killed three of my men and wounded five; and it killed and wounded some artillery men and horses who happened to be passing along the road, as well. The snow outside is red with their blood today. It was a small shell, too.

Two casual shells, a few nights ago, fell simultaneously, and killed twenty-two and wounded thirty-two men of the South Irish Horse at Ste Emilie – a short way down the road. But that is not likely to happen again. The fact is we have only just come to these parts, and it takes time to dig in. Each day we improve our position.

144

The Major-General told me, the other day, that the casualties of the Division, up to the time we left the Bullecourt region at the beginning of this month, had totalled 19,580.

19 December 1917 [Tombois Farm to Island Traverse, Lempire]
The Brigadier has just rung up and said they have granted my leave for the 23rd; so I shall sail on the 24th and should be with you that evening.

RCF goes on leave for two weeks on 23 December.

NOTES

1. Monsignor Arthur Ryan, close friend of Major Willie Redmond, for whom he published a commemorative book shortly after his (Redmond's) death, in 1917; Ryan became a familiar figure on the Western Front as his visits, and those of other Catholic chaplains, increased. As the war progressed, the ratio of Catholic chaplains to soldiers rose sharply; see Terence Denman, 'The Catholic Irish soldier in the First World War', *Irish Historical Studies*, Vol. XXIVII, No. 108, 1991.

2. This incident involved an FE 2d of No. 20 Squadron, which was set on fire at 9,000 feet over nearby Ploegsteert Wood. The pilot, Sergeant Thomas Mottershead, was engulfed in flames as the plane went down, while his observer, Lieutenant WE Gower, attempted to dowse him with a fire extinguisher. Mottershead's bravery in attempting to land his plane undoubtedly saved the life of his observer. He was posthumously awarded the VC; HA Jones, *The War in the Air, Vol. III*, OUP, 1931.

3. T/Major Peter Kerr-Smiley (1879–1943); Unionist MP for N. Antrim, 1910–22; commissioned 21/Lancers; served Boer War, 1901; T/Major, 14/Royal Irish Rifles.

4. Redmond's charm won many friends, across all political divides. Lady Parsons, wife of the founder of the 16th (Irish) Division, was a great friend and influential supporter.

5. Lieutenant-General Sir Alex Hamilton Gordon; born 1859; Afghan campaign, 880; Boer War 1899–1901; commanded Aldershot 1914–16; commanded IX Corps 1916–18.

6. Major-General, later Sir Oliver, Nugent (1860–1926); educ. Harrow; Hazara Expedition, 1891; MID, 1891 & 1896; DSO 1896; Boer War 1899–1900, MID; promoted Lieutenant-Colonel, 1906, KRRC; ADC to the King, 1909–15; GOC 41st Brigade, 1915; Major-General, GOC 36th Ulster Division, 1915–18; strong Protestant credentials, having raised the Cavan UVF in 1914; the historian Cyril Falls reported that he had a violent temper, while Brigadier-General Frank Crozier, who served under Nugent, found him 'a tough man but a fine soldier'; for Nugent's political and military role, see Nick Perry, 'Politics and Command: General Nugent, the Ulster Division and relations with Ulster Unionism 1915–17', in Brian Bond et al, *Look to Your Front*, Spellmount, 1999.

7. They would be afforded the same ritual of having their rosary placed around their neck before burial.

8. The family house, 1 Gordon Place, Kensington, London.

9. Captain IH Garvey; died of wounds, 20 February 1917.

10. The Stokes mortar came in a variety of firing tube diameters – 3 inch (in

service from August 1915), 4 inch (late 1915) and 6 inch (early 1917). The mortar could project a bomb nearly 400 yards; it was controlled at brigade level, hence Pereira's veto.

11. Lieutenant-Colonel MJ Sweetman (1864–1922), of Co. Wexford; married to RCF's sister; East Yorks. Regt.; close friend of Stephen Gwynn.

12. There are no details of this extraordinary episode in the battalion War Diary (PRO WO95/1970). The month of February 1917 has been removed or lost. Similarly, there is no record in the War Diary of the 47th Brigade (PRO WO95/1969).

13. The officer was 2nd Lieutenant PLN Gordon-Ralph; captured 19 February, 1917; repatriated, 7 December 1918.

14. In fact Captain Fitzgerald survived.

15. Lieutenant-Colonel RH Monk-Mason; born 1871; 2nd Lieutenant, Royal Munster Fusiliers, 1892; Lieutenant-Colonel 1/RMF, 1915; wounded Gallipoli, 1915; DSO, 1917.

16. Plumer's popularity was not a recent phenomenom. He had gone out to Africa in 1899 as an unknown officer, and returned a household name. He destroyed his papers after the Great War, to protect his reputation; see Geoffrey Powell, *Plumer – The Soldiers' General*, Leo Cooper, 1990.

17. Lieutenant-Colonel HFN Jourdain (1872–1968); commissioned 1/Connaughts 1893; T/Lieutenant-Colonel 1914; commanded 5/Connaughts, Dardanelles 1915; 29th Inf. Brigade, August–September 1915; 6/Connaughts 1916–17; transfered 16/RWF, July 1917; Anglo-Irish Protestant who was a regular and felt himself better placed to command the battalion. He tried to alienate Pereira and Hickie as well as battalion officers, from RCF, without success. His private diaries reveal his bitterness towards RCF, which often resulted in violent rows at battalion headquarters. His large entry in *Who's Who* (always compiled by entrant) illustrates the problem. RCF makes little reference to him; see Jourdain Diaries, especially 27 March, 21 April 1917, Jourdain Papers, 5603/12, NAM, London. Jourdain later wrote the regimental history of the Connaughts and edited their magazine, *The Ranger*.

18. Three days later America committed her first act of war by sending six torpedo boat destroyers to European waters.

19. Under SS143, *Instructions for the Training of Platoons for Offensive Action* (February 1917), the platoon had evolved into an independent tactical unit; see Paddy Griffith, *Battle Tactics of the Western Front – The British Army's Art of Attack, 1916–18*, YUP 1994, pp. 76–9.

20. HE Cardinal Francis Bourne (1861–1935); educ. St Edmunds, Ware; Bishop of Southwark, 1897; Catholic Archbishop of Westminster, 1903–35.

21. In 1987, on the 70th anniversary of the distribution of the crucifixes, a Memorial Mass was said at Locre Church in memory of the officers and men of the 6/Connaught Rangers. The celebration was attended by RCF's surviving daughters and their families, and the Burgomaster and Aldermen of Ypres.

22. The Catholic Church, and especially their priests, were often considered to be more in touch than the Anglican clergy with the front-line soldier. One explanation is that most Catholic priests (unlike their Anglican counterparts), were working-class, like most of their congregation. Ultimately, Catholicism was more professional in its pastoral work in crisis situations, and 'although the Church of England had many rituals, they had no authorised form of sacramental confession and absolution', see Alan Wilkinson, *The Church of*

England & the First World War, SPCK, 1978, pp. 132–4; Jane Leonard, 'The Catholic chaplaincy', in David Fitzpatrick (ed.), *Ireland and the First World War*, Mullingar, 1988.

23. Captain JL Esmonde (1893–1958); son of Dr T/Captain John Esmonde, RAMC, who died at divisional camp, 1915; Nationalist MP for North Tipperary, 1915–18; one of the youngest of the Irish Party MPs to join the British Army; initially appointed to 16th (Irish) Division Officer Cadet company; commissioned Tyneside Irish; served 10th Royal Dublin Fusiliers.

24. In fact, support for Home Rule was rapidly evaporating, and by the following year, most Irish Nationalists had switched their support from an Irish government within the Empire, to one outside the Empire, as espoused by Sinn Fein. This was Ireland's main legacy from the Great War; see Thomas Hennessey, *Dividing Ireland – World War I and Partition*, Routledge, 1998, p. 236.

25. For an analysis of discipline and punishment in the 16th (Irish) Division, see Lynn Speer Lemisko, 'Morale in the 16th (Irish) Division, 1916–18', *Irish Sword*, Vol. XX, No. 81, 1997.

26. Field Punishment No. 2 consisted of pay forfeit, extra fatigues and pack drills, for a period of twenty-eight days. The man could not smoke and was confined to a diet of biscuits and water. FP No. 1 usually involved the humiliation and discomfort of being chained to a wagon wheel for two hours a day. Beyond this lay the prospect of a Court-Martial.

27. The ballad of the Irish Chieftain who became King of all Ireland in 1002.

28. IX Corps were allocated tank support from 2nd Brigade, Heavy Branch Machine Gun Corps, comprising A and B Battalions. Twenty-eight new Mark IV tanks were used in the centre attack, with old Mark Is being utilised as supply tenders. Messines saw the baptism in action of the new Mark IV, whose improved frontal armour provided protection against German 'K' armour-piercing rounds. The Heavy Branch was officially renamed The Tank Corps on 27 July 1917.

29. An 'Operations Order – Appendix II' is attached to the battalion War Diary, detailing the raid. The object of the raid is stated unimaginatively as, 'to kill Germans'. To guide the men back, a shower of gold and silver rain rockets was used; see PRO WO95/1970.

30. The raid was carried out against German trenches to the south of Petit Bois. Each bomber carried twelve grenades, each rifleman had 170 rounds. 2nd Lieutenants WA Hamilton and DJ MacSherry, L/Corporal R Serplice and Private W Shaughnessy, were killed in the action. 2nd Lieutenant Robertson was wounded; PRO WO95/1970.

31. At Messines, nineteen mines were exploded – not quite simultaneously. They contained a total of a million pounds of explosive and created craters 100 yds wide and twenty-five yards deep. Over four miles of tunnelling had been excavated, by pick and shovel, to achieve this. Two mines failed to explode. Of these, one exploded in 1955 but the other still remains dormant.

32. The centre of the IX Corps attack comprised the 16th (Irish) Division on the left, with the 36th (Ulster) Division on the right. The village of Wytschaete formed the divisional boundary.

33. Major TRA Stannus; 4th Leinsters; acting CO, 7th Leinsters; DSO 1917; died of wounds, 17 June 1917.

34. 2nd Lieutenant, A/Captain JP Roche, MC; RFA, att. 47th Trench Mortar Battery; killed in action, 7 June 1917.

35. Willie Redmond died of his wounds in the 108th Field Ambulance unit. He

suffered shrapnel wounds to the arm and leg, which although not serious, seem to have caused his death through shock. He had premonitions of his fate, seeing it as a noble sacrifice for Ireland; see Stephen Gwynn, *The Last Years of John Redmond*, Edward Arnold, 1919.

36. Captain Henry Harrison (1867–1954); educ. Westminster School and Balliol, Oxford; Nationalist MP (Irish Parliamentary Party), Mid Tipperary, 1890–1902; 3/Royal Irish Regiment, 1915; writer and steadfast early supporter of Charles Parnell.

37. The artillery that Plumer had at his disposal was awesome. A total of 2,226 howitzers and guns pounded the German positions – one gun to every seven yards of front.

38. Should be Messines.

39. Redmond's body was taken to the convent chapel at Locre. General Hickie managed to find a rare coffin for the burial, which was witnessed by officers from both the 16th (Irish) and 36th (Ulster) Division. Locre Hospice was virtually destroyed in 1918, but Redmond's grave survived and despite official attempts to remove it, still remains isolated today – 'a lonely grave'; see Terence Denman, *A Lonely Grave – The Life and Death of William Redmond*, Irish Academic Press, 1995.

40. Captain CA Brett, whose 'Recollections' provide interesting detail on the composition, not only of the battalion, but of its headquarters staff. He notes that in 1915, 'the battalion was 95% Catholic. 'As a Protestant, I took the Church of Ireland Church Parade, which usually was 10 men and 3 officers.' Brett Papers, 7608–40, NAM, London.

41. Stephen Gwynn was always viewed with suspicion by Sinn Fein. His forebears were an extraordinary mix of Landed Unionist, Nationalist and Suffragette. While his wife converted to Catholicism, he remained a Protestant, with a brother who was a Major-General. His son, Denis, who worked at the British Ministry of Information during the Great War, became involved in the row over the exposure of the Casement 'Black Diaries'.

42. Sinn Fein's rise was assisted by the growing perception that Gwynn and his fellow Nationalist MPs had little influence over the British Government.

43. RCF's medical records enquire as to any disciplinary action taken against the perpetrator of the accident. A report solemnly blames the horse; PRO WO 339/48941.

44. For an analysis of the political, as well as military manoeuvres at Passchendaele, see Robin Prior and Trevor Wilson, *Passchendaele – The Untold Story*, YUP, 1996.

45. Originally part of the Zulu state, the Swazis fought in 'full dress' costume during campaigns in South Africa. RCF observed detachments of Swazis during the Matabele rebellion.

46. In order to straighten the German line, thereby releasing desperately needed divisions from the Somme front, Crown Prince Rupprecht ordered a withdrawal on 9 February 1917. The operation, code named 'Alberich', aimed to pull back troops within five weeks, to a deeply constructed defensive position called the Siegfried Position (the British called it the Hindenburg Line). Rupprecht's Chief of Staff, von Kuhl, exceeded his brief and laid waste to the evacuated territory; see Captain Wynne, 'The Hindenburg Line', *Army Quarterly*, January 1939; also The Wotan Position', *Army Quarterly*, July 1939.

47. A 'MEBU' (*Mannschafts-Eisen-Beton-Unterstand*) was a reinforced concrete bunker, where machine-gun crews or mortar detachments could shelter from bombardment. When all was clear, they clambered on top to fire at the

attackers. There are still Mebus intact today, though half buried, especially in the stretch of line between Bullecourt and Héninel; for a guide to their design, construction and use, see Peter Oldham, *Pill Boxes on the Western Front*, Leo Cooper, 1995.

48. The 'First Attack on Bullecourt' had taken place on 11 April 1917, and the major battle, known as 'Second Bullecourt', commenced on 3 May 1917, and lasted two weeks. The battle engulfed the surrounding villages and cost the British and Australians 20,000 casualties. Cyril Falls, the military historian, recalled: 'One witness was astonished. He never saw a battlefield, including Ypres, where the living and the unburied dead remained so close, for so long.' see Jonathan Walker, *The Blood Tub – General Gough and the Battle of Bullecourt, 1917*, Spellmount, 1998.

49. Known more commonly as the Royal Garrison Artillery (RGA). Originally formed to man fort coastal guns protecting the Royal Navy, the RGA came to play a prominent role in the Great War. By 1918 over a third of British guns were classed as either 'heavy' or 'medium'; see Bidwell & Graham, *Fire-Power: British Army Weapons and Theories of War, 1904–45*, Allen & Unwin, 1982.

50. When the Imperial War Graves Commission systematically removed the remains and gathered them in military cemeteries after the war, relatives were offered the original wooden crosses. Only 11,325 requested them. The remainder were shipped home, often being placed in the parish churches of the fallen; *Annual Report of the War Graves Commission*, 1922/23 (London, 1923).

51. A eulogy to Raymond Asquith, the son of the Prime Minister, appears in John Buchan, *These for Remembrance, Memoirs of 6 Friends Killed in the Great War*, Buchan & Enright, 1919.

52. Lieutenant GYL Walters; Irish Guards, attach. MGC; died of wounds, 15 September 1916.

53. Each sniping post had to submit a daily report of enemy activities along its front. A post would usually comprise an observer with periscope as well as his sniper. The observer would pick out isolated targets, not groups, who might offer retaliation.

54. There are very few graves in the district for soldiers killed in the Battle of Bullecourt in 1917. Such was the intensity of the battle, on such a narrow front, that few bodies could be safely retrieved. Bodies of the enemy might be bundled into shell-holes, the site being marked but unnamed.

55. Anita Mary, RCF's second daughter.

56. Poignant reminders of civilian life were not unusual on battlefields. The famous 'head-on' combat photograph of German soldiers of Hutier's Eighteenth Army at Villers-Bretonneux reveals an iron bedstead on a trench parapet.

57. The 'Livens' projectors were usually fired by a Royal Engineers detachment. The canisters, when filled with gas, could deliver a deadly charge much more accurately than the older method of opening valves on gas cylinders. Other popular contents of Livens canisters were cold tar and raw sewage.

58. The Redmond family had a long association with Wexford. Willie Redmond gained the Wexford Borough seat in 1883, at the age of 22. He had a long association with East Clare but in the by-election following his death, Eamon de Valera, of Sinn Fein, captured the seat.

59. Lieutenant-Colonel E Roche-Kelly; born 1881; educ. Downside; Boer War, 1901–2; OC 6/Royal Irish Regt.; MC & DSO, 1917; OC 1/Border Regt., 1927.

60. Father ST Wrafter MC was one of three chaplains attached to the 47th Brigade; the others were Fathers Maurice O'Connell and CT Brown.
61. The term 'Boche' was first used in 1914, from French slang *boche*, rascal; 'Fritz', from the German nickname for Friedrich, arrived in 1915, but soon fell out of use; 'Jerry' was used in 1917 and remained popular during World War II.
62. Charlie Chaplin remained the most popular film entertainer of the war. His constant battles on screen with the ridiculous elements of military life made him a hit with soldiers. Chaplain's most successful comedy was *Shoulder Arms*, released just before the Armistice.
63. Edith Feilding made sure the children had plenty to occupy them in the basement during Zeppelin and Gotha bombing raids. Bombs fell within several hundred yards of the house.
64. Whilst many regular officers believed that polished kit at all times enhanced morale, many temporary officers were more tolerant; see Gary Sheffield, 'Officer-Man Relations and Discipline in the 22nd Royal Fusiliers 1914–18', in *Look To Your Front*, Spellmount, 1999 p. 144.
65. RCF refers to the attack, by all three brigades of the 16th (Irish) Division, against 'Tunnel Trench', part of the Siegfried Position, still held by the enemy. It ran north-west from Bullecourt to Fontaines-lez-Croisilles. This was a diversionary attack to the main Battle of Cambrai which commenced on 20 November 1917.
66. After Brigadier-General Pereira retired from the army, he resumed his travels. His major achievement was to journey from Peking to Lhasa, Tibet, in 1921. Despite being lame from an old hunting accident, he carried out the expedition mostly on foot, a distance of over 7,000 miles; Pereira Papers, Royal Geographical Society, London.
67. Up to January 1918 92% of recruits from the province of Connaught were Catholic. Similar percentages applied to Leinster and Munster. In Ulster, 27% of recruits were Catholic; see Patrick Callan, 'Recruiting for the British Army in Ireland during the First World War', *The Irish Sword*, Vol. XVII, No.66, 1987.
68. This part of the German position around Bullecourt was a hybrid of German defence systems. In the northern part of the Siegfried Position, the new policy of 'elastic defence' was strictly enforced. This meant lightly held fire-trenches, with a network of strongpoints behind, with reserves held deeply in the rear. But in the Bullecourt sector, the front fire-trenches, which included Mebus, were formidable. In Tunnel Trench, there were four Mebus, about 150 yards apart – Neptune, Pluto, Jove and Mars, sited in forward saps.
69. Captain Brett was subsequently wounded in the attack and invalided home. He therefore luckily escaped the carnage of the 1918 German Spring Offensive; see Brett Papers, 7608–40, NAM, London.
70. Captain TMHS Tuite; born 1891; awarded MC for action at Tunnel Trench.
71. Having captured an enemy emplacement or bunker, the new occupiers would find it difficult to hold against enemy counter-attack. Often the structure was 'blind' – the only opening being the entrance, which was originally placed at the rear, to avoid fire. This now faced the attackers.
72. These half-suits of body armour were issued two per Company, and were only worn in defensive positions, by sentries and machine-gun teams. Weighing approximately twenty-five pounds, most troops found them difficult to wear and awkward when handling weapons. They were much in evidence in this part of the German front and the museum in nearby Bullecourt has a fine example.

73. Lieutenant-Colonel GAM Buckley (1866–1937); educ. NZ and Cheltenham; NZ Defence Force, 1900; member of Shackleton's British Antarctic Expedition, 1908; Captain 12/Hants. Regt; OC 7/Leinsters 1915; MID, three times; DSO, Guillemont, 1916; invalided home from France, 1918.

74. Brigadier-General HG Gregorie; born 1878; 2nd Lieutenant, Royal Irish Regt., 1900; South African War, 1900–2; MID twice; promoted Major, 1915; T/Brigadier-General, 1917–18; DSO, Great War.

75. The Germans tended to bury their dead in mass graves; for a study of differences between the British and German way of commemoration, see George L Mosse, *Fallen Soldiers*, OUP, 1990; and Jay Winter, *Sites of Memory, Sites of Mourning*, CUP, 1995.

76. Major RM Raynsford (1877–1965); 2nd Lieutenant, Leinster Regt., 1897; Boer War 1900–2; promoted Major, 1915; OC 5/Connaught Rangers and 10/Devons; DSO, 1918; Lieutenant-Colonel, 1925; retired 1926.

WAR LETTERS TO A WIFE

PART II : 1918

SERVICE WITH THE CONNAUGHT RANGERS

6th Battalion (1 January–1 April)

8 January 1918 [Front Line, Lempire]

Once more I have vowed that never again if I can help it will I travel by the 'leave' train. I had forgotten to bring a candle, so the cold being bitter and the windows broken, I shivered in the darkness.

It is beyond my powers adequately to describe the horrors of the 'leave' train, the scandal of which still continues after 3½ years of war. After fifteen hours on the train, I reached my transport lines near Villers Faucon at 2 pm in a blizzard, having had nothing to eat since last evening.

9 January 1918 [Front Line, Lempire]

The terrible weather still holds, the frost having lasted practically since I left here on the 23rd December to go on leave. The blizzard continues, and the trenches are half full of snow. I have spent a good deal of today and tonight in them, and find that both officers and men retain their usual cheerfulness and patience in spite of their appalling hardships.

10 January 1918 [Front Line, Lempire]

A few minutes before four o'clock this morning the enemy tried to raid one of my Lewis gun posts which is placed, necessarily in an isolated position, well out in No Man's Land, about 150 yards in front of the fire-trench, in a sunken road which crosses both lines of trenches. The raiders came across the snow in the dark, camouflaged in white overalls.

The double sentries on duty in the sunken road heard, but in the darkness did not see, a movement in front of them. Hesitating to shoot, they challenged. The immediate reply was a volley of hand-grenades. Private Mayne, who had charge of the Lewis gun, was hit 'all over', in many parts, including the stomach. His left arm was reduced to pulp. Nevertheless, he struggled up, and leaning against the parapet, with his uninjured hand discharged a full magazine (forty-seven rounds) into the enemy, who broke, not a man reaching our trench. Then he collapsed and fell insensible across his gun.

The second sentry's foot was so badly shattered that it had to be amputated in the trench. The doctor has just told me that he performed this operation without chloroform, which was unnecessary owing to the

152

man's numbed condition, and that while he did it the man himself looked on, smoking a cigarette, and with true Irish courtesy thanked him for his kindness when it was over.

Words cannot express my feelings of admiration for Private Mayne's magnificent act of gallantry, which I consider well worthy of the VC. It is, however, improbable that he will live to enjoy any decoration that may be conferred upon him.

12 January 1918 [Villers Faucon]

The incident of the morning before last had so filled one with pride of the battalion that I confess I have been aghast at receiving the following memorandum, which has been circulated in the Division:–

'Another instance has occurred of an enemy patrol reaching within bombing distance of our line. This must not occur again. Our patrols must meet the enemy patrols boldly in No Man's Land,' etc., etc., etc.

How simple and how grand it sounds. I think I can see the writer, with his scarlet tabs, seated in his nice office 7 or 8 miles behind the line, penning this pompous admonition.

So Private Mayne, it seems, will go unrecognised and unrewarded. In the meantime he has died, and I can only say, 'God rest his soul'.[1]

15 January 1918 [Villers Faucon]

My darling Joan,

Thank you for your letter which I got today. I went straight into the trenches where I found my Regiment when I arrived here. The trenches were very nasty too. The ground was frozen so solid that it was impossible to dig deep, and the trenches were consequently very shallow – some were only 3 or 4 feet deep and half full of snow; so wherever you went, you were in full view of the Germans. In fact it wasn't safe to move about in daytime, unless it was foggy.

My Headquarters, where I sleep, are in a deep mined dug-out, almost 25ft or 30ft underground. I don't like this kind of dug-out but it is all we have to go to sometimes. I like the surface ones better.

Mother told me of the egg you bought for her. That was very nice of you.

Goodnight, darling Joan,

Your loving Daddy.

27 January 1918 (Sunday) [Ronssoy]

Today is the Kaiser's birthday, and we half expected that things might happen, but there has been a thick fog, and all has been as silent as can be.

'Am I offensive enough?' is one of the questions laid down in a pamphlet that reaches us from an Army School some 30 miles behind the line. It is for the subaltern to ask himself each morning as he rises from his bed. Most laudable! But, as the Lewis Gun Officer remarked today, it is one of the paradoxes of war that the further you get from the battle line, the more 'offensive' are the people you meet!

The Brigadier called today, to say he had sent in my name for three weeks attachment to the French Battalion Commanders' School at Vadenay, near Chalons-sur-Marne.

The battalion is getting very weak, and something will have to be done before long.[2]

28 January 1918 [Tombois Farm, Lempire]

We came up into the Front line this evening, relieving the 1st Royal Munster Fusiliers, and this morning I went round the trenches – the same that I left to go home on leave on the 23rd December.

The change is remarkable. I left the trenches frozen like rock. I find them, today, half full of sticky mud; twice as wide and half as deep, owing to the caving of the sides; two layers of trench boards buried 2 feet deep in glutinous mud. It is a labour to walk in them, and today being a clear, sunny day it was not an occasion for easy cuts across the open.

Even so, for long stretches of these trenches you are under full view of the enemy – about 500 yards away. But he does not shoot, which suggests that his trenches are no better than ours, and that he does not want us to shoot at him.

It has been very misty the last few days. The enemy is wonderfully quiet. You scarcely hear a sound. Just a shell or burst of shells, or a bullet now and then, and that is all.

I got my orders today and leave for Vadenay on February 2.

2 February 1918 [Continental Hotel, Paris]

I got up at 4.15 this morning and caught a train at Roisel, reaching Amiens about ten o'clock. There I had lunch, bought a few things, and of course visited the Cathedral.

The contrast between the destruction I have left behind and this wonderfully majestic work of man was quite bewildering. High Mass was being sung as I went in, and as the great organ thundered out again and again, it made the air and even the ground throb.

I reached Paris at 4.30, and leave again tomorrow at noon. I have just been to Gaby Deslys' Revue at the Casino, and as it is past midnight I will go to bed.

8 February 1918 ['Court Supérieure d'Infanterie', Vadenay]

It is like being at school again. We go to the lecture room at 8.30 each morning, and are lectured to – in French, of course – for 3 hours, or more! In the afternoons we are motored to see different Army Schools, etc.

I am much struck with the thoroughness and efficiency of these

Frenchmen, and the serious way – in contrast to ours – that they go about the war. I wonder if they overdo it. But it is an interesting and valuable experience, and I am being most hospitably treated, and am already getting into the French ways of eating and living.

The one discomfort is the cold, since this is a woodless and coalless country, and one cannot get a fire very often. The French do not seem to mind, or else have got 'habitué' (as they say) to this kind of hardship. Gardner (the only other English officer) and I slink back from our evening walks with any old end of timber we can find, discarded from the Back Area defences, to warm our frigid billet.

P.S. The other day I met Nungesser[3] – the greatest of the French airmen. He walks with a limp, having been wounded many times.

17 February 1918 (Sunday) [Vadenay]

After the long interval of a fortnight your letters are now beginning to arrive in droves. Twenty-seven came yesterday, of which fifteen had been opened by the French censor!

What sad news about poor Vyvyan Harmsworth's death.[4] I saw him last at that luncheon at Miss Capel's house in Park Place, last August, with his father and Eugène Schneider – the head of Creusot.

The father will feel it terribly. To think that two of his three sons are dead. It seems such a short time since our visit to Highcliffe, when they were boys. How times have changed. Poor Bart, too.

Vyvyan was a fine fellow. With his wealth and backing he could have had his pick of the Staff jobs. But he was not built that way. He was always with the fighting portion of his regiment – except during the times when he was recovering from his wounds.

20 February 1918 [Vadenay]

Yesterday afternoon I at last satisfied my ambition, and flew in an aeroplane. It was a glorious day, and, piloted by a little French corporal, we mounted to something over 5,000 feet and cruised for three-quarters of an hour at that altitude. It is a wonderful feeling. We were so high above the captive balloons that they looked like beans (which is their shape).

All was going well when, suddenly, a crack and a whizz: something was wrong in front. Bits of metal came flying back, missing the pilot, but making a hole in each of the wings. A piece 2½ feet long caught up in the stays and fluttered there. The propeller made a hesitating turn or two, then stopped, and I knew only that we were 5,000 feet above the ground. I began to wonder what would happen next.

The pilot steered the machine round and round in little spiral curves towards the earth, while I sat and watched the landscape getting closer and more defined, and as a precaution, fixed the strap which is provided for the purpose, around my waist. As we neared the treetops we got rather wobbly (my pilot was manoeuvring for position and was keeping the aeroplane level), but finally we landed smoothly on the very aerodrome we had started from. I felt much relieved.

They tell me it was a rare accident. It was caused by a valve of the engine, which was of the rotary type, blowing loose, and cutting the steel housing of the motor. It was some pieces of the housing that had come flying back.

The engine was of course wrecked; but I have had my fly, though I dare say I am not so keen to repeat it just at present.

1 March 1918 [Ronssoy]

I have now returned to our battalion which is still in the line (in support for the moment), and our plans are very indefinite.

For me it does not matter. I have had my rest, but the men are getting tired. This is, I think, their 38th day up. Indeed, the whole Division sorely needs a rest, and above all, training.

General Hickie has gone home sick, and General Hull[5] temporarily commands the Division. In my Brigade I am the only Battalion Commander left of those who were with it on the 20th of last November. Indeed, one battalion in the Brigade has gone through two new CO's since that famous day.

5 March 1918 [Hamel, Tincourt]

We were unexpectedly relieved and marched back last night to this village. Our erratic movements are doubtless due to the expected German attack, of which the papers have been so full for weeks past.

I leave you to imagine the state of the men's bodies and clothing after so long a time in the line, almost without a wash.

I was glad to get back to the battalion, and found that all had gone well during my absence, and that every one was happy in spite of the tiring and trying time they had gone through. There had not been many casualties, and very few had been killed, though one splendid man had lost his life in what I fear was a foolish attempt to explore No Man's Land in daylight.

6 March 1918 [Tincourt]

I went to see an army oculist today at a place about 16 miles from here. On my way back, sitting on the box seat of an ambulance, I met a string of cavalry horses returning from water. I was admiring the boots of the subaltern who was walking in front, and thinking what a pleasant contrast they were to the ill-fitting slipshod things one sees in the trenches, when I glanced up at the officer's yellow woollen waistcoat, and then at his face. Who do you think it was? – Osmund,[6] smiling all over, whom I had not seen since that day at Windsor, when he came over from Sandhurst; and who has now grown into a man.

I stopped and was taken off to have tea at his camp at Doingt, with his Colonel (Durand), his Squadron Leader (Whitehead), and Peto[7] – a subaltern – whom I must have met as a child when staying with his father (Basil Peto, MP) and his mother, at Guildford.

Afterwards, I walked back here – about 4 miles, and Osmund came part of the way with me. He is just the same delightful enthusiastic boy he always was. He had been doing an infantry spell in the trenches, and had been on patrol, and was bubbling over with his experiences. He is of the sort who sees only the good in people, and all his geese are swans. He ended up by saying, 'The family is doing quite well: You've got the DSO, and Uncle Vincent[8] has the MC, and I've got my second pip!'

It is eighteen months today since I took over the command of this battalion.

15 March 1918 [Villers Faucon]

I got up at 2.30 this morning and marched the battalion forward to the Reserve trenches behind Ronssoy, as counter-attacking party, against the enemy's offensive which is still expected daily. It was very cold – the ground white with frost. At 10 am, no attack having been delivered, we marched back to billets.

This morning I saw an aeroplane shot down from a great height. It rolled over and over till it reached the ground – a nasty sight.

This evening a German aeroplane dashed over and brought down the Villers Faucon balloon, in flames. We saw the occupants jump safely out with their parachutes, but the enemy, in spite of furious 'Archy' and machine-gun fire, also got away.

17 March 1918 [Villers Faucon]

We again marched forward at three o'clock this morning to man Bois Switch and the Ronssoy sunken road. It is a wearing life, and all are feeling the strain. We are still the counter-attacking battalion.

Our pyrotechnicians are testing some wonderful new parachute lights, which illuminate the whole country for miles around, and to some extent enliven these early morning watches.

This is St. Patrick's Day, and, as you know; a great feast-day for the Irishmen, which they look forward to all the year round. Their duties today kept them from attending Mass (which means much to them). They have now returned from the daily wait behind Ronssoy and the subsequent cable-burying, and are having an extra good dinner, which they are too tired to enjoy.

I enclose some shamrock which has been sent to the battalion from Ireland.

24 March 1918 [Bray]

I have had no opportunity to write during the last three days. As you will have learned, the much advertised offensive crashed upon us last Thursday, since when we have been fighting a rearguard action, almost continuously. A retreat was the one possibility that had never occurred to us, and, unfortunately, it involves a kind of manoeuvring in which we are unversed, in spite of all our experience. For the time being the enemy has turned the tables in a manner which it is difficult to realise.

We have had no regular sleep for a week or more, and all are worn out, and to some extent dazed by the fatigue and strain.

After several days of uncanny silence, the enemy's artillery opened at about half-past four on the morning of the 21st. The forward areas were drenched with poison gas, and the back areas, to a distance of over five miles behind the front line, were shelled with the most savage fury. It was upon intensity of fire more than accurate shooting that the Germans relied, for not only had they refrained from registering beforehand, but there was a dense fog, which entirely prevented any kind of observation.

At the opening of the battle, two Brigades of this Division were holding the line in front of Ronssoy and Lempire.[9] The third – my own – was in Divisional Reserve, in wooden huts at Villers Faucon, 4 miles behind the firing line. Here we got our full share of the shelling, and at 8.30, after several narrow shaves, my Headquarters were hit.

The shell which hit the house crashed through into the cellar, blistering the floor and bending the wall of the ground-floor room, yet avoiding those of us who were in it; and, while it buried the officers below under a couple of feet of bricks and mortar, they escaped with nothing worse than bruising. The cottage, however, was so shaken that another hit would have brought it down, and I decided to leave it.

As things began to look more and more serious, Father McShane, the young chaplain, went round the battalion, and gave absolution to all.

While the men were having dinners, Ronssoy was reported lost, and I received instructions to march the battalion forward, and to report for orders to the Brigadier-General commanding the 49th – one of the Front line Brigades.

We were on the move by 12.30. The enemy was still shelling heavily, and we had several casualties as we went forward through the barrage. We passed two huge 12-inch howitzers on the broad-gauge railway, already abandoned. The adverse trend of the fighting became still more apparent, as we passed the 18-pounder positions, from the vigorous efforts that were being made to get away the guns and howitzers. With their usual dash, the Field gunners were struggling to move these guns, but though they had been pulled out of the pits, they were in many instances destined to go no further, there being no horses left alive to draw them.

As we reached the firing line, the trench was being heavily and effectively shelled. A few hours before, it had been a Reserve trench; so far behind, in fact, that it was only partly dug. There were considerable gaps; and as there was no communication trench leading up to it, the only approach was across the open.

We found it occupied by a few living stragglers – remnants of the garrisons of the forward positions, and strewn with the bodies of the dead who had already fallen to the enemy's shell-fire.

Among the severely wounded, there lay already one of my Company Commanders (Denys Wickham) – an admirable officer who has weathered two years of the worst of the war. I stopped a moment with him – long enough to see that he was being looked after, and moved on. The orders I had been given on the way up by the Brigadier of the 49th Brigade were to counter-attack without delay, with the 1st Royal Munster Fusiliers, who, he said, would co-operate on my right flank.[10]

As the Companies assembled for the counter-attack, the hostile shelling seemed to increase, and more than once there was a direct hit upon a bay, killing or wounding every man in it. A whizz-bang skimmed the parapet and hit the parados where I was standing, splashing my face with earth with such a smack that for a moment I thought my cheek was shot away. I felt and found only a drop of blood. With my usual luck a graze was all there was to show.

As I recovered, a recently joined subaltern came to me and reported that Cummins[11] – second in command of his Company – and several men with him, had just been killed by a shell, and that the men on either side were shaken; which was indeed scarcely to be wondered at, seeing that many of them (a draft of 180 had joined the battalion only a day or two before) were experiencing their baptism of fire. I told him he would have to carry on just the same, and I must say that the plucky and unhesitating manner in which this boy turned back to his job was very admirable.

At the same time, I must confess that the news he had brought was the greatest possible blow. Cummins was one of my most tried and trusted officers: though young, he was, in times of danger and difficulty, always to be relied upon. Moreover, he loved and was loved by his men. No wonder, with his reputation, that some of his men were shaken! Though he lay dead only a few yards along the trench from where I stood, even I shrank from visiting the spot.

These were the conditions under which the counter-attack was prepared.

It was delivered at 3.45 pm, by two Companies, with one Company in support and the fourth in reserve. It was pressed with great gallantry, and had it been supported on the right, as had been promised, it is probable that it would at least have resulted in a local setback to the enemy's advance.

The assaulting Companies (A and D) reached the sunken road bounding the western edge of Ronssoy Wood. As Captain Norman led forward the supporting Company (C), he saw what he at first supposed to be the battalion which should be co-operating on his right, but soon discovered it to be the enemy, lining the Factory Ridge to his right front; as well as parties of the enemy approaching along the Ronssoy–Ste Emilie road, evidently with the object of getting round the flank of the leading Companies.

He immediately engaged the enemy, forming a defensive flank along the Ronssoy–Ste Emilie road, but soon fell, wounded. Lieutenant Russell[12] then took command, but fell almost immediately, mortally wounded.

Simultaneously, the only other officer with the Company – McTiernan – was mortally wounded, and with the greater part of the Company having become casualties, the remainder were forced to fall back upon the trench they had started from. The Commander of one of the other Companies, Captain Crofton[13], was killed while leading his men forward, while the Commander of the other – Lieutenant Ribbons – who had succeeded Wickham, was made prisoner.

Two tanks took part in this counter-attack, but both were soon knocked out, one receiving a direct hit from a shell which killed all the occupants.

At 5.15 pm, I was ordered to report at 49th Brigade Headquarters, which were at Ste Emilie, in a deep mined dug-out in the grounds of what once had been the château. I made my way there between the shell-holes, many of which were so recent that they were still smoking. The bombardment continued violently, though rather wildly, and as I neared my destination, the swish of machine-gun bullets mixed with the general din.

My first duty was to report to the Brigadier[14] the result of the counter-attack. He was apologetic, and explained that his orders for this operation should have been cancelled: they had, he said, been cancelled in the case of the Munsters, but he had been unable to communicate with me. Then he added: 'I hope you will not think hard of me.'

There was no answer to this – at least no civil answer. I could see no reason for his having failed to communicate with me; nor, having failed, could I excuse him for having cancelled his orders to the Royal Munster Fusiliers to counter-attack, knowing that we were counting upon their co-operation.[15]

The General then told me that his Brigade was reduced to about sixty men, and that he had been ordered to withdraw; and this he immediately proceeded to do.

I now came back under the orders of my own Brigade, whose Headquarters were in a chalk quarry some 400 yards to the north-west of Ste Emilie.

Throughout the day that followed, owing to our heavy losses in guns the previous day, we were practically without artillery support. At 3.30 am, all stood to, but in spite of a thick fog which seemed entirely to favour the enemy, daylight arrived without any sign of further activity on his part.

It was beginning to look as if we might be going to have a restful day, when, at about six o'clock, three German prisoners (an officer and two other ranks) were passed back from the fire-trench. They spoke English fluently, and upon being questioned as to whether it was intended to renew the attack during the morning, replied that it was.

The information we had extracted was at once sent back to Brigade, and in less than half an hour, its accuracy was confirmed by the sudden outburst of the enemy's barrage on a similar scale to that of the previous day. This was followed in due course by the German infantry, who swept forward, wave after wave, in overwhelming hordes.

My own Companies, had already suffered severely, and had lost three Captains and two seconds in command out of four, during the counter-attack of the preceding afternoon – not one officer escaped.

There being no communication trench, the firing line was, from the moment the attack started, cut off from all behind it, and though two of the battalion signallers made a gallant attempt to cross the exposed strip of ground that separated Headquarters from the Companies, they succeeded in delivering their message only at the cost of one of their lives, the other being wounded.

On this occasion it was necessary to employ signallers, as all the runners

161

were out, but I feel I must record the wonderful bravery of the runners – both Battalion and Company – at all times, but especially when the conditions have been most exacting and have demanded supreme courage and almost superhuman devotion.

In the course of a battle it is often necessary to send a runner with a message under circumstances which involve certain death or wounding, yet never have I seen one of these carefully chosen men waver or hang back. No matter how dangerous the errand – and he well knows what is before him – the runner on duty never wants calling twice. Give him his message, and he will pick up his rifle and be off, often to his death. I have seen so many officers and men go off like that smilingly to their death in this war, and, looking back, it certainly does seem sometimes as though a special buoyancy of spirit animates those about to die.

In the afternoon, a general retirement was ordered to a prepared line (the Green line), in front of Tincourt, some miles behind the original front line. We reached it at the cost of a few casualties from shell-fire. I must say I had hoped to find some fresh troops there, but there were none. Indeed, the trench was practically empty.

The battalion was now reduced to the Headquarters Company and thirty-four stragglers.

At dusk I was ordered to line the Tincourt–Templeux La Fosse road (my left on Tincourt Wood), with the 1st Munsters on my left and the 2nd Leinsters on my right; the latter (reduced to the strength of about a Company) having been temporarily placed under my command. My instructions were to cover the retreat of the remnant of the 49th Brigade.

I made my Headquarters for the night in an exceedingly comfortable three-roomed hut in Tincourt Wood, formerly the abode of an officer of the Divisional Staff, whose Headquarters had been here.

Its appearance suggested that some sudden and deadly cataclysm had overcome the occupant while he was having his breakfast, the remains of which, together with one or two half-finished cups of tea, still littered the table. The floor had a carpet: expensive oil lamps, crockery, and a profusion of knick-knacks lay about: but there was no sign of any effort having been made to save these treasures, so rapid, apparently, had been the owner's exit.

The next morning (yesterday), the 49th Brigade began to fall back soon after daybreak, and the arrangements for the withdrawal to the Bois des Flacques line were carried out without difficulty and in good order. The operation was assisted in its initial stages by a fog, and the retirement was covered by a heavy artillery barrage, as well as by a number of tanks, two or more of which, however, succumbed to engine trouble and had to be destroyed by their crews and abandoned.

The position which we now took up was an old line of trenches on the top of a steep ridge. Behind us, in the plain to the west, lay Doingt and Peronne.

As we arrived in sight of these places, some buildings were already ablaze, and I also saw one or two explosions – evidently the work of our own troops – which suggested that preparations were being made for a further retreat.

Early in the afternoon, the enemy's line of skirmishers topped the skyline, some 2,000 yards in front of our position. This was followed by the assault troops, who soon had gathered in large numbers in the woods, and wherever the ground gave cover. Simultaneously, a heavy long range machine-gun fire was opened upon us.

The leading skirmishers, pressing forward like hounds on a hot scent, were very bold, and in the face of a fire which was moderate – owing to the necessity of economising ammunition – persisted in their advance across the exposed valley that separated us.[16]

About this time an enemy aeroplane flew low over our line and dropped a flare. This was mistaken for one of our own signals by our artillery, who immediately put over shrapnel, which killed two of my men, and wounded a third.

At about 1 pm, I saw the battalion on my immediate left leaving the trenches in a body, and I sent a runner to ask for an explanation. Their second in command returned personally with the runner. He said he had received orders from Brigade to fall back. I suggested that there must be a mistake, and he replied that he would go to Brigade Headquarters and ascertain definitely the acting Brigadier's wishes. I myself went and saw Colonel Crockett, to find out if he knew anything. Then, seeing no reason for a retirement, I ordered two platoons of the 13th Royal Sussex Regiment, which happened to be available, to fill the gap.

As I was returning to the fire-trench I was met by my Adjutant (Captain Ritchie Dickson), who said that during my absence an order had come from Brigade to evacuate the line we were holding, and to fall back upon Biaches. He added that Major Raynsford was making the necessary arrangements.

Major Raynsford had passed the order on, in writing, to the 2nd Leinster Regiment and our own battalion, but when I saw him, a few minutes later, he had just been shot through the body, and was being carried back under considerable difficulty on a ground-sheet. Four men, each holding a corner, were staggering under his weight, and one of these, as he saw me coming up, called out: 'It's all right, sir, you can trust us to get him out': and so they did. They carried him under fire, a mile or two till they came across a motor machine-gun carriage, and they placed him upon this and sent him away to safety.[17]

I formed up the few men of the Connaught Rangers at the foot of the hill on the edge of the village of Doingt – the same village where I had taken tea with Osmund so short a time before, and in conjunction with Colonel Crockett and his men, and Major Whittall's sappers, fire was brought to bear upon the enemy, who were already descending the near side, and whose machine-guns were already shooting from the slopes of the ridge we had just occupied.

We then fell back through Doingt and Peronne, halting parties at convenient points to cover the withdrawal of the remainder. I will not say that the retirement was not ragged. It was. But though it was followed by the enemy's machine-guns and shell-fire, his advance was sufficiently delayed to enable us to reach an old line of trenches crossing the Herbecourt road, almost without casualties.

An engineer officer was at each bridge in Peronne, waiting to blow it up after the passage of the infantry, and at the first I left a party, under Ritchie Dickson, to assist in this operation. These rejoined the battalion safely during the evening.

At midnight I received orders to march back to Bray, and at 6.30 this morning, we bivouacked in a field a few hundred yards east of the village, where we found Brigade Headquarters, and where I got a couple of hours of much needed sleep in the Brigadier's tent.

The friends I met expressed surprise at seeing me. For the fourth time during my military career I had been reported killed.

30 March 1918 [Rouen]

I hope you got my wire saying that I was safe, in hospital. We have crammed years of life into a week, during which my usual Providence protected me, though the Battalion – indeed the whole Division – is practically gone.[18]

Not one of the officers doing duty with the Companies came out of the second day, and, since then, the small remnant left has suffered still further.

I had to leave them on the evening of the 27th – the seventh day of the battle. Just as they were holding up the enemy rather well, I fell and dislocated my left elbow joint, while running forward to get the Lewis guns on to a target of retiring Germans.

I was under chloroform[19] for forty minutes yesterday, while they tried to pull the telescoped bones back into position, but another X-ray photograph today shows that I have to go through it again this afternoon.

31 March 1918 [Rouen]

I concluded my letter of March 24 with our arrival at Bray that same morning. During the day, the battered remnants of the battalion were reorganised into two Companies. By the addition of stragglers, and officers and men recalled from courses, leave, etc., our fighting strength had been raised to 7 officers and 180 other ranks.

In the afternoon, the Brigadier (General Gregorie)[20] returned from leave, and the Brigade was detailed for the protection of the bridges over the Somme, it having been reported that hostile cavalry had crossed the river, south of Peronne, and were making their way in a westerly direction.

By 10 pm, I got my men into position at Sailly Lorette, the village allotted to me, and during the night, charges of gun-cotton were laid by the Sappers, preparatory to blowing up the bridges in case of necessity.

Sailly Lorette is an old-fashioned and picturesque village, perched on the slope and summit of the steep escarpment which here forms the northern bank of the Somme, and, in less disturbed times, no more attractive place could be desired for tired troops to billet in.

I passed a woman on the road, setting off towards Amiens, with a few cattle and a wagon-load of household things. I stopped and spoke to her. She had, she told me, three farms in the neighbourhood, and was leaving 100,000 francs' worth of property behind to the tender mercy of the Hun.

On the river bank, I met a man with two little boys – his sons, he said – whom he had brought in a barge from Peronne. They had been through the bombardment. 'Could I tell him how near the Germans were now?'

A frail old man and his wife of seventy or more were trundling a heavy wheelbarrow containing their belongings up the steep ascent which leads from the river towards Amiens. They asked if I thought it would be safe for them to rest for a little while. They had travelled all through the night, with nothing to eat. Fortunately, I had a packet of chocolate, so I gave them that.

'La guerre, no bon,' one of them said to me in the new French; and the thought repeatedly occurred to me – 'Thank God, at least, that our people in England have been spared this'. It was some satisfaction that I was able to lend a couple of the battalion horses to help some of the oldest women to get away.

We were ordered away during the afternoon to Cérisy, a mile and a half higher up the Somme, to guard the bridge there, news having come through that the enemy was now threatening from the north of the river. As at Sailly Lorette, arrangements had been made to destroy the bridge at this village, should the necessity arise.

My sleep was interrupted during the night that followed. At two o'clock, two officers of the Labour Corps burst into the room where I was sleeping and called out excitedly: 'Do you know that the Germans have broken through on the north bank of the river, and that you are the last people left?'

Having delivered this alarming message they disappeared – I am sorry to say before I had awakened sufficiently from the corpse-like sleep, to have them arrested.

Though these officers' fears were obviously genuine enough, there was, during the few days of which I write, too much of this kind of thing. The previous night, for example, two sappers had rushed past the sentries with a similar tale, and there is no doubt but that the enemy inspired many of these incidents. In fact, he made systematic use of spreading panic behind our lines. Unhappily, there are always plenty of nervous people in the army, as well as out of it, who can be safely relied upon to spread false news, if only it is bad enough.

I have been told that at this time it had been intended to take out the Division, which, as you now know, had been very badly cut up on the 21st and 22nd. Be this as it may, the Fates ruled otherwise. The enemy was pressing hard and with considerable success on the northern side of the river, and during the morning of the 26th, the 47th Brigade was ordered to move and take up a line in front of Proyart, a village 3½ miles south-east of Cérisy.

By two o'clock, or shortly after, we were in position, in a railway cutting which happened to be handy, and elsewhere digging in where no natural cover was available. We (the Connaught Rangers) were in the centre, with the 1st Munster Fusiliers and the 2nd Leinsters on our left and right respectively. On the left of the Brigade was the 48th Brigade, and, on the right, the 39th Division.

At 3.50 pm, it was reported, and it soon also became apparent from the enfilade fire, that the enemy had broken through the 66th Division on the right of the 39th. Later, the position on this flank improved, but it was then reported to me that the Brigade on our left had withdrawn. This information I passed on to Brigade, and I was informed that the gap would be filled before dawn.[21]

Nobody slept that night. The battalion frontage was patrolled continuously. Parties of the enemy were observed digging some 800 yards in front of our line, and I sent an officer with a Lewis gun to hamper them.

At 2.30 am, I was visited by one of the Staff Officers of the Division, who greeted me with the cheering news that strong French reinforcements were already at Lamote miles behind us, and that they would be passing through us to the counter-attack within the next six hours. He added: 'So you have only to stick it a short time longer'.

This would have been all right if it had been true. Unfortunately it was not.

Not only were there no fresh fighting troops – either French or English – at Lamote, but I saw none when, fifteen hours later, I travelled back to Amiens, and even beyond: how this officer came to make so inaccurate a statement is still a mystery to me.

Before daybreak some men were reported to have refilled the gap on the left of the Brigade, but these appear to have gone again almost immediately, and as soon as it was light enough to see, small parties of the enemy could be observed between our Brigade and the river, making their way towards Mericourt and Morcourt.

When I first saw this movement I sent a message to Captain Goodland

(1st RMF), who was on the left, asking him to send a patrol to intercept it, if possible; and I also got a section of Field Artillery and two Vickers guns to sweep the ridge where the enemy was accumulating. Later, as the movement continued, and the parties of the enemy passing round our flank grew larger and bolder, I sent a Lewis gun under 2nd Lieutenant MacWeeney to try and get round them.

For several hours the Germans continued to stream through the gap on the left in ever-increasing numbers, and at 10.15 am, the position had become so acute that the officer commanding the 1st Munsters reported that he was compelled to accommodate himself to the new situation, and that he was falling back.

A hurried conference was then held, as the result of which Colonel Weldon (2nd Leinsters) ordered a withdrawal in echelon, commencing from the left, to a position on the line Morcourt–Framerville.

The right covered the retirement of the left during the initial stages. Covering parties were also left temporarily behind as the retirement continued. That it had become necessary was proved by the machine-gun fire which met us, as we fell back, from the direction of what had been our left rear, in which locality large bodies of the enemy had already collected.

My usual good fortune pursued me on this occasion, though, as we walked back in the face of the gusts of bullets – being pursued in addition from behind by the enemy's shell-fire – the chances of surviving at times seemed very small.

A sight that met us as we passed through Proyart has photographed itself upon my mind. An old man on a high dog-cart, drawn by a crazy-looking horse, rather like the horse Don Quixote used to ride, drove solemnly and reluctantly through the village. He was the last inhabitant to leave. He had a long white beard and wore one of those high black Flemish caps, and the heavy shells falling upon the houses around him, sending up clouds of smoke and brick-dust, left him and his horse apparently quite unconcerned. It looked as though he had clung almost too tenaciously to his home, but I believe he got out all right. At any rate, I watched him pass safely along the first mile or so of the road towards Amiens.

The Colonel of another battalion told me afterwards that, at this same place, he saw an old woman and a little child, stumbling through the fields, hand in hand. The former was too feeble, and perhaps had also been a little too obstinate, to leave her home till the very last moment. Now, perhaps too late, she was devoting her whole energy to saving the child; and, as each shell fell, both threw themselves upon their faces on the ground.

On reaching the new position, I occupied an old trench which runs past the junction of the Proyart and the main Amiens roads. As a general retirement was by this time in progress, I formed my men up on the main

Amiens road together with the 1st Royal Munster Fusiliers, and a good many battle stragglers from other regiments who had attached themselves to us.

With this force, which must have been close upon 400 strong, I then reported to General Bellingham[22] (commanding the 118th Brigade), whom I met on the road. At General Bellingham's request, I lined up with the 39th Division in three lines of old trenches which cross the Amiens road. Here, until I left, some four or five hours later, we held up and inflicted losses on the enemy, who appeared repeatedly in force in the villages of Rainecourt and Framerville, in front of us.

A considerable number of aeroplanes – both German and British – took part in this action, shooting at each other's infantry, and assistance was rendered to us by the artillery.

Finally, a counter-attack was delivered by two fresh Companies, which were brought up specially by motor lorry. This proved too much for the Germans who turned and fell back hastily through the now blazing villages.

It was in running across to the Lewis guns to direct their attention to a bunch of the enemy I had observed, that, at about 4.15 pm, I stumbled over some overgrown trip wire, and dislocated my left elbow. The men thought I had been hit. So did I. And it cost me a good coat, which the stretcher-bearers ripped open with a knife in their usual reckless fashion, hunting for the wound.

This was the end of the battle, so far as I was concerned. I waited half an hour, feeling very sick, until General Bellingham (who had been away at the telephone) returned. Then I handed over the command to Ritchie Dickson, the senior of the only two officers left of all we had gone into battle with on the 21st.

The last sight I saw was that of one of our aeroplanes crashing vertically to earth from a height of some 400 feet. It fell, head-first, like a stone, and sent the dust flying like a dud shell. Both pilot and observer must have been killed instantly.

With my servant, Doyle, I made my way towards Amiens. As we neared Lamote – after a circuitous walk of nearly 4 miles, our troops were falling back in droves across the road, from the direction of the Somme. Our men, as they fell back, were being pursued by a furious shell-fire. The road, which was being treated as a special target, was littered with dead horses, and was horrible to look upon.

We came upon a motor lorry, which was just preparing to move off: It was filled with wounded, but I got a seat on the step, while Doyle climbed inside.

For the next few minutes we ran the gauntlet through a storm of shells. The conductor stood on the step and bawled encouragement to the driver like a Cockney at a boat-race. The driver fairly sweated in his efforts to push the clumsy vehicle along at a faster speed than that for which it was designed. It was an exciting race, but we got through, and, after several changes, travelling part of the way on casual motor-cars which we picked up on the road, and part by ambulance, we eventually reached the Casualty Clearing Station at Nampes. Near Villers Brettoneux (where the line now is), a Major of the Heavy Artillery, on whose car we were riding, gave us some port, some chocolate, and a bag of biscuits. These, since we had not had a proper meal for close on thirty hours, Doyle and I devoured ravenously. As we passed through Amiens, I noticed marked signs of the heavy bombing the town had received from aeroplanes the night before.

The Casualty Clearing Station which we found at Nampes had moved back with the general retirement, and the tents composing it had barely been pitched when we arrived.

The marquees were faintly lighted by wax candles, and were crowded with herds of wounded. The bad cases lay upon stretchers, which almost hid the ground. So numerous were these that it was often necessary to step over one.[23] The walking wounded packed the gaps and overflowed outside as well. The doctors and nurses, though they must have been half dead with fatigue, worked cheerfully and unceasingly at the highest pressure.

After being bound up, I was directed to the railway station, to wait for the ambulance train. Here I was fortunate in finding a very generous Railway Transport Officer, who invited me to pass the night in his office, and gave me a meal of eggs and bread and butter, and some rare old rum.

When at last the train arrived, at 3.30 in the morning, it was of so luxurious a type – the latest Red Cross marvel – that the long and tiresome wait was fully compensated for. I was immediately put to bed, and at about 1 pm, reached Rouen.

And here I am, in No. 2 Stationary Hospital, where I have slept, practically for three days, waking up only to take food or to be chloroformed. I was chloroformed twice before my elbow, which had been out of joint for 72 hours, was got right.

RCF returns to England on 1 April 1918. He is admitted to Dorchester House Hospital, Park Lane on 2 April 1918.

NOTES

1. Private Mayne was posthumously Mentioned in Despatches.
2. Like all divisions, the 16th (Irish) was in the process of restructure at this time. Battalions were reduced from twelve to nine in each division. High casualties and falling recruitment meant twelve Irish infantry battalions were disbanded between November 1917 and February 1918; see Terence Denman, *Ireland's Unknown Soldiers,* Irish Academic Press, 1992; and Patrick Callan, 'Recruiting for the British Army in Ireland during the First World War', in *The*

Irish Sword, Vol. XVII, No. 66, 1987.

3. Lieutenant Charles Nungesser (1883–1927); served as cavalryman and was wounded twice before joining French Air Corps; specialised in aerial bombing before gaining fame as a fighter pilot; credited with forty-five kills; killed in 1927, while attempting to fly the Atlantic.

4. Captain Hon. HAV StG Harmsworth MC (1894–1918); eldest son of Viscount Rothermere and nephew of Lord Northcliffe; 2/Irish Guards; wounded three times and eventually returned to England, where he died of wounds, 12 February, 1918; his brother, Vere, a Lieutenant in the Drake Bn, RND, was also killed in action, 13 November 1916.

5. Major-General Sir Amyatt Hull (1865–1920); a strong-willed commander who nevertheless acceded to General Gough's demand for a heavily defended front-line. This left the 16th (Irish) Division dangerously undermanned in the 'Battle Zone' area. Hull's son, Sir Richard, became a Field-Marshal and CIGS, 1961–4.

6. Lieutenant OF Stapleton-Bretherton (1898–1918); educated Downside; 9/Lancers; killed in action at Hervilly Wood, Roisel, two weeks later on 22 March 1918; only son of Edith Feilding's brother, Frederick S-B. Edith Feilding lost one brother (Robert) killed in the Boer War and another (Captain Wilfred), killed in action, 11 November 1914.

7. Lieutenant (later Captain) CHM Peto (1897–1980); 2nd son of Sir Basil Peto MP; 9/Lancers, wounded and MID; Brigadier in WWII and later MP.

8. Captain Vincent Stapleton-Bretherton MC (1888–1982).

9. The 48th and 49th Brigades. The 16th Division had taken over these positions from the French but the defences in this salient were poorly dug and wiring, inadequate. The British were using the 'flexible defence in depth' system, recently inherited from the Germans, deploying troops in 'advanced', 'battle zone' and 'rear zone' positions. Despite being ill trained in these sophisticated tactics, General Sir Hubert Gough (5th Army) insisted that two brigades should man the advanced positions. This left the 'battle zone' vulnerable to flank attacks; see Tim Travers, *How The War Was Won – Command and Technology in the British Army on the Western Front, 1917–18,* Routledge, 1992, pp. 50–74.

10. Lieutenant D MacWeeney MC, 6/Connaughts, blamed the 49th Brigade for the failure of this suicidal attack. He recalled afterwards, 'to even contemplate a counter-attack showed rigidity of mind worthy of the Crimean War . . . combined with an inability to see the situation was long past a local solution, ensured the destruction of the battalion'; see MacWeeney Papers, 7707–12, NAM.

11. Lieutenant, T/Captain FK Cummins; 6/Connaught Rangers; MC, 1917; killed in action 21 March 1918.

12. Lieutenant AHE Russell; att. 6/Connaught Rangers; died of wounds, 22 March 1918.

13. Captain TH Crofton MC; att. 6/Connaught Rangers; killed in action, 21 March 1918.

14. Brigadier-General P Leveson Gower (1871–1939); cousin of the Duke of Sutherland; commissioned, Derbyshire Regiment, 1891; Tirah Expedition, 1898; Boer War 1899–1901; GOC 49th Brigade, 1916; gassed 1917; DSO, 1917.

15. Practically every officer with the battalion became a casualty on 21 March. Lieutenant MacWeeney calculated that of the nineteen officers in action, six were killed, six wounded and five captured; MacWeeney Papers, 7707–12, NAM.

16. One of the main reasons for the German success on 21 March 1918 was the sheer speed of their assault. The British forward positions had been expected to hold for forty-eight hours – in the event, they collapsed after ninety minutes; see Martin Samuels, *Command or Control – Command, Training and Tactics in the British and German Armies, 1888–1918*, Frank Cass, 1995, pp. 265–9.

17. Major Raynsford was moved back to the Lucknow Casualty Clearing Station. The CCS was only designated for 600 stretcher cases, but by the time he arrived, there were already 2,500 cases awaiting treatment; see Tom Johnstone, *Orange, Green and Khaki – The Story of the Irish Regiments in the Great War, 1914–18*, Gill & Macmillan, 1992, p.379.

18. The following month what was left of the 6/Connaughts became a training unit. They were then incorporated into the 2/Leinsters and the battalion was formally disbanded in August 1918. The remainder of the 16th (Irish) Division were contracted into a brigade and used for training purposes. When the 16th Division was returned to France in July, it was no longer an Irish division (it included just one Irish battalion – the 5/Royal Irish Fusiliers).

19. Chloroform, ether and nitrous oxide were the main general anaesthetic agents available. With experience gained during the war, leading to improvements in administration techniques, general anaesthetics became safer.

20. As RCF had mentioned as early as 16 March, an enemy offensive was known to be imminent. It could hardly have helped the brigade's defence for its commander to be absent on leave at this critical time.

21. RCF attributed the collapse of the 16th (Irish) Division to the tiredness of the troops. But much of the problem can be traced to Corps level, for it was mainly the divisions lying on Corps boundaries that suffered. Corps-to-Corps staff communication was weak and when, for example, Congreve's VII Corps lost control of the retreat, disorganisation rapidly spread down to divisional and brigade level; see Tim Travers, *How the War was Won*, Routledge, 1992, pp. 72–7.

22. Brigadier-General EHCP Bellingham (1879–1956); commissioned Royal Scots, 1889; Boer War 1899–1902; OC 8/Royal Dublin Fusiliers, 1916–17; DSO, 1917; GOC 118th Infantry Brigade; captured 27 March 1918 and repatriated December 1918; succeeded to baronetcy, 1921; joined Royal Air Force in World War II.

23. It has been estimated that the overall British casualties for 21 March 1918 amounted to 7,500 killed, 10,000 wounded and 21,000 taken prisoner – a total of 38,500. By contrast, the Germans lost 11,000 killed and 29,000 wounded (inc. lightly). RCF estimated that his battalion alone lost twenty-two officers and 618 OR out of 700 in the line; see Martin Middlebrook, *The Kaiser's Battle*, Allen Lane, 1978, pp. 320–3.

WAR LETTERS TO A WIFE

PART III : 1918

SERVICE WITH THE 1/15TH LONDON REGIMENT

1st Civil Service Rifles (16 August onwards)

RCF is passed fit to resume active service on 6 August 1918. He leaves via Charing Cross Station on 7 August and arrives at Boulogne on the same day. Owing to the destruction of the 6/Connaught Rangers, he has to wait in Etaples for the allocation of a new battalion.

16 August 1918 [Etaples]
I picnicked today with Mrs Worswick and her sister (they are running a soldiers' club), and Lady Sinclair (Marigold Forbes, daughter of Lady Angela), who is just turning twenty-one, has been married six weeks, and whose husband is in the 2nd Life Guards. Afterwards we bicycled to Paris Plage, and bathed.

While I was drying myself, an orderly discovered me and handed me orders to report at Etaples Station at 5.40, to proceed and assume command of the 15th London Regiment – the 1st Civil Service Rifles.[1]

This, to say the least of it, was unexpected, since officers are usually kept waiting for weeks, and sometimes months, in the Commanding Officers' pool, as they call it.

20 August 1918 [140th Infantry Brigade HQ]
I left base at 2.20 on the afternoon of Sunday. At Canaples, we detrained, and in the early morning a car was sent for me. After a drive of 12 or 15 miles, I was dropped at my new Divisional Headquarters at Heilly.

The Divisional Commander, General Sir George Gorringe,[2] was just starting off in his car to visit General HB Kennedy[3] (60th Rifles), my new Brigadier, and took me along with him. I found that my new battalion was in the front line, but as it was coming out tonight, the Brigadier asked me to sleep at his Headquarters.

I went up in the afternoon, with the Brigade Major, who turns out to be Captain L M Gibbs,[4] Coldstream Guards ('Laggs' Gibbs), to visit the battalion, and was introduced to the officers. This was on the opposite side of the Bray–Corbie road to the spot where I was encamped with the Guards Entrenching Battalion in 1916. At that time it was a very safe place. It has now lost that reputation, which is reflected in the name given to it by the soldiers, which is 'Toot Sweet' Valley.

I still write from Brigade Headquarters, which are in tents, on the battlefield of twelve days ago. They are about a mile from Sailly Lorette, ever memorable to me on account of its associations with the retreat of last March. Last evening, after visiting the battalion, I walked into that once beautiful village, and revisited my old Headquarters of March 24. Much fighting has since taken place there, and the village and church are completely destroyed, and the houses where I slept and messed are gutted.

The country around this camp is still littered with the residue of the battle of August 8. The dead have not yet all been collected, and I judge from what I have seen, that our people killed many Germans.

21 August 1918 [Marett Wood, Méricourt]

I dined again with General Kennedy last night, as the battalion was not due to arrive back from the trenches till 2 or 3 am. The 'family feeling', which I have always told you is so necessary for successful war, is certainly strong in the Brigade. As for the Brigadier – I never met a more companionable man. There is nothing whatever of the Staff Officer about him. In fact, though he himself has to wear red tabs as a Brigadier-General, he has a saying that 'once a man has put on red tabs it is only a matter of time before he becomes a *******', which is a view not uncommonly held in the fighting line.

This is the 1st Prince of Wales' Own Civil Service Rifles (1/15th London Regiment) – one of the 1st line London Territorial battalions. The Brigade is the 140th – the same that relieved us (1/Coldstream) – on June 1, 1915, at Le Rutoire. The Division is the 47th.[5] The Corps, the III.

I find that I am succeeding Eric Segrave,[6] who has got a Brigade. Strange coincidence, isn't it, that I should find myself filling the shoes of one of my best and oldest friends? It makes things very much easier, as not only am I sure to get a good name in advance from Eric, but you may be sure that he has left a good battalion behind him.

26 August 1918 [Bonnay]

We have been at it, hammer and tongs, the last few days, but I got out last night for a breather, having been on my feet almost continuously for four days and nights. Things have gone well, and there is no doubt but that we are killing a lot of Germans considerably more than they are killing of us. Besides, we are capturing large numbers of prisoners. I am with a splendid crowd. They are like little lions – these London men.

I have a new second in command, who joined last night – Major Desmond Young, of the 60th.

*   *   *

29 August 1918 [Carnoy Craters]

We pushed on forward again this afternoon, and I am writing from what was, on July 1, 1916, the German front line – a place of desolation; it is familiar ground to me.

We have already come across two 'booby traps' this evening, one of which killed two good men. The padre has just told me that one of them had been sentenced to seven years for stealing pearls, but was let out when the war came, to join the Army. He got a DCM and a MM. So he made good.

The enemy is moving fast, and is miles away, and will take a bit of catching, I fancy.

4 September 1918 [Behind St Pierre Vaast Wood]

Tomorrow morning we are off again after the enemy. Let us hope he will go back kindly.

The standard of courage among these London lads is so high, that men who would be considered brave elsewhere do not seem particularly brave here. In fact, they would look like shivering rabbits beside some of them.

We are very fortunate in our padres. The RC Chaplain is Father Benedict Williamson. His real name is, however, known to few, since he is invariably spoken of as 'Happy Days'[7], a nickname he has earned from his incurable optimism. Formerly, he was an architect. He is a Catholic by adoption – not heredity. He is a remarkable character. He carries the Host with him always, and administers it to any of the troops whenever they may desire it. The shell-holes serve him as chapels. He is, so he has told me, a believer in 'religion by print', on the principle that print does not argue with the reader, and the reader cannot argue with print. Each time the words are read, the same thing is repeated – over and over again – till, at last, the most determined sceptic may be brought to admit that there is something in it after all.

The C of E Padre – Farebrother[8] – messes with the battalion. He is not so long from Eton, and is quite charming.

8 September 1918 (Sunday) [Heilly]

So much has happened since I said Goodbye to you at Charing Cross that the sequence of my letters has got out of joint, and it will be difficult to pick up the thread.

I will, therefore, go back to August 21, on which day I actually took over the command of this battalion. The following morning, at 4.40, the Division was to take part in the 4th Army offensive,[9] to be resumed that day. The battalion assembled for the attack shortly before Zero, and I moved my Headquarters to a dug-out on the railway, north of the Bois des Tailles, which had been allotted to me by Brigade. From the railway embankment I watched the opening of the barrage.

How often have I tried to describe to you that grandest and most spectacular of all the shows ever staged by man – the crash of a thousand guns bursting suddenly out of the silence of the night: the continued roar: the rapid intermittent flicker on the clouds: the trembling earth beneath you:– while you listen anxiously for the rattle of the enemy's machine-guns – that nasty sickening sound which you are just able to distinguish amid the din, and which tells you that he is not taking it lying down.

After a few minutes, the enemy artillery began to put it back on us, some of his shells bursting unpleasantly close to where I stood. All went well on this occasion. Although there was considerable reply from the machine-guns, the operation was entirely successful, and by 2 am, parties of prisoners, chattering like monkeys, began to reach my Headquarters.

Some 300 were captured, including two very dapper looking unwounded officers, one of whom knew a little French. As he spoke he smiled amiably, occasionally appealing to his friend – when asked a question – and laying his hand caressingly on his shoulder. A finicky kind of creature he looked, and mighty glad to be out of it. No fool either, you will perhaps say. We also captured a number of machine-guns and some trench mortars.

At 4.45 in the morning, I went forward to the Companies. With my guide – a runner named French – I led off along the railway cutting. Presently we stepped out across the open. It was all right until we got to within 300 yards of the Bray–Albert road. Then the stuff began to fly. An SOS alarm rocket went up from some of our troops in front, signifying a counter-attack by the enemy. It was a false alarm but, none the less, the machine-guns began to rattle, and soon we found ourselves advancing through quite a storm of bullets which whistled past or sent up little spurts of dust as they spattered the ground around us. What a fool I am, thought I, to have followed this boy's short cut across the open instead of practising ordinary discretion and sticking to the railway. He was unimposing to look at, with spectacles and a smile:– in peacetime a clerk in some office: but I never saw anyone more callous to danger than he. He won't last long, I decided, and sure enough he has been hit since, though I hope and believe not seriously.

We walked on. As we neared the road a wounded man lying on the grass, a hundred yards away, called out for help. My runner, Lewington, and Private Wells – a servant – went out from the road and brought him in a few minutes later, still under heavy machine-gun fire. I helped them to lift him on to a stretcher. He had been hit badly in the stomach, so that his vitals were protruding. But, as he lay, he muttered plaintively, 'Oh, if I could only come across the man as did that'. He was carried off to the Aid Post.

Throughout the day, the enemy continued to pound our lines, but though the men were only lightly dug in they stuck it, and well before midday the situation was soundly in hand.

Shortly after noon, I received orders from the Brigadier concerning an advance to be made during the coming night, to a line some 2,500 yards further forward. The Civil Service Rifles were to attack on the right of the Brigade and I went forward with the Adjutant (Captain Paul Davenport MC)[10], to pass these orders on.

Owing to a misunderstanding, two of the Company Commanders had mistaken the rendezvous, so Davenport and I spent an hour and a half or more, waiting with the remaining Company Commanders, under furious bombardment all the time.

It is a good thing that Battalion Commanders and Adjutants should have their share of this sort of thing to remind them of the troubles of the firing line, and it is a pity that the experience does not more often go higher. As usual, however, the damage done on this occasion was trivial in proportion to the expenditure of ammunition, though one direct hit was obtained a few yards down the road from where we stood, killing and wounding some good men, including a sergeant who was due to go home for a commission, and who, unfortunately, was killed.

General Kennedy sent me a couple of bottles of Veuve Cliquot, 1906, with his final orders for the attack that evening. He is the most thoughtful and generous of Brigadiers, and the act was typical of him. I felt, however, that the Company Commanders deserved it more than I, and so sent the champagne on to them. When I saw them later, I asked how they had enjoyed it, and was told that they had given it to the sergeants:– I was not greatly pleased, as that was not what I had intended.

This wine was some of the last remaining of a priceless collection which the General had bought from the French during the retreat last March. I do not think there is anyone else in the army who would have had the wit to think of such a thing at such a time. When the enemy was advancing on Epernay it occurred to him that there ought to be some good wine going cheap, and he actually sent a motor lorry, in the midst of all the confusion, to buy up what he could for his Brigade.

To return to the attack of the night of the 24th/25th. Zero hour was to be 2.30 am. The battalion assembled for the attack on the Bray–Fricourt road. Near to the assembly position lay many of our men, killed during the previous day or two. Here was a group of ten, evidently all mown down by the same sweep of some machine-gun. There, individual dead and groups of two or three, and, thankfully to say, there were German dead as well.

The casualties from our attack, amounted to some thirty-five, including two officers – one of whom had his foot blown off, and most, if not all, were caused by our own barrage. It is surprising how calmly such accidents have come to be regarded, even by the infantry who are the sufferers. But the sense of comradeship and understanding between the two arms is almost perfect nowadays. Each appreciates the difficulties of the other's job, and the Infantry Commander has often to resist a strong temptation to complain of too close shooting for fear that, next time, the artillery-man in his anxiety to avoid accidents may lift his guns too much. It is generally better economy to risk a few casualties from our own fire than that the artillery should shoot too much for safety. More casualties may be caused in the attack by the machine-guns of the enemy remaining in action between our infantry and our barrage, than are ever likely to result from accidents through closer shooting.

From the infantry point of view, the task of following closely behind the barrage is not the easy matter that it sounds in the lecture rooms behind the line. Owing to the 'error' of each gun, the so-called 'barrage line' is in reality an irregular and varying belt, perhaps 150 yards in width. It requires much individual judgement on the part of the men to advance at exactly the proper speed – neither too fast nor too slow. It is a difficult business in daylight, and much more so in the dark, especially in the heat and turmoil of an engagement.[11]

At half-past four in the morning I left Happy Valley to visit the Companies. A thick fog had settled down which completely blotted out the landscape. It was obvious directly I came across my men that the battalion had not reached its objective: but how to find the objective in the fog, that was the trouble. I knew that Bronfay Farm – a famous landmark well known to me in 1916 – stood close in front; but as it was impossible to see further than 20 yards, it was difficult to find the place.

However, after a time the sun burst through the fog, and to my delight revealed Bronfay, and I was able to direct the battalion to its proper position.

Then I returned to Happy Valley, where my Headquarters were, passing on the way a wounded German officer who spoke some English and who told me he had lain out through two of our bombardments. He was lucky to be alive. Others belonging to his side were lying about, less fortunate than he. I imagine they were mostly men left behind by the retiring enemy to do destruction work. Hand charges of high explosive lay beside some of them. There were also machine-gunners, those brave picked men whom the enemy leaves behind to cover his armies in retreat.

Beside the guns lay many of the gunners, dead; and wherever I looked – whether on the banks or among the dug-outs, or among the bushes, I saw dead Germans – boys many of them, lying singly and in groups. There were also a number of German wounded. God knows how long they had lain there. They had crept into the dug-outs, some of them: others were still in the open. They were quite exhausted. One scarcely breathed at all. Another (very young), whose sufferings had clearly reached the limit of endurance, muttered prayers that the end might come quickly. Between us we got them collected, including the English-speaking officer I mentioned earlier. A doctor dressed their wounds and they were sent to the rear.

The patience and dog-like resignation of the wounded is one of the miracles of the war. It is most striking.

In the afternoon General Kennedy brought up Major Desmond Young, my new second in command, and at the Brigadier's urgent wish I left him in charge of the battalion, which was withdrawn from the front line the same night and bivouacked.

At 7 am on the morning of the 30th, we marched to Maurepas Ravine, where we halted, and scattered in shell-holes. The German 'Heavies' were busy all that day, and at 3.15 pm, a big shell burst on the further slope of the ravine – quite half a mile away – and a piece hit Davenport, who at the time was walking between myself and Knox, the American doctor. So I lost my Adjutant. He is now in England, and a great loss he is, since he is a most able, courageous and valuable officer.

The matter is of interest as indicating the enormous spread caused by the instantaneous – the so-called 106 fuse – which is so much used nowadays both by the enemy and ourselves. Such shells burst instantaneously, as the nose touches the ground, and the pieces fly horizontally to a great distance. They make scarcely any crater at all, and, consequently, it is unlikely that there will be much cover for advancing infantry on the battlefields of the future.[12]

We spent the night and the following day and night in the Ravine, sleeping and feeding comfortably in musty smelling huts provided by the enemy. These were built of wood, of which he seems to have had a plentiful supply, and showed every sign of hasty abandonment. The musty smell of the German huts and dug-outs is very peculiar, and will, I feel sure, remain familiar to my nostrils till my dying day.

At 3 pm on August 31, I got orders for an attack to be delivered by the Brigade at 5.30 the following morning, in conjunction with the 141st Brigade on the right and the 55th Brigade (18th Division) on the left. The objective was to be an old line of trenches skirting the south-west edge of St. Pierre Vaast Wood.

I watched the opening of the battle from outside the door of my shelter with Colonel Kaye, commanding the 17th London Regiment, which forms part of the Brigade, and having stood there some ten minutes we parted, I stepping down into my dug-out, he into his, which was immediately opposite. Two seconds later a shell fell on the exact spot where we had been standing, crashing in both doorways. The lights went out and for a few moments all was dust and darkness. Then, when the candles had been lit, we counted the cost. Colonel Kaye's American doctor was the first to be dragged into my dug-out. His face and clothes were white from the chalk dust raised by the explosion, and one of his legs was blown off. It was the first time he had ever been under fire. As he lay he gave instructions as to how he should be handled. He was got away to the rear, but he did not survive more than a few hours. The same shell killed the gas sentry outright, hit my signalling sergeant (Moore) so badly that he died after a short interval, and wounded several runners.

In the meantime, the attack was going well, and prisoners began to come back within five to ten minutes after Zero. One of my Company Commanders (Lieut. Lascelles) and another officer (a South African – 2nd Lieut. Kirk), whose first day in action in France it was, were killed early during the advance, but otherwise losses were slight, and by 7.30 am, all objectives had been reached and were being consolidated.

Large numbers of prisoners and machine-guns were captured, the battalion's share amounting to 200 prisoners, and some ten machine-guns. Included among the former were two doctors, whom we impressed, while others were as usual made to act as stretcher-bearers. A motor ambulance was also captured.

Later in the morning, I got orders to the effect that the battalion would be relieved during the night and would take part in an operation the following morning, in support to the 74th (dismounted Yeomanry) Division.

The plan, which was complicated and ambitious, was that the 74th Division should attack, their objective being Nurlu. Our Brigade was to follow in close support, the Civil Service Rifles on the left. After crossing the Canal du Nord, the Brigade was to wheel to the left, forming a defensive flank on the high ground to the north-east of Moislains.

The battalion advanced in two waves, Desmond Young, second in command, leading. I with my acting Adjutant, Captain Whiteley, followed with the rear Companies. From the start we came under heavy artillery and machine-gun fire as we moved down the slope to the south-west of Moislains.

In spite of casualties amounting to over half its fighting strength, the battalion – or what was left of it – succeeded in establishing itself in a trench close to the west of the village, with some men from other battalions of the Brigade and a few Yeomanry.

I will try and picture what I saw. Speaking of my own battalion, most of the men are very young – in fact, quite boys. They wear khaki shorts with grey hose-fops turned down over their puttees. On their sleeves they have canary yellow hearts as a distinguishing badge.[13]

The sun began to rise very brightly as we started, and gave us our direction, which was due eastwards. Almost immediately the enemy opened with a heavy artillery barrage which he soon supplemented with machine-gun fire. In all directions among the advancing battalion, the shells started to burst, and the casualties soon began to accumulate. Knox, the American doctor, opened an aid-post in an open trench which we passed over, where he dressed the wounded throughout the day under shellfire. The battalion continued its advance. The machine-gun fire grew heavier and heavier. It came from the front and from both flanks. With their khaki 'shorts' showing about 4 inches of bare knee, the men went forward, looking, as Desmond Young said, like a lot of boys going to a football match. The runners pushed their bicycles.

It was a truly wonderful sight: each man with his shoulders squared to the objective, walking with bayonet fixed, apparently unconcerned, through the deadly fire; many dropping; the remainder carrying on; needing no pushing or exhorting; each individual acting as a host in himself. The stretcher-bearers went about coolly, at the walk, from one wounded man to another. I remember one stretcher-bearer in particular – a boy of about nineteen, who was wounded later in the day – and who was really admirable in his utter sang-froid and disregard of self.

The last hundred-yard lap was the worst, and had it not been that the ground was pitted with shell-holes, not one of us could have got across it alive. Towards the end, two men fell beside me – not more than a couple of feet away – one so badly wounded that he died almost immediately. Then we reached the trench I have spoken of, and, though the enemy tried hard to throw us out by every means at his disposal, we managed to stay there. Some bombers got behind us whom we were unable to tackle properly, owing to our having run out of bombs.

For a time the situation looked precarious. The shelling, too, was very furious for some hours; but in the end things settled down, and though we were a small party and semi-isolated, we became more or less established.

At about 9 am, having failed in our efforts to get communication with the rear, Colonel Dawes, commanding the 21st Battalion, went back, and, at 1 pm, still having been unable to secure communication, I went back myself, leaving Desmond Young in charge of the men of the Brigade that still held the forward trench.

I made my way to the nearest telephone which was in an old limestone quarry on the Rancourt–Peronne road. There was a sort of communication trench that I was able to follow. At intervals along the trench lay the dead and wounded, many of them. I passed a group of five signallers, evidently killed by the same shell, and another of seven or eight men swept down together by machine-gun fire.

I saw Knox as I passed his aid-post, and told him of the wounded; and he and Farebrother, the Chaplain, went out later with a party and fetched them in.

At my position of assembly (in Dallas Trench), in addition to the usual dead horses, there was an abandoned German field battery – the whizz-bang that we have learned to know so well – with two gunners, dead, beside it. Speaking of horses, I have never seen so many dead horses as during this recent semi-open fighting, and we, too, have paid our toll in this respect, the battalion having on one single day (September 1) lost seven horses killed and three wounded.[14] Dead horses and derelict tanks have been a feature, and I have counted as many as nine or ten of the latter without changing my position.

In the middle of the night I was awakened from a much needed sleep. General Kennedy was on the telephone. He gave me directions for a further advance to be made in the morning, and his way of doing this was characteristic.

'Got your map?' he asked.

'Yes, General.'

'See line-so and so?'

'Yes, General,' said I, hurriedly picking out the map readings he gave me with the aid of a candle.

'Well, you start from there at 8 am. Your objective is this line . . . ,' and he gave a further line of map readings. Then he switched off.

He never fusses, thank God: and he leaves all details to the men whose duty it is to do the job. And that, I venture to think, is the proper way to fight battles.

At 8 am (September 6) the battalion was again formed up for the attack. It looked like a nasty bit of country on account of some thick woods we had to go through, but all went well. Desmond Young and I had been taking it in turn to go forward with the battalion, and it was my turn this day.

The men advanced just a little too far, having passed over the crest of a ridge, where they had come under full view of the enemy. The latter was taking full advantage of the conspicuous target presented, and was pounding unmercifully with artillery and machine-gun fire. This, however, was only for a minute or two. The battalion, under Captain Eccles, turned and walked some 50 yards back over the crest, and as it reached the reverse slope each man again turned and faced the enemy. Gibbs and I watched the movement, and the coolness and deliberation with which it was carried out was admirable.

Having seen the battalion into position I returned to my advanced Headquarters. I was soaked with sweat (it was a sweltering day), and I took off all my upper garments, to cool.

I found Desmond Young justifiably pleased with himself, having discovered a fine piano in Bois Epinette – one of the woods we had taken – in what had evidently been a German Corps or Divisional Headquarters. It was the only thing left behind. It weighs about half a ton, but he got it away in the mess-cart, and we have lugged it about ever since, and have had plenty of music out of it. It will ultimately help to furnish the Regimental Depot at Somerset House.

During the night we were relieved, and bivouacked, and yesterday we were brought here, by motor-bus, to Heilly, on the Ancre. Our casualties had amounted to the following:[15]

Aug. 24–30	Officers.	Wounded	–	3
	NCOs and Men.	Killed	–	7
		Wounded	–	48
Aug. 31–	Officers.	Killed	–	5
Sept. 6		Wounded	–	8
		Missing	–	1
	NCOs and Men.	Killed	–	70
		Wounded	–	229
		Missing	–	18
				389

P.S. While waiting yesterday morning for the buses to arrive, with some of my officers, I explored the battlefield of September 2.

We retraced the last lap of the attack, and identified the trenches through which the enemy had tried to outflank us. We found their bombing posts, with the stick-bombs still lying on the fire-step, ready to throw. They had paid their toll. All had indeed gone well, but that last exposed slope was a sorry sight. There were our Lewis guns, many of them still mounted and pointed towards the enemy positions – the gunners beside them. The dead lay thick, their packs opened and the contents scattered; their letters and little souvenirs they had carried, thrown out by the ghouls of the battlefield, littered the ground beside them. Beside one boy lay a black earthenware cat, his mascot, which had not saved him. We had certainly paid heavily for this little scrap of trench.

We buried an officer and twenty-four men of the Civil Service Rifles there and then, and many others of the Brigade were still left lying. There was no time for anything elaborate, so the poor bodies with their blackened faces were just lifted into shell-holes or into the trench, one or two or three or four together, and earth was put over them. Then a rifle, with bayonet fixed, was stuck into the ground, butt uppermost, to mark each grave – with the names on a bit of paper attached to the trigger-guard.

Then, after Farebrother had read the burial service, we left them, and the same afternoon reached the Ancre, in which we bathed.

This evening I had my first opportunity of seeing the battalion quarter guard mounted. It is the practice in the battalion for the band to play at guard-mounting when out of the line, ending up always, as the old guard marches away, with the hymn 'Abide with Me'. It is a pathetic tune, I think, and always makes a lump come into my throat.

9 September 1918 [Heilly]

My Headquarters are below the old château, with its wonderful red-brick wall, in a house, where, in 1916, a restaurant was kept by some refugee French ladies. We used at that time to come over to it – some 3 or

4 miles from the Guards Entrenching Battalion in the Bois des Tailles, to get the only good meals which were procurable within range.

It was funny to find myself back in this house – now deserted, after two years, and to find it so changed and wrecked, though still good enough to put up in. My bedroom, which is upstairs, has a shell-hole through the ceiling, and the only bit of furniture in it when we arrived was an iron bedstead, so bent and broken that I had made plans to sleep on the floor.

However, after dark, I noticed something going on outside, and, on enquiry, found that the servants had found a fine French mattress in the village, which they were hauling up through the window for my use. It was entirely their own idea.

12 September 1918 [Auchel, Pas de Calais]

We marched from Chocques, this morning, headed by the band – a sadly depleted battalion, less than two Companies strong, in spite of drafts from home that have joined during the last few days.

We have come to Auchel, a big coal-mining village, where there are shops and estaminets and women and children, and where the officers will have sheets, and every NCO will have some sort of a bed to sleep in.

It is a great contrast to the scenes we have left in the shocking wilderness of the Somme. Everybody has his tail well up, and though I question if you would think much of our village if you saw it, both officers and men might easily have arrived in Paris or London, so beaming are their faces. We are to remain here a fortnight, to refit and receive reinforcements.

Our band is thirty-three strong. We do not risk it in battle unless we are absolutely tied up for stretcher-bearers.

14 September 1918 [Auchel, Pas de Calais]

The men are loving their time here. They sit in the Estaminets[16] – an atmosphere you could hardly breathe in – smoking, and singing, and airing their French. It is just the sort of change they want after all they have gone through – a taste of town life, however remote from the ideal.

15 September 1918 [Auchel, Pas de Calais]

This morning General Birdwood[17] attended a Brigade open-air service, held on the Auchel aerodrome. He brought with him Talbot (son of the Bishop of Winchester), who preached. When he had finished, General Birdwood addressed the Brigade; then the battalions marched past him, and the Battalion Commanders were introduced.

The newspapers have always made such a hero of him that I was prepared to be disappointed: but he certainly has a clear eye and a taking manner both with officers and men: and he talked sound common sense in his address to the Brigade, which is more than one always hears on these occasions.

In appearance he is straight and upright, and he has far less 'red tab' about him than the most junior member of his staff. He does not even wear a 'red hat'. Moreover, he is evidently not punctilious about his clothing, for the spikes of the buckle of his belt were missing, and the latter was done up anyhow.

So huge is the scale on which this war is being fought that it is a great event to see one's Army Commander.

I remember once being asked when on leave, what the men thought of Haig – by a very intelligent man, too. It was during one of the bad times. He asked me this question, and added: 'If, by now, they don't look on him as a demigod, it proves that he is not the right man and ought to go'.

You might as well ask what the private soldier thinks of God. He knows about the same amount of each. Though I have been in every army in France, even I have never seen the Commander-in-Chief. I have only seen my Army Commander on four occasions in over three years – Plumer twice, and Birdwood twice.[18]

16 September 1918 [Auchel, Pas de Calais]

I have just dined with Wyndham Portal. After dinner was over, we watched a performance by Leslie Henson's[19] concert party, in an aeroplane hangar.

Leslie Henson has come out here from 'Theodore & Co.,' having been given a commission in the RAF, and 'does his bit' by entertaining the troops. It is a fine thing for them and goes far to keep them happy. There were, as usual, some good female impersonators, and the show was altogether splendid.

Last night General Kennedy came to dinner in the mess, and the cook made a very successful effort. We had a string trio playing in the next room.

There is some first-class talent in the battalion. Knox, the American doctor, has a voice which is not only, by nature, of extraordinary quality, but is perfectly trained: so, with our captured piano, we have plenty of music. In addition, there are the Divisional 'Follies' who are always good.

One of their jokes, which goes down well with a front-line audience, is: 'What is a Patriot?'

Answer: 'A man who sheds your blood for his country!'

General Morland,[20] the Corps Commander, visited us this morning and I took him round the battalion, which was out training. It is a sad sight to see it so reduced. To be added to our losses since I joined under four weeks ago, the battalion had already lost 140 men and officers in the trenches during the four days preceding my arrival.

That makes a total of 529, which is nearly equivalent to the fighting strength of a battalion, nowadays.

*   *   *

17 September 1918 [Auchel, Pas de Calais]

I dined with Colonel Dawes, and was given the best dinner of its kind I have had in France. Dawes is only twenty-seven, but has commanded a battalion, except when he was wounded, since August, 1916. He is quite deaf in one ear, having had a bullet through it.

Otherwise, I spent the day intensively, writing up the official narrative of the recent fighting, which, thankfully, I have now finished, as well as the recommendations for award – that thankless and most difficult of all the duties, apart from the heavy work of rebuilding the battalion, which fall to a Battalion Commander after every battle.

Honours are not, as you might logically suppose, awarded in bulk to a battalion, in proportion to its merit, and left to the Colonel and his Brigadier to distribute in such manner as they think fit. Would that they were! No. They have to be dragged out of the Higher Authorities like back teeth. In each individual recommendation a 'specific act' must be cited, which, if there is to be any chance of favourable consideration, must be made to 'stand out'.

It must be couched in the flamboyant language of the Penny Dreadful, and the result often is that the most deserving cases get cut out by the Authorities, far behind the line. Their function is to decide these matters, and who, as a rule, have no personal or first-hand knowledge of the men or the conditions upon which they pass judgement.

It has been said that the pen is mightier than the sword, and I can truthfully say that, under our system, if a battalion is to get its proper share of honours, it is essential that its Commander should have at his disposal – not necessarily a truthful but at least a flowery pen. No matter how brilliant the performance, it must be dressed up in language which would startle the performer – generally a modest man – could he see it, so gaudily must the lily be painted.

Apropos of which a story is told of a certain CO who once recommended one of his men for a Military Medal. The recommendation was turned down, the 'story', presumably, not being considered good enough. The CO was disappointed, since the case was a particularly deserving one, but, nothing daunted, he tried again. He rewrote the story, racking his brains for the most extravagant language he could muster. His success exceeded his wildest expectations. The man got a VC.

Lord! How I hate the system! I get letters from fathers, appealing for their sons. Mr. McCreery, from Ireland, points out that Corporal McCreery has been fighting in the trenches for two years, and more, and it would do him so much good when he returns to the RIC, to have something to wear. But these things are not for such as he.

I have known men – good men too – eating their hearts out through want of recognition. How petty this sounds. Yet a ribbon is the only prize in war for the ordinary soldier. It is the outward visible sign – the ocular proof – to bring home to his people, that he has done his job well: and, say what you may, a man's prowess, when the war is over, will be assessed by the number of his ribbons.

Personally, I often wish that this form of reward did not exist, seeing that ribbons must be distributed by men, not gods. By the way, if they were given by God, how many an iridescent breast would cease to sparkle;– and the contrary!

Then, think of the Foreign decorations! These are handed over to our War Office in batches, at more or less regular intervals, by all of the Allies. How many ever reach the front line? I have known perhaps half a dozen to do so in my experience.

It is a thousand pities that these things should be as they are, since the natural effect is that the bitter aloofness that too often exists between the fighting and writing sections of the army, keeps growing.

Lately, there has been talk of limiting the award of fighting honours for action in face of the enemy. Will the rule be observed rigidly? I wonder. In any case, the decision comes late, since it may be presumed that most if not all those of the Staff that count have already got what they want, though some of them are doubtless hard to satisfy.

As for wound stripes, I don't know who invented <u>them</u>. Personally, I think they are un-English, besides being absurd. There are a few people who seem to make a hobby of collecting them. It is not difficult. It is only necessary to be gassed, however slightly, in order to appear in the casualty list. I have even heard of a case where a scratch on a wire entanglement was considered sufficient. The absurdity of the whole thing is that a 'wound' of such a kind – so far as wound stripes are concerned – ranks equally with the loss of a leg or eye. Or two legs and two eyes for that matter, so long as they are all lost at the same time.[21]

18 September 1918 [Auchel, Pas de Calais]

I have a surprise for you. We leave for the Italian front on Saturday. I was told this yesterday in confidence. Today it is official. Of course, if the enemy makes a move between now and then it may be off: otherwise, we go.

I will not disguise the fact that the prospect of a change of climate and 'entourage' has caused delight among the troops, as it has to myself. We shall be four days on a troop train. I say I am glad, but, truthfully, I shall feel a little sorry at leaving France. It is a cursed war, and I dislike the whole business as much as anybody. Yet I love it: it has been the breath of life to me, and I shall always look back upon the time I have spent here with great happiness.

Eric Segrave – who is now a Brigadier – motored over to see us today. He is just the same as he was nineteen years ago. He got quite sad when it was time to leave. He simply worships this battalion, and looked almost homesick as he went off to rejoin his Brigade, though the latter belongs to the 51st Division, which our enemies reckon to be one of the best in France.

He says commanding a battalion is four times more difficult and ten times more interesting than commanding a Brigade. He says: 'Of course they un-gum Brigadiers. There are so many Brigadiers and so few Brigades. But good Battalion Commanders are very hard to get'.

All the same, a good many Battalion Commanders have been un-gummed during the last few weeks.[22]

28 September 1918 [Foufflin-Ricametz]

My darling Joan,

I have been bad at writing, haven't I? But, if you only knew the life I have been leading – first fighting for sixteen days, four days without sleep, then reorganising the battalion after its heavy losses; then travelling and marching. But I have made a point of keeping up my letters to Mother. I think I have three letters to thank you for.

By the way, I sent off a packet of chocolates a day or two ago. There were two packets for each of you elder ones. And, a few days before that, I sent you a pamphlet of optical illusions which I thought would amuse you.

Uncle Edmund[23] has sent me a beautiful great chestnut horse from Abbeville which I shall take away with me to _____. He is perfectly splendid and is admired by everybody. Our Brigade Major, who is a Coldstreamer, told me today that it was the best horse he had ever seen in an infantry regiment in France. If Uncle Edmund is still at Heathfield, will you tell him all this.

Wasn't it splendid getting the prayer book back? But what a pity it was not with me during the recent fighting.

Your loving Daddy.

1 October 1918 [Foufflin-Ricametz]

After several orders and counter-orders, the move to Italy is off, and we are going back to the line. The transport moves today. The rest of us start tomorrow. I feel sorry for myself, but I can tell you I felt ten times more sorry for the men when I inspected the battalion this morning.

8 October 1918 [Le Maisnil]

There is no continuous front line nowadays. A railway embankment separates us from the enemy, who has burrowed into it in parts, and occupies some of the culverts which run through it. We hold the line by posts, and so does he, and the interesting thing is that neither side knows for certain exactly where the other's posts are.

This afternoon I visited the outpost line with my orderly, Corporal Douglas. On the way we passed a little group of five dead machine-gunners. An unlucky 'whizz-bang' had hit their emplacement, killing the five and wounding a sixth, so badly that he is not likely to recover.

10 October 1918 [Le Maisnil]

I write in a wooden hut, built by the enemy. It is one of a group which he forgot to burn in his retirement. It is surrounded by a fence, 12 feet high and composed of twenty strands of barbed wire. It is provided with a battery of concrete cauldrons, and I can only suppose was made for herding prisoners of war. Well, anyhow, we are in it now, though not as prisoners.

I sent for the piano today, and after dinner we had music. Small, the Intelligence Officer, who is a wonderful pianist, played, while the doctor sang. It seems funny to think of first-class music in a wooden hut, 3,000 yards behind the firing line. That would not have been prudent six months ago.

13 October 1918 [Maisnil]

The weather is cold and wet and dismal. I went for a long walk with Farebrother this (Sunday) afternoon, and explored again the old front line.

We passed the ancient wall of one of the earliest Carthusian monasteries in France, a hundred yards or less in front of which our old fire-trench runs, while the support line cuts across the great enclosure, and a main communication trench meanders through it. In the middle is the monks' fishpond, and between the latter and the wall are the graves of some of our soldiers.

We walked on in a south-westerly direction, to where No Man's Land becomes narrow and has been mined. Some Australian dead of perhaps two years ago – or rather their bones, recognisable by the shreds of uniform – still lie there, and we will bury them tomorrow. Beside them lie their rifles, shattered since by shell-fire, and the bombs they carried when they went out to the attack in which they lost their lives.

14 October 1918 (Midnight) [Estaires]

Again, we are for Italy. We were relieved by the 57th Division this evening and have marched back well behind the line;– a march which we continue tomorrow. I wonder if this is my exit from the war. The latest 'peace' news rather suggests that it may be so. Well, if it is over, how glad we shall all be. Yet, it has been a wonderful experience, and, strange though it may seem, I have enjoyed it. The very frightfulness of it all has punctuated and emphasised the happy intervals. Is it selfish to say this? In doing so I do not forget the long-drawn and weary anxiety that it has meant for you.

The battalion which relieved us was the old 1st Royal Munster Fusiliers, with whom, as you will remember, I was in the 47th Brigade, and whom I last saw on March 27 last, during the retreat towards Amiens. They have again suffered heavily since that day, their Colonel (Kane)[24] and most of the other officers I knew having been killed during the month that has just passed. However, I was glad to find Nightingale[25] and Marsden (second in command and Adjutant) still with them. We marched away from Le Maisnil in the moonlight, the band playing.

Farebrother went out this morning with two pioneers and buried the Australians whom we found yesterday. He buried twelve.

15 October 1918 [St. Venant]

For two days, until we reached the old German front line of the summer of this year, we had marched over country and through towns as big as Portsmouth or Southampton, not one house of which has escaped the destroying hand of the enemy. Not even the most humble cottage has been overlooked, so 'thoroughly' has the work been accomplished.

During the latter part of the march we passed women who had just returned following up the enemy's withdrawal, to inspect the damage done to their homes.

It was very harrowing to watch them. Some of the very young seemed cheery enough, but the others wore sad faces as they searched the ruins with their handkerchiefs to their eyes, picking out bits of broken crockery or any kind of rubbish, and collecting, with the utmost care, old, ragged, shell-torn or half-burnt clothing;– stuff, one would think, fit only for the incinerator.

It is tragic, and, if the people who were responsible for these cruel outrages are to be let off, it is all wrong. Let anyone who may have doubts on this point, picture his wife or mother returning to her home to find every particle of furniture, everything of any value, gone; the rest buried under a heap of brick-dust, produced – not by shell-fire or the accident of war – but wantonly, by organised gangs of destroyers employing high-explosive. And this description applies to hundreds of square miles of territory, including endless villages, towns, and cities. Thank God, I say on this occasion, we British are not famed for being 'thorough'.

16 October 1918 [St. Venant]

We hang about, at present in perfect safety, amid the ruins of St. Venant. Little groups of two or three women in black, with a few children, keep returning to search among the ruins. Occasionally, they find their home not quite destroyed, and then they set to clear away the wreckage and scrub the floors, and rig up what bits of furniture they can find. It is wonderful to watch their industry and patience. What a pity that such sights are not always on tap, when one is worrying about the trivialities that often loom so large in ordinary life! What a tonic it would be.

These women seem to live without sustenance. They cannot have much money and if they have, there is nothing to buy. There is no fuel except the rafters of the houses, and food must be exceedingly scarce. Yet they carry on, and show no outward sign of distress. They are doing all this without

189

'man' help, or practically so. I have seen one or two French soldiers on leave, but that is all.

17 October 1918 [Fontes]

We marched again this morning still further back, to Fontes, where I write from an extremely cheerful billet, with electric light, and such a bed. I was pleased to find, on arrival, that my Adjutant, Davenport, who was wounded on August 30, had rejoined the battalion.

Before leaving St. Venant, I presented the poor lady with whom I had been billeted with a nice chair which we have been carrying about the last few days, having 'salved' it from a German Mebu near Le Maisnil. The battalion pioneers also patched up her windows with pieces cut out of an old sheet, and mended her chimney, which had been hit by a shell, so that she could light a fire.

She had lost most of her belongings – 'Volé,' she said, 'par les soldats Anglais'. She took me and showed me her safe, upstairs, which I must confess had been broken open very scientifically, though fortunately, as she explained, without gain to the looter, since only unpaid bills were in it. As I was leaving she came up rather remorsefully and apologised for having said it was 'les Anglais' who had done the damage. 'She had been mistaken'. It was 'les Ecossais'. She little knew she hit me either way.

Perhaps it may have been true, but you must not judge too harshly. The battle line was immediately in front of the town when the incident must have happened, and the enemy was advancing fast in overwhelming numbers. No doubt some men argued: 'If there is anything to be had, it is better that we should have it than the Germans.' After all, it is culpable not to destroy valuable material when it appears certain that it must fall into the hands of the enemy. But one would prefer that the soldiers kept their hands clean.

19 October 1918 [Fontes]

When last I referred to the subject we were definitely for Italy. Today Italy is definitely off. If a private commercial venture were run on these lines, I wonder how long it would last!

20 October 1918 (Sunday) [Fontes]

In a few days we are to take part in a triumphal march through Lille!

Since I first came to France and was put in the trenches in front of La Bassée, I always said: 'When the entry into Lille takes place, I hope I shall be there': and, today, I find myself detailed for it.

25 October 1918 [Fontes]

I have been reading Haig's despatch dealing with the March Retreat. It appears we were in the very centre of the German attack, yet the 16th

(Irish) Division is not mentioned, and how the General who commanded the 5th Army at that time could have made the omission, is difficult to understand.[26] Nevertheless, the report is intensely interesting to me. Ronssoy, Ste. Emilie, and Villers Faucon, which stand out so prominently, were the scenes of our fighting on March 21 and 22, and of our counter-attack at midday on the 21st.

Proyart, which also figures with such importance, was the place where we stood on March 26 and 27. What then remained of the Division was lined up a hundred yards in front of the village. There was no other Division so near as ours; yet another Division, and not ours, is mentioned. Perhaps this is because it was by that time so reduced as to be considered negligible. Yet that is no excuse.[27]

I tried to describe to you at the time how our left was in the air, but until I read Haig's report, I never realised how critical the position really was during those two days.

From the report I now learn that the Army on our left – against whose right flank we had stood – had fallen back miles; and when I saw the Germans filtering past our left, they were not passing through a gap a few hundred yards wide (as I thought), but through a gap five miles wide! Well, all I can say is that the enemy, on that occasion, threw away a golden opportunity, and how any of us survived was a miracle of God.[28]

26 October 1918 [Lomme]

We are in the western outskirts of Lille, having come here by train today, and I with my Headquarters am billeted in an imposing – almost baronial – house. It looks as if it ought to be in the centre of a big park, instead of lining a suburban street, as it does. The house is empty except for ourselves and some refugees who live in the kitchen. In normal times it is, no doubt, the home of one of the formerly wealthy manufacturers of this great city, whose practice it is to build the palaces in which they live, near their works, and among the more humble habitations of their work people, which seem almost squalid by comparison.

Until a few days ago, as you know, these parts were in the hands of the enemy. Until three days ago, many of the inhabitants had not tasted fresh meat for twelve months, and had depended for their sustenance on the American Relief Committee, whose white bread, I am assured, was often eaten by the enemy, who substituted black bread in its stead.

From Perenchies, where we detrained, we had a 3-mile march in the dark. The guns in front – on the far side of Lille – flashed distantly, and reminded us of our destination.

As we reached the suburbs, our band struck up the 'Marseillaise'. It was happy inspiration, and I shall never forget the scene which it provoked. The people came running from their houses – old and young, men, women and children – carrying lamps and candles. They followed the battalion, clapping and cheering. It was the first time for over four years that they had heard troops marching to that tune. And the 'Marseillaise' is a fine tune to march to, and in spite of not being a Frenchman, I feel the thrill of it each time I hear it.

Tomorrow (Sunday) we devote to 'polishing up' for the great 'march-through'.

27 October 1918 [Lomme]

Today, after lunching with Dawes I walked with Farebrother and Knox into Lille – on special pass, since the town is 'out of bounds' for troops. The 5th Army, represented by our Division, which was opposite the city during the enemy's withdrawal, will make its official entry tomorrow.

It is a novel and unique experience for most of us to walk into a town, every inhabitant of which looks at us like a mother at her sons. The ladies welcomed us with smiles. The children were more demonstrative. They rushed at us and seized our hands. They clung on to us till they had completely satisfied their curiosity – a process which took some time, since many of them can scarcely have been fledged when the war started, and they had certainly never seen an Englishman in uniform before. A little red-haired girl followed us like a lapdog, half-way through the town.

The stories I have heard today of how these poor people have, for over four years, been bullied, have aroused in me a bitterness which I have never felt before, and which, somehow, we did not get in the trenches. It is extraordinary, now, to think backwards and to picture the grinding down of the inhabitants of this great city behind the German lines and in front of where we stood during all those years.

Today, the enemy has gone, and in going has given us some curious illustrations of his mentality. He did not dare flatten Lille as he has so many other cities; but, in leaving, presumably as an emblem of his hatred, he has used the upstairs rooms of many of the houses as latrines. In a bedroom of a great house of this suburb of great houses where we are billeted, where the Brigadier has his Headquarters, and where I dined tonight, a certain article was found in a bedside cupboard. It had been used for a purpose for which it was not designed, and on the cupboard door was chalked a notice in German which, translated, read something as follows: 'Here is a breakfast for an Englishman, made by a good German'.

What do you think of that for 'Kultur'?

Lille, as you know, is (or was) a city of <u>huge</u> factories. So far as I know, every single machine has either been removed to Germany or systematically destroyed. One owner of a mill told me today that when the destroyers came to break up his plant he asked 'for what reason'? They said they wanted iron. Yet they did not take away the iron, which still lies where it formerly stood, blasted to bits ! Was it pure lust of destruction, or part of a pre-arranged plot to injure France commercially? Probably, a bit of both.[29]

These people have become so isolated from the rest of their fellow-countrymen. Why they hardly know the word 'Boche'; and de Caux – our Brigade interpreter – tells me when he entered Lille the first day, wearing his French shrapnel helmet, people asked him 'was he a pompier (a fireman)?' They had not seen a French picture paper since the war began. Yet they live in a town as important as Manchester!

28 October 1918 [Hellemmes-Lille]

Today, in glorious sunshine – the first almost for nearly two months – we marched through Lille. We billeted last night outside the walls, in the western suburb known as Lomme, and this morning, after passing through Lille from west to east by way of the Rue Lequeux, we passed through the Grande Place – where wooden stands draped in red, white and blue had been erected, and where the Army Commander, General Birdwood, stood:– then, following the Rue Carnot, we marched on through and out of the city by the Louis XIV gate, where the bridge has been destroyed and the road mined by the enemy.

The day has provided a truly wonderful experience. For miles we marched through decorated streets, through immense crowds of cheering citizens: It is a miracle when, in so short a space of time, so many flags can have been obtained. I hear that the very morning the inhabitants awoke to find the enemy gone, women were to be seen running about the streets waving tricolours which had been hidden during the four years and more that Lille has been held in captivity. Each battalion was headed by its band today, ours playing English airs as we passed through the suburbs, and bursting into the 'Marseillaise' when we reached the more fashionable parts, with electrical effect upon the people crowded on the pavements. We entered the Grande Place to the tune of the 'Sambre et Meuse' – the great French marching song; again changing to the 'Marseillaise' as we left it.

The ladies and children gave little souvenir flags to the men, but they fought a little shy of me. Perhaps my rather conspicuous position at the head of the battalion, mounted on a charger which, as you know, is about 17 hands high, put them off. But I was determined not to be outdone, so asked one particular lady if she would give me the flag she was carrying 'pour mes enfants'. This she not only did, but rushed into a house and presently brought out a bunch of little hand-painted paper flags, so that I have been able to send one to each of the children and enclose one herewith, also, for yourself.

On our arrival at Hellemmes-Lille, from where I write, I received a hearty welcome from my host and hostess, M. and Madame Paul Lefèvre. The former speaks English, having lived for seven years at Bolton, in Lancashire. He is a cotton spinner, and is manager of a huge English-owned factory in which the battalion is billeted. The factory has been robbed of every particle of its machinery – like the rest. To give you an idea of the size of this factory I may say that the whole battalion, including the transport (fifty-seven horses plus vehicles and personnel) are quartered in it.

During the German occupation my host and hostess were separated by way of reprisal. He was sent to Vilmar, in Russia, and she to Holzminden, in Germany. Neither was told where the other was. He said he was told it was because he was an Alsace-Lorrainer, and that he was a hostage. No other reason was given. He was kept in a church at Vilmar for seven months, with 50 centimetres in width of ground to sleep upon; and he is a fat old man, well on in the fifties. Think of that![30]

29 October, 1918 [Hellemmes-Lille]

My dearest Joan,

I enclose a little paper flag that was given to me as we marched through the streets of the second city of France yesterday – I was riding at the head of my battalion – on the occasion of the official entry of the British Army. We had a lovely day for it – the first I think for nearly two months.

Do you soon go to Rough Down? Do you remember our carving a 'J' on one of the seats one Sunday afternoon.

Your loving Daddy.

29 October 1918 [Hellemmes-Lille]

This afternoon I again rode into Lille, entering by the Louis XIV Gate, by which we left the city yesterday. A great crater yawns in the roadway opposite this gate, and a wooden trestle made by our engineers replaces the bridge over the moat, which, like the other bridges leading eastwards, has been blown up by the enemy.

On reaching the town, as I found no horse or wheeled traffic other than some belonging to our army, I sent my horses home and walked, so as to be in company with the inhabitants, every one of whom was on foot. No, not quite. I saw a hearse drawn by what poor Osmund would have called a 'skin': indeed, it was less than a skin. It was a skeleton. That was the only horse or vehicle that I saw in Lille today, left behind by the Germans after their merciless occupation of the city.

Knox, the doctor, does quite a large practice among the local inhabitants, as we pass from one place to another, most of their own doctors being away at the war. Anyhow, they come in numbers. Influenza is rampant, and the people find their way to our aid-post. A few days ago a little boy came along who had blown off two of his fingers and damaged an eye, playing with a detonator which he had picked up somewhere. I fear there will be many more such accidents in Northern France and Belgium.

1 November 1918 [Froyennes]

We left Hellemmes-Lille on Wednesday, the 30th, and after we had left we received a rapacious bill from M. Lefèvre – for coal briquettes alleged to have been consumed during our stay in his house! As we had provided him and his wife with provisions the value of which would have bought any few briquettes we may have burned many times over, this was an unpleasant surprise.

I with my Headquarters officers then stayed one night at Chereng, where the battalion billeted in what had been a fine house before the war. I slept in a big bedroom with a white up-to-date enamelled bath attached; but, as every single window throughout the entire building had been broken by aerial-bomb explosions, it was very cold. A woman servant who was in charge told me that one of the bombs (unfortunately ours) had blown off her mistress's leg, and that she was still in hospital.

Last evening, we came up into the front line. It is really becoming a very interesting – not to say extraordinary – war. The country is well built over and both the enemy and our own outposts occupy houses, sometimes not more than a couple of hundred yards apart, from the windows of which they furtively watch one another's movements, and observe the effect of the hurricane bombardments in which we both occasionally indulge.

I may say that it is a style of warfare which provides plenty of incident, and gives considerable scope to the adventurously inclined since without actually going into a house, it is impossible to find out whether it is occupied by the enemy. In one house a curtain was reported by a sentry to be moving in a suspicious manner. When I arrived on the scene, a lively discussion was going on about it. A few minutes later, I heard a hammering sound. It was Desmond Young banging at the door of the house with a pick-axe. He got into this house, too, to find it empty, though he was nearly killed by a sniper in the garden, who saw him through the window. He certainly deserves to get something worth having out of this war.

It is indeed what you might call 'Opéra bouffe' warfare.[31] We are waging it amid charming scenery – the prettiest I have seen in Belgium:– in a rich land of opulent houses and châteaux and great schools and convents; and, incidentally, I may say that every movement we make is observed by the enemy from Mont St. Aubert – a remarkable hill, crowned by a church steeple, that dominates the surrounding country so completely that without going indoors, or behind a wall or hedge, it is practically impossible to get out of sight of it.

The sangfroid of the villagers who have remained is extraordinary. They do not even send away their children, which rather suggests the courage of ignorance, and it is horrifying to see the poor little things playing about, unconscious of the dangers threatening them. It is all so unnecessary. Apart from the 'crump' there is a frequent hail of 'bits' from the anti-aircraft shells, besides the constant possibility of a bullet fired at, or from an aeroplane. Yet not a woman or child has any protection, except the cellar. They go about with bare heads and without gas masks. Yesterday, as my Adjutant (Davenport) and I arrived opposite our new Headquarters, a 5.9-inch shell greeted us, landing in a ploughed field, about 40 yards away. Expecting a second shell we stepped behind a cottage. A woman came out to have a look. I said: 'Ne serait il pas plus sauf pour vous dans la cave.' To which she replied: 'Et pourquoi pas pour vous?'

Towards the firing line, is a great pretentious and rather grotesque white building – in which Prince Ruprecht of Bavaria,[32] Commander of the German 4th Army Corps, had his headquarters for two years. I have been all over it this afternoon and seen the rooms in which he dined and slept, and the bath in which he washed, till a fortnight or three weeks ago. The building has been pierced several times by shells, but on the whole is in good condition.

I dreamed last night that there was an armistice and was woken by the sound of shells.

2 November 1918 [Froyennes]

Last night was very noisy – a night of reciprocal hate; with the result that early this morning the civilians were at last beginning to stream back, pushing handcarts, carrying bundles, and leading children by the hand. And a good thing too, since many of them – so I am assured – are spies. On one handcart I saw a baby, two years old or less, which had come practically from the line of outposts. Think of it. After a night, too, that even the old stagers had found distinctly hot.

Do they not care for their children? or are they just ignorant of the power of shell-fire or the effect of gas? – against which neither they nor their Government appear to have made the smallest provision.

I went on to Prince Ruprecht's white château, in the stables of which I have an advanced platoon. This château suffered considerably from shell-fire last night. Then, after visiting the outposts, I returned towards Froyennes.

As I was about to visit the support Company Headquarters in the village, I noticed a house with a big fresh shell-hole in the wall, through which some very clean looking women were shovelling brick-dust. I knocked at the front door and walked in. I found myself in a convent. Just inside the doorway stood a group of nuns. I made some remark about the shell-hole, and was eagerly invited in 'to see'. They seemed quite delighted that anyone should take an interest in their welfare. Indeed, though it is difficult to believe, they seem to have been left to their fate by whoever the male Belgian authorities were, either in the village or behind it, who were responsible for their safety.

The room I was taken to was the usual convent 'parlour' – that is to say what was left of it – with the usual crucifix and the holy pictures: but again I was struck by the fact that this room, though wrecked, was being perfectly swept up by perfectly clean and starched women, just as you see them in Kensington Square. I was introduced to the Reverend Mother and soon found myself engaged in animated conversation with the nuns, in my appalling French. One of them produced the nose cap of the shell that had done the deed. I said, by way of sheepish conversation, that it would make a good souvenir. She made a face and said: 'C'est Boche', and added that if it had been one of ours it would have been different – which I thought was very nicely put.

Then she went on to explain that this was a hospital. You know how bad my French is. All I could see was that a shell had burst on their ground-floor – luckily a shell with an instantaneous fuse, which therefore had not penetrated the cellar. But I asked her, lamely: 'Avez vous des malades, donc?' to which she replied in French: 'Come and see.'

The Reverend Mother and this nun then led me down into the cellar, and as we reached the entrance, the Reverend Mother said: 'N'est'ce pas une scene triste?' And I looked and saw what I think was the most pathetic sight I have ever looked upon. There were two cellars, end on end, lit up by an oil lamp, and in both were packed beds, all occupied, and in the narrow spaces between the beds were the sitting 'malades'.

Directly I entered, the eyes of all lit up as if some deliverer had come. I was introduced, and they all murmured 'Mon Colonel'. 'Bon jour', etc., etc. It was a shock to me. I was in a hospital for dying nuns. Scarcely one of them could have been less than seventy, and many must have been much older. There were two that spoke English. One had been for some years in a convent at Highgate. She kept saying, in stilted English: 'You will see that we are in a very unsatisfactory situation.'

Another, at the far end of the second cellar, who they told me had not left her bed for over five years, also knew a good deal of English and held her thin hand above her bed for me to shake, calling out over and over again, 'Thank you', 'Thank you'. I should have broken down if I had tried to talk much to them. I asked how many they were. They replied, forty-four. I promised to try and get ambulances to take them away, and I will do so. I hope that no more shells hit their cellar in the meantime.

I can still hear their voices as I left them, saying (I cannot repeat the French): 'You will do what you can for us, won't you; we are in such distress.'

P.S. It is now nearly a quarter to midnight, and I have already got a promise of ambulances sufficient to carry away eight lying-down cases during this night, and eight more tomorrow morning. The remainder I will see away somehow, but transport is very scarce, and those that can walk will probably have to walk some miles.

Is it not tragic to think of those poor old saints herded together in their dreary dungeon, with the shells bursting above their heads? You should have seen them in their beds:– snow-white linen and starched night-caps, so beautifully washed; as if there wasn't a war within a hundred miles.

3 November 1918 [Froyennes]

In the course of my rounds this afternoon I still found civilians near the firing line. From the stable of Prince Ruprecht's white château, the enemy had been trench-mortaring vigorously with heavy stuff, and one of my men had been killed in the field in front. Yet the family that lived there, which included several small children, had not gone. They were, however, dressed up to go, in their best clothes, and conspicuous among them was a tiny boy in a vermilion suit.

5 November 1918 [Hardie-Planque Farm, Cornet]

I had been up in the line until nearly 2 am, but I went up again. I found one of my advanced posts in the process of being severely hammered with 'pineapple' darts and by heavy trench mortars which, as you know, have a range of only a few hundred yards and therefore are proof positive that the enemy is near. The men of another post, I found sniping merrily at the German machine-gunners opposed to them, some of whom were occasionally showing themselves on a railway embankment by the river.

During the afternoon I was visited at my Headquarters by Colonel Montgomery, GSO (1) of the Division. He seemed a little nettled that the Germans should still be there.[33] However, after dark, the Germans themselves once more demonstrated their bad taste, and at the same time their presence, by raiding one of our posts. They did it with determination, too, employing a heavy covering artillery barrage.

7 November 1918 [Hardie-Planque Farm, Cornet]

Today it looks as though we may have peace within a few hours! So near does it seem that we have a sweepstake on the hour when hostilities shall cease! In the meantime, the enemy continues to crash away, night and day, and so do our people, but nothing falls near here.

How strange it will be when the fighting stops. I am already beginning to look back upon the last 4½ years as a sort of dream, in which there stands out a single tall figure in black:– always the last to have been seen by me when leaving for the war, and the first on coming home for leave. I will leave you to guess whose is that faithful, patient figure.

10 November 1918 (Sunday) [Barberie]

Yesterday morning the enemy was reported actually to have gone back, and it was not long before we received orders to move forward again to Froyennes.

As we passed Prince Ruprecht's château on our return to Froyennes, we found six men of the Brigade lying there. They had been killed while on patrol duty; the last of the Division, and perhaps almost of the Army, to be killed in the war. They belonged to the 17th London Regiment.

NOTES

1. The Civil Service Rifles were originally formed in 1859 as a volunteer unit. In 1860 they invited the Prince of Wales to accept the Honorary Colonelcy of the Regiment, which was known thereafter as 'The Prince of Wales' Own'.
2. Major-General Sir George Gorringe (1868–1945); Dongola Expedition, 1896, DSO; Boer War, 1899–1901, ADC to Lord Kitchener; Major-General, 1911; GOC 12th Indian Division, Mesopotamia, 1915–16, wounded; GOC 47th Division, 1916–19; promoted Lieutenant-General, 1921.
3. Brigadier-General HBPL Kennedy; 2nd Lieutenant, 60th Rifles, 1898; Boer War 1899–1902; Captain, 1904; Major, 1915; DSO, 1916; Lieutenant-Colonel, 1917; Brigadier-General and GOC 140th Infantry Brigade; MID seven times.
4. Captain LM Gibbs (1889–1966); 2nd Lieutenant, 2/Coldstream, 1910; Captain, 1917 and Brigade Major, 140th Brigade, 1918; DSO, 1918, MC and bar; ADC to Lord Rawlinson, C in C India, 1922–5; OC 1/Coldstream, 1930–4.
5. The 47th (2nd London) Division arrived in France in 1915 and was engaged at Aubers Ridge on 9 May 1915. In the same year the division fought at Festubert, Loos and Hohenzollern Redoubt. In 1917 they distinguished themselves at Messines and Bourlon Wood.
6. Lieutenant-Colonel WHE Segrave (1875–1964); commissioned HLI, 1898; Major, 1915; Lieutenant-Colonel, OC 1/15 London Regt., 1917–18; DSO & 1 2nd Bar; Brigadier-General, GOC 152nd Brigade, 51st Division.
7. A week after RCF's letter, Father Williamson's happy character was severely tested when he was summoned to attend the execution of a Private of the 47th Division, condemned to be shot for desertion. In Williamson's memoir, *Happy Days in France & Flanders* (Harding & More, 1921), he recounts the grim event in some detail, but the convicted man remains anonymous. It was undoubtedly Private P Murphy (aged 20), 47th Bn MGC, executed on September 12 1918, at Labeuvrière Monastery.
8. Rev. Felix S Farebrother; educ. Eton, Trinity Oxford 1910; Canon, St Martin's, Epsom, 1919; later Vicar of Warnham, Sussex.
9. Officially named The Battle of Albert, 21–23 August 1918. Albert, which was utterly destroyed, fell to the 18th (Eastern) Division on 22 August.
10. Captain P Davenport; MC & MID three times; Adjutant 1/Civil Service Rifles, June 1917–April 1919; wrote the history of the 1st Battalion in the Great War, in *The History of the Prince of Wales' Own Civil Service Rifles* (privately printed, 1921).
11. During the last eighteen months of the war, the rolling or 'creeping' barrage became remarkably sophisticated. It often consisted of up to six lines of shells all lifting together, bolstered by machine-gun and gas barrages.
12. The 106 percussion fuse was introduced in the Spring of 1917. While RCF, as a regimental officer, lamented the loss of shelter for attacking troops, GHQ saw the reduction in the number of craters as an aid to speeding up attacks.
13. Apart from comfort, the object of wearing shorts for summer dress, was to reduce lice infestation. The 47th Division employed a series of coloured playing card symbols as battle patches. The symbol denoted the battalion,

and colour (yellow, green, red), the brigade; see 47th Division War Diary, PRO WO95/2705.

14. It has been estimated that the number of horses and mules employed by the British Army towards the end of the war exceeded 1 million. During the British advances in 1918, huge numbers of these animals were used to move artillery and divisional trains forward, exposing greater numbers to death or injury; see Captain Sidney Galtrey, *The Horse and The War*, Country Life, 1918.

15. For further details on casualties, see the battalion War Diary, PRO WO95/2732.

16. Estaminets were basic French cafés or inns, where troops could unwind, drink cheap beer or devour a plate of chips. Usually run by a family, whose daughter would add a welcome diversion for the men; for a sketch of life in the 'estaminet', see Captain JC Dunn, 'September 1917' in *The War the Infantry Knew 1914–1919*, PS King, private edition, 1938.

17. General William Birdwood (1865–1951); educ. Clifton, Sandhurst; Boer War, DAAG to Kitchener, 1899–1902; Lieutenant-General and GOC Anzac troops, Gallipoli 1915–16; GOC I Anzac Corps, Western Front, 1917–18; GOC Fifth Army, 1918. Early favourite of Kitchener, who seemed to appreciate his 'neat' appearance – in this context, RCF's remarks about 'Birdie's' untidy kit are surprising. He was no tactician, but was a very effective PR man and smoothed over Anglo/Australian quarrels, though he was not universally loved by the Australians as some contemporaries state. Haig had doubts about him, but still gave him command of the Fifth Army, after Gough's degumming.

18. RCF's comments confirm the fact that few men or junior officers had contact with, or opinions about, the senior commanders. Reputations of Army commanders were largely created after the war; see 'The General and his Troops' in *Army Quarterly*, October 1961, and FM Montgomery, *Memoirs of Field-Marshal Montgomery*, Collins, 1958, p.35.

19. Leslie Henson (1891–1957); actor and producer; wartime West End credits included 'The Admirable Crichton' and 'In the Trenches' (1916); joined the army and transferred to the RAF in 1918; prolific stage performer in 1920s and 1930s.

20. Lieutenant-General Sir Thomas Morland (1865–1925); commissioned KRRC, 1884; spent early military career in West Africa; Brigadier-General, 2nd Brigade, 1910–13; Major-General, GOC 5th Division, 1914–15; T/Lieutenant-General, GOC X Corps, 1915–18; XIII Corps, April, 1918; later C in C, Army of the Rhine, 1920. Gough was dismissive of Morland, but Haig rated him from days at Aldershot, as 'one of our best'.

21. Gold wound stripes were awarded for each wound and were displayed on the lower left sleeve of the tunic.

22. To be 'un-gummed' was to be sacked and sent home. A variation of the French word *dégommé*, unstuck. In the Boer war, an officer was 'stellenbosched' (sent back to Stellenbosch) or in the French Army, 'limoged' (sent back to Limoges).

23. Edmund Stapleton-Bretherton of Heathfield House, Hampshire; brother of Edith Feilding; born 1881; T/Major and Director of Remounts (service which supplied horses to newly created units, and organised the treatment and replacement of wounded horses).

24. Captain RRG Kane; DSO, 1915 & Bar, 1919; A/Lieutenant-Colonel 1/Royal Munster Fusiliers; died of wounds, 1 October 1918. When Guy Nightingale took over command after Kane was killed, the battalion had been reduced to

seven officers and 261 men.

25. Lieutenant Guy Nightingale left an interesting collection of letters to his mother and a vivid diary from Gallipoli; see PRO 30/71/5.

26. General Gough, the Commander of the Fifth Army, was sacked on 3 April 1918. A 'head' was needed by Lloyd George and Sir Henry Wilson, and various Liberal politicians had old scores to settle with Gough, going back to the 1914 'Curragh Incident'. If Haig's despatch counted on GHQ input, it was likely to be inaccurate – Gough complained that none of the staff visited him during the chaos, Herbert Lawrence (Chief of Staff) even telling Gough on March 21, that the Germans wouldn't attack again the following day. 'He just purred like a damned pussy-cat,' recalled Gough; Gough to Lloyd George and Liddell Hart, Reform Club, 27 January 1936. Liddell Hart Papers, LH11/1936/31, King's College, London (KCL).

27. The despatch is very much at odds with Gough's own story, recalled in his book, *The Fifth Army*, Hodder & Stoughton, 1931. He heaped praise on the 16th (Irish) Division, citing their action during the battle as 'a very notable and gallant performance' and 'a truly wonderful example of courage and initiative'.

28. For a study of the retreat of the 16th (Irish) Division, see Tom Johnstone, *Orange, Green & Khaki – The Story of the Irish Regiments in the Great War 1914–18*, Gill & Macmillan, 1992 pp. 378–90.

29. RCF's assumption was correct. Two German organisations were formed to cripple the French economy in occupied territory: the *Abbau Konzern* methodically destroyed factories and mills: the *Wumba Waffen und Munitions-Beschaffungs Anstalt* stripped French machinery for sale to German companies.

30. During 1916 25,000 people were deported from Lille, to provide forced labour, but the intervention of the King of Spain later halted this practice. In 1918 the authorities recommenced deporting – the women to Holzminden and the men to Vilna (Lithuania). RCF appears to have misspelled the name.

31. Form of French comic opera. RCF alludes to a lightweight military action.

32. Son of King Louis III of Bavaria; a competent tactician in a Prussian dominated OHL (GHQ); descendant of King Charles I, and as head of the House of Stuart, a claimant to the British throne.

33. Lieutenant-Colonel Bernard Montgomery (1887–1976), showing typical impatience with the enemy; later became Field-Marshal and 1st Viscount Montgomery of Alamein; towards the end of the Great War, served as Chief of Staff, 47th Division; sometimes confused with Archibald Montgomery, Chief of Staff, 4th Army, 1916–18.

WAR LETTERS TO A WIFE

PART IV

Epilogue

12 November 1918 [Officers' Club, Hotel Royal, Lille]

Yesterday, we were to have pushed on and captured another town, which would have been a bloodless victory, since the enemy was retreating so fast that it was difficult to keep pace with him; and, since my battalion had been detailed as advanced guard, the day would unquestionably have provided plenty of amusement. A screen of cavalry (19th Hussars) was to have advanced in front of us, and this in itself would have been a novel experience, being the first time, I imagine, since 1914, that such a thing has been possible on the Western Front.

However, a stop was put to the proceedings by the signing of the Armistice, which took place in the morning, as you know, and my orders were countermanded, and the battalion sent to La Tombe.[1]

I woke up again, yesterday, with a temperature, and, as the doctor thought I might be sickening for influenza, he suggested a rest for a few days. So, in the evening, I was taken in an ambulance to a hospital in the Rue Jean Sans Peur, Lille. I had eaten nothing for twenty-four hours. But when I reached the hospital, and found myself in a long gloomy dormitory with the man in the next bed in delirium, I felt I was not bad enough for that. It seemed probable that even if I had not already got influenza I soon should have it in such surroundings. So I escaped, and got a comfortable bedroom, with a bath, at the Officers' Club at the Hotel Royal, where I slept, and from where I write.

15 November 1918 [La Tombe]

Yesterday morning I was sent for by the Major-General to explain a report – undeniably justified – which he had received, complaining about my desertion from the hospital in the Rue Jean Sans Peur. He was very nice about it, and forgave me.

In the afternoon I rode to the top of Mont St. Aubert. It is one of those hills typical of Belgium – like Kemmel, or Mont des Cats; and, like the Mont des Cats, is capped by a Church.

When we were before Tournai, ten days ago, this wonderful point of vantage was, as I told you, in the hands of the enemy. His artillery

202

observers sat in the point of the steeple, well above the bell, and watched our positions, well knowing from their experience of that period of the war that we should not shell the church. I climbed up into this observation post. The chairs the observers had sat on were still in place in front of the loopholes. It was almost like being in an aeroplane, so steeply and suddenly does the hill rise from the surrounding plain, and so extensive is the view. In front – most conspicuously – stood the great school where one of my posts had been, and to the left, under direct observation through an avenue between the trees, was the Countess's red château.

16 November 1918 [Leuze]

This morning I again rode round the line of posts of ten days ago – the line of the last stand of the enemy before his final retirement.

On the right bank of the Scheldt, just in front of the great school building, there is a German military cemetery. The Germans have been much more decorative in these matters than we. In the middle is an eagle of stone, on a high pedestal, and at the heads of some of the graves are carved memorials, also in stone. Even the wooden crosses are more elaborate than we make them.[2] Sandwiched in between the German graves, here and there, is an English grave. Altogether, I saw three, and the name on one was Fielding – a private of the South Wales Borderers. The crosses over these English graves are precisely the same as those on either side of them. But there is always a distinction between a dead German and a dead Englishman. The former 'rests in God' (Ruht in Gott); the latter just 'rests' (Hier ruht ein Englander).

We are on the trunk road to Brussels, and tramping along this road, from the direction of Germany, we see an almost continuous stream of refugees and men and women deported by the enemy, thousand upon thousand. This has been going on for practically a week now. They push or pull handcarts, or are harnessed to horse carts and even wagons, which are loaded with their belongings, and all are profusely decorated with the flags of the Allies.

17 November 1918 (Sunday) [Leuze]

Yes, as you say, the sudden and complete collapse of the Germans is almost bewildering. The feeling among the soldiers here was, on November 11, rather one of awe and inability to appreciate the great relief that had so suddenly come to them. There was no visible change in their demeanour and I do not think many felt much inclined for jubilation.

As for the French of Lille and the Belgians of Tournai, the signing of the Armistice meant nothing to them. Peace was proclaimed – so far as they were concerned – on the day the enemy withdrew, and our patrols entered their cities. I cannot help hoping that in the excitement at home no English man or woman has failed to feel humbled by these terrific events, or has forgotten to give proper thanks for the Empire's wonderful escape – indeed, for the escape of all humanity: And I hope that the children – for whom most of all, the war has been fought, however little they understand these things today – may have had the duty of thanksgiving impressed upon them; not just to say 'thank you' once in their prayers, but each morning and evening, again and again, for years to come.

As the padre said today: 'England has won this tremendous victory after trying for four years to lose the war'.

God knows how true that saying is! Think of the strikes at home, and the bickering, and the muddles.

P.S. It will probably be asked why our advancing army was called off just as it was on the verge of finally routing the enemy. I suppose the reason was that as we advanced, we were each day putting so many more miles of destroyed roads and railways between our fighting troops and our sources of supply.[3]

23 November 1918 [Palace Hotel, Brussels]

This morning I called upon the British Minister, Sir Francis Villiers, at the Legation, which has just reopened. Mr. Gahan, the English Chaplain, was there. We spoke about Nurse Edith Cavell, whom as you will remember, Mr. Gahan attended, and I asked him if she had actually received the brutal treatment that has been described.[4] He said, 'No – that was invented by certain journalists'. I asked if she had received a fair trial. He replied that she had. He went on to say that she was quite content with her sentence, and felt no resentment on account of it. She had expected no other result. The surprising thing, he said, was that the Germans had left her alone so long as they did – that she was not arrested earlier for helping Allied soldiers to escape.

In those early days of the war, he said, the people of Brussels were very amateurish and did all kinds of reckless things, not knowing the risks they ran. They were inclined to look upon the Germans as slow-witted and easily fooled. Edith Cavell was to a large extent betrayed by the loose, boastful talk of the people she had helped to get away. Some Belgians, too, threw her over at the last, and she was left to bear alone the full brunt of a military offence which in reality had been shared by many others. But it had been agreed upon beforehand that it should be so.

Mr. Gahan added that more responsibility had been placed upon her shoulders by her friends than any woman should have been allowed to bear. Indeed, after she had received her sentence, she told him she was relieved that it was over.

The sentence was carried out quietly and decently in the early morning. She was accompanied by the German Chaplain – a good man, he said – and she bore it without a flinch.

We failed to get away this evening owing to the breakdown of the compression gear of the car, so went to a music hall. I loathe Puritanism, as you well know, but I think a little of it would do that place no harm.

The show ended with the Allied National Anthems, the audience standing up and joining in.

The last turn was the 'Star-spangled Banner'. Though Knox, who was with me, had been singing energetically enough, this so stimulated his patriotic fervour that he burst into fortissimo. His magnificent voice drowned the singing of the audience. They dropped out gradually, and by the end of the second verse he was singing by himself, accompanied only by the performers who were massed on the stage.

But he was too much even for them, and, one by one, they too gave up, until in the end, he was performing a solo, the eyes of all riveted wonderingly upon him.

He is a tall, good-looking fellow, and it was a striking finale to the performance.

4 December 1918 [Ferfay]

My dearest Joan,

I have been very busy, improving our billets which were in a dilapidated condition when we took them over. We are starting an officers mess in a château, but as every stick of furniture had been looted and the windows broken, it will take days to make the place habitable.

I went to Brussels to look for traces of Uncle Wilfred[5] on the day that King Albert re-entered the town for the first time in 4½ years. I found all the inhabitants dancing and singing in the streets. They didn't know what I was – whether Belgian or English or American. They didn't even know their own soldiers by sight in the khaki uniform, which of course they adopted only since the war began. I have never had such a triumphant entry into any place before. One lady even rushed up and flung her arms around my neck and kissed me.

Your loving Daddy.

12 December 1918 [Ferfay]

This afternoon, having borrowed a motor ambulance, I undertook to show Knox and another American Army doctor who is visiting us from Paris over the old Cuinchy–Loos battlefield. It is a melancholy business and I doubt if it is worth the candle, but it is very interesting.

On the way we visited the ruined square of Bethune; thence the Cuinchy Brickstacks and the Railway Triangle and the famous mine craters.

We scrambled over the trenches on either side of the string of craters. It was a new and impressive experience for our visitor, who now saw this kind of landscape for the first time. And this is a fair specimen. Again, I had no difficulty in tracing the old positions, which indeed have scarcely changed during the war. The old listening posts remain, and the advanced line – where you stood so close to the enemy that you had to creep like a mouse – looks almost as I left it in 1915.

Then we went on, through the ruins of La Bassée, to the Chalk Pit of Loos. So destroyed is this portion of the Lens–La Bassée road that we had to take to our feet. The ground around the Chalk Pit has been much disfigured by shell-fire, and the wood that grew beside it, as well as Bois Hugo – from which we met such heavy fire on September 28, 1915 have completely disappeared. So also has the building alongside the Chalk Pit, in the cellar of which our wounded lay.

Puis 14 (bis), where Harold Cuthbert was killed, is recognisable by the shreds of shell-torn machinery that lie about. Hohenzollern Redoubt is gone, blown into the sky. It is represented, today, by some huge mine craters.

I began to feel sorry that I had undertaken to bear-lead the American sightseer. He is a good enough fellow, but was too entirely absorbed in the collection of souvenirs. I remember one of my officers, Barron, during the battle at Croisilles, telling a private whom he found relieving a German prisoner in a dug-out of his watch – if he wanted souvenirs– to go and get them in the firing line. How much less right has a mere sightseer to souvenirs? It is horrifying to see this sacred ground desecrated in this way, and still more so to think of what will happen when the cheap tripper is let loose. With his spit he will saturate the ground that has been soaked with the blood of our soldiers.

This particular man, not knowing what he was doing, would pick up a bone (it is lucky he did not notice any of the boots that still lie about with the broken off foot inside) and would call out, 'Oh, look, a human tibia' – or whatever kind of bone it might happen to be. Like a veterinary man I took round the trenches at Fricourt in September, 1916, he would pick up a battered British helmet – the owner of which had obviously been killed; or a shattered rifle butt, which as likely as not, had belonged to one of the men of my own Coldstream battalion of 1915, it was so decayed.

I could overhear Knox whispering to him behind my back to put these things down. <u>He</u> knows. It is the way of the world, no doubt, but I pray I may see no more of it. I know that these things will be collected, and hoarded, and no doubt boasted of, by tourists, – things that no one who has fought would have in his possession. Fortunately, the Salvage Corps is busy at work, collecting and burying such trophies.

The entry to the old lime kiln, where Arthur Egerton and Dermot Browne were killed, is entirely obliterated, but I found the vertical flue, through which, by means of a piece of telephone wire, we extricated 'Bing' Hopwood and the rest of the Headquarters Company, who had been buried at the same time. I looked for the grave in which we buried Egerton and Dermot but could not find it.

Before we left I thought I would give our visitor a <u>respectable</u> souvenir, and picked up a German hand grenade. It had been lying about so long that I did not think it could possibly have any sting left. However, I pulled the safety cord to make sure, and immediately there followed a hissing sound. I called to the two doctors to take cover and threw the bomb, which a second or two later went off with a loud explosion.

A splinter drew a spot of blood from our visitor's hand, at which he said, jokingly, 'Anyhow, I shall be able to tell them at home that I've had a wound'.

Then we went on, through the ruins of Loos, past the great 'crassier' upon which the famous pylon (the Tower Bridge as it was called) now lies flat.

It was then getting dark, so we came home.

18 January 1919 [Ferfay, Pas de Calais]

I arrived here yesterday, to find demobilisation the order of the day. We sent off an officer and 26 men today. The party for demobilisation is paraded each day at 2pm, when I say goodbye and shake hands with the men, and the band plays them down the road. A crowd of the undemobilised waits about to see them start.

28 January 1919 [Ferfay]

What was left of our band played the demobilisation draft away today. It played for the last time and was then itself demobilised.

3 February 1919 [Ferfay]

The raging desire still continues to be demobilised quickly. Never-theless, I feel pretty sure that, for many, there will be pathetic disillusionment.

In the trenches the troops have had plenty of time for thought, and, as 'Happy Days' said the other day, there has grown up in their minds a heavenly picture of an England which does not exist, and never did exist, and never will exist so long as men are human.

After all, there was a good deal to be said in favour of the old trench life. There were none of the mean haunting fears of poverty there, and the next meal – if you were alive to take it – was as certain as the rising sun. The rations were the same for the 'haves' and the 'have nots', and the shells fell, without favour, upon both.

In a life where no money passes, the ownership of money counts for nothing. Rich and poor alike stand solely upon their individual merits, without discrimination. You can have no idea, till you have tried it, how much pleasanter life is under such circumstances.

In spite – or partly perhaps because of the gloominess of the surroundings – there was an atmosphere of selflessness and a spirit of camaraderie the like of which has probably not been seen in the world before, at least on so grand a scale. Such is the influence of the shells!

The life was a curious blend of discipline and good-fellowship; wherein men were easily pleased; where there was no gossip; where even a shell when it had just missed you produced a sort of exultation;– a life in the course of which you actually got used to the taste of chloride of lime in tea.

In short, there was no humbug in the trenches, and that is why – with all their disadvantages – the better kind of men who have lived in them will look back upon them hereafter with something like affection.

18 February 1919 [Château de Ferfay, Pas de Calais]
Up to the present, I have been billeted at the house of the caretaker of the château of this village – M. Flament. Today I came to sleep at the château, in a room which I have furnished roughly.

The officers' mess has been in the château since December 16. It belongs to the Comte d'Hinnisdal, but, so far as I can gather, is not used by the family as a permanent home until after they are dead, when they are brought here and buried in a vault near the house. Over the vault is a chapel, in which a pensioned one-legged priest says daily Mass for the dead Hinnisdals below.

The château is one-room thick, and so constructed as to be cut by the wind from whichever side it blows, and I cannot help feeling that the family is well advised in avoiding it during their living days. As the result of the war it is now in a wretched condition, leaky and unkempt, stripped of all furniture, bare and comfortless.

During the war it has been one of our Corps Headquarters. It has never come within the range of battle, which therefore renders curious a story which has been repeatedly told to me, and which I think may be true. While digging a practice trench not so very long ago, some dead English soldiers were found, their burial-place unmarked and unrecorded.

There has been much speculation as to the meaning of this burial, and the explanation which seems to be generally accepted is that the bodies are those of soldiers who were shot for cowardice.[6]

Though I have never actually come across it, I seem to have been reading all through the war of soldiers being shot for so-called cowardice, and I would like to say to you that I disapprove in almost every case, of this method of dealing with a trouble which is generally the result of nervous collapse, and may be uncontrollable. The best of men have their ups and downs in war, as in peace. I will go further and say that there are men who are capable of the bravest actions, and yet whose nerve may break down under certain conditions of strain, especially when they have been kept too long in the battle line.

It may be argued that it is as reasonable to shoot one man for a temporary lapse as it is to give another a VC for a momentary heroic impulse. Perhaps it is. Both alternatives, I think, are open to criticism. The true test of a soldier is his average behaviour under the tearing stress of war during a long period. It is the same in all walks of life. Of course, as you know, the justification for these shootings is believed to be that they deter other soldiers from running away. Surely, that is a poor reason to give in our army!

The most deplorable feature of the business is that the court which tries these soldiers is often composed of men who have not themselves experienced, and therefore cannot visualise the supreme test to which, after all, the culprit did once submit himself, and that probably voluntarily. There are many who have not done as much.

I do not fail to appreciate the horror it must cause the judges – to give their sentence. There is no blame to them. Under the existing system, it is their duty.

But, when I think of the great contrast between the culprit – a front-line soldier – and the Court which sometimes tries him, I am reminded of the hale and hearty men who, in the early days of the war, used to tub-thump about England, exhorting their fellow-countrymen to 'join the Army' and 'do their bit'.

And I call to mind a certain subaltern I once knew – a lawyer in private life – who never did an honest day's work in the trenches; yet who, after four days of scrim-shanking in the front line, managed to get sent home:– and was soon promoted to the rank of major, and told off to prosecute conscientious objectors!

31 March 1919 [Château de Ferfay, Pas de Calais]
We continue to get orders and counter-orders, and the homecoming of the Cadre seems likely to be by the Channel Tunnel!

It is, indeed, a miserable business, and has spoilt the whole war for me. Officers and men slink to their homes, one by one – as 'Happy Days' (who left today) used to say – as if they had lost the War, instead of won it.[7]

11 May 1919 [Felixstowe]
We crossed from Le Havre in a crowded transport, on which we passed the night. Besides ourselves there were about 1,500 Canadian troops. I shared a cabin, but the men had scarcely room to breathe.

We hung about Southampton all yesterday, and finally got away about a quarter to five in the evening. The long train of transport never failed to draw attention to us as troops returning from France, and in the good old English way, the people turned out of their houses, and thronged the streets as we passed, and cheered and waved their handkerchiefs.

It was nice to think that at last, after all the years of war, these men were getting some personal and first-hand recognition from their fellow-countrymen. And they thoroughly enjoyed their home-coming.

I have sometimes heard soldiers in the trenches speak as though they thought the people at home were callous, and thoughtless of their sufferings. But there was no sign of callousness yesterday.

I had not seen this side of England before – at any rate from my present view-point, and for me, a tinge of sadness was mingled with the joy of home-coming as I looked on.

NOTES

1. The Armistice was finally signed at 5 am in a railway carriage, in a siding in the Forest of Compiègne. It came into force at 11 am and by 8 pm that evening, the Kaiser had reached sanctuary at Amerongen Castle, Holland.
2. These seem more like the elaborate cemeteries from the Franco-Prussian War. While the design of British Great War cemeteries linked the dead with Christian sacrifice, German cemeteries were starkly different. Flowers were usually forbidden, and mass graves were preferred, symbolising the nation rather than individuals.
3. Perhaps the lessons learnt from the collapse of the German Spring offensive were still fresh in everyone's mind.
4. The British Matron of a Red Cross hospital in Brussels, Edith Cavell was executed on 13 October 1915, for helping allied soldiers escape to the Dutch border. Her death received much coverage in the British Press. Her body was returned to London after the war.
5. Captain WS Stapleton-Bretherton; brother of Edith Feilding; 4/Royal Fusiliers; killed in action 8 November 1914, at Veldhoek Château, Menin Road ; no known grave and listed on the Menin Gate Memorial, Ypres.
6. Multiple executions were rare. The largest number shot at one time was five – all members of the 3/Worcesters, on 26 July 1915. The offence was 'desertion'. They were buried in the Ramparts at Ypres.
7. RCF kept in touch with the priest and later wrote the Foreword to Williamson's memoir, *Happy Days in France & Flanders*.

Index

(Rank shown held at time of first mention)